TRANS.CAN.LIT

TRANS.CAN.LIT
Resituating the Study
of Canadian Literature

Smaro Kamboureli
Roy Miki, editors

Wilfrid Laurier University Press

We acknowledge the support of the Canada Council for the Arts for our publishing program. We acknowledge the financial support of the Government of Canada through the Book Publishing Industry Development Program for our publishing activities.

Library and Archives Canada Cataloguing in Publication

Trans.can.lit : resituating the study of Canadian literature / edited by Smaro Kamboureli and Roy Miki.

Includes bibliographical references and index.
ISBN 978-0-88920-513-0

1. Canadian literature—20th century—History and criticism. 2. Canadian literature—21st century—History and criticism. 3. Literature and globalization—Canada. 4. Canadian literature—Minority authors—History and criticism. 5. Literature and state—Canada. I. Kamboureli, Smaro II. Miki, Roy, 1942–

PS8061.T73 2007   C810.9'0054   C2007-903511-6

Cover design by P.J. Woodland. Text design by Catharine Bonas-Taylor.

Every reasonable effort has been made to acquire permission for copyright material used in this text, and to acknowledge all such indebtedness accurately. Any errors and omissions called to the publisher's attention will be corrected in future printings.

∞

This book is printed on Ancient Forest Friendly paper (100% post-consumer recycled).

Printed in Canada

CONTENTS

SMARO KAMBOURELI

PREFACE

Preamble

Canadian literature: a construct bounded by the nation, a cultural by-product of the Cold War era, a nationalist discourse with its roots in colonial legacies, a literature that has assumed transnational and global currency, a tradition often marked by uncertainty about its value and relevance, a corpus of texts in which, albeit not without anxiety and resistance, spaces have been made for First Nations and diasporic voices. These are some of the critical assumptions scholars have brought to the study of CanLit, as we have come to call it for the sake of brevity, but also affectionately, and often ironically as we recognize the dissonances inscribed in the economy of this term. Whether it is considered an integral part of the Canadian nation formation, an autonomous body of works, a literature belonging somewhere between nation and literariness, or a part of "world literature," CanLit has been subject to a relentless process of institutionalization. Sometimes subtly, sometimes crudely, it has always been employed as an instrument—cultural, intellectual, political, federalist, and capitalist—to advance causes and interests that now complement, now resist, each other.

This is not a process peculiar to CanLit. From the literary traditions of Germany and France to those of Brazil, India, and Australia, literature has been mobilized as a discourse that, no matter the diversity of its particular aesthetic and formal configurations, has served the geopolitical and socio-cultural ends of institutions that are often at odds with what it sets out to accomplish. The conditions under which CanLit is produced and the ways in which it is appropriated differ from one context to another, but one element is constant: literature is inextricably related to certain practices of polity. It may be understood and employed as a special category, as it is in English studies, but this category unravels when literature is seen to operate as an inter- and intra-, as well as a discursive, cultural site of exchanges. What this means, among other things, is that literature functions as a sphere of public debates, but is never fully harmonized with them, thus registering the limits of cultural knowledge and politics. Complicit and compliant, literature is also purposefully defiant and joyfully insolent. Hence an incommensurability delineates literature, and this condition is also reflected in how it is read.

CanLit, then, is not a term to be taken at face value. It resonates with the same ambiguities characterizing literature at large, but also with the complexities—even nervousness—associated with its own history and location. The specific trajectories of CanLit bespeak a continuing anxiety over intent and purpose, its ends always threatening to dissolve. This accounts for its intense preoccupation with its own formation: its topocentrism; its uneasy relationships with the British, the Commonwealth, and the American; its uneven responses to the (post)colonial and its so-called minority literatures; its desire to accommodate global cultural contexts; its obsessiveness with identity; and its institutionalization and celebration through cultural, social, and trade policies. These diverse preoccupations attest to CanLit's specificity, but also to its nervous state.

Though not always read or theorized as a discourse related to the formation of the Canadian nation-state—its early fantasies of homogeneity, its strategic cultural and language policies, and its fetishization of its multicultural make-up—CanLit is marked by a precariousness suggestive, in part, of the nation-state's politics of remembering and forgetting, on the one hand, and the positivism with which Canadian literature has been supported and exported by government agencies, on the other. Such a politics of representation has its own storied tradition to which the idiom of the CanLit imaginary is vulnerable. Still, if the state posits Canada as an imagined community, CanLit is both firmly entangled with this national imaginary and capable of resisting it. The body literary does not always have a symmetrical relationship to the body politic; the literary is inflected and infected by the political in oblique and manifest ways, at the same time that it asserts its unassimilability. A similar multifarious yet intransigent condition also marks CanLit's institutionalization within academe. From the belated and gradual fashion in which it has entered the curriculum of Canadian English departments to the ways it has become a popular field of study, from the various critical debates as to how it should be read to the professional and disciplinary determinants that influence its teaching and study, CanLit has reached a certain deadendedness; yet it also displays a resistance to being entirely subsumed by the very processes and institutions that influence its course.

CanLit is, then, at once a troubled and troubling sign. Troubled because "Canadian" minus any qualifiers evokes the entirety of the geopolitical space it refers to, but it also siphons off large segments of this space and its peoples into oblivion at worst, and circumscribed conditions at best. Nevertheless, the term conveys a semblance of plenitude. Notwithstanding the various attempts to instigate and maintain a dialogue between anglophone and francophone literatures in Canada, CanLit has, more or less, always functioned as a referent to Canadian literature in English. What's more, even within the parameters of this English idiom, CanLit's feigned plenitude has been forged by means of occlusion and repression, marginalizing particular idioms of English, as the language has been othered by indigeneity and diaspora. If CanLit has revamped itself, and is employed today as a referent to a body of works that includes Sto:lo, Okanagan, Cree, Ojibway, Métis, South Asian, Japanese Canadian, Trinidadian Canadian, and Italian Canadian authors (to mention just a few examples of literatures that have a minoritized history), it remains a tradition that bears the signs of its troubled trajectory. Its alteritist configuration may have compelled it to question some of its institutionalized and institutionalizing practices, but it has also recast its semblance of plenitude in new guises, if not with greater force. With what was illegitimate now legitimized, CanLit may be in a position to applaud itself for the "progress" it has made, but it also runs the risk of wresting difference and otherness into a Canadian trope: rendering otherness as familiar and familial, thereby situating it within the history of its present. While CanLit as an institution reflects this process whereby the other becomes the same, normative and therefore transparent, it also insists on positing itself as a discursive site where the other can deflect its assigned familiarity, its status as a vanishing object. Despite the various ways in which it is managed, CanLit has the potential to challenge the presumption of its intelligibility and, in turn, defy the notion that Canada is an imagined community. It is in this sense that CanLit is a troubling sign: never fully released from the various ways it is anchored, it can disturb and alter the conditions that affect it.

CanLit may thus be instrumentalized by and concerned with the Canadian state, but it also contests the stateness, and boldly points beyond it, to an elsewhereness that is not yet legible, that defamiliarizes the tropes that produce transparency and its accompanying contentment and complacency. An alternative cognitive space, this elsewhereness demands epistemic breaks that require new tools to comprehend its materiality; it calls for an understanding of temporality and space that questions the assumption that knowledge is residual, always anterior to what has come before, the product of the same epistemological gestures that have cultivated the categories of "proper" subject and "other" in the first place. This elsewhereness inscribed in CanLit intimates that Canada is an unimaginable community, that is, a community constituted in excess of the knowledge of itself, always transitioning. Thus CanLit demands a transformation of the codes and means of its self-representation and its representation of others. It is to this summons for developing new terms of engagement with CanLit and Canada as an un/imagined community that the TransCanada project responds.

The TransCanada Project: Its Inception and Process

The TransCanada project was conceived three years ago at Alexis, a Greek restaurant on Broadway West, Vancouver. A short walk from Roy Miki's house, it is where we usually go for a late evening talk when I visit him and Slavia. Over the years that we've been going there, we have conjured up different scenarios explaining how Alexis has managed to remain in business since it is always virtually empty; but that spring of 2004, while a boisterous young crowd watched sports in the next-door pub, we conjured up Trans-Canada. It was not a project devised out of the blue. We had been concerned about the state of CanLit for a while, and we speculated on the current debates, and the possibilities they created, the consequences of which, no matter how exciting, often dissipated almost before they had the chance to make a dent in the field, gone adrift in the frenzy that has come to be a permanent feature of our profession.

There was no doubt in our minds that what had been happening to and what continues to characterize the production and study of CanLit was—is—symptomatic, on the one hand, of how the humanities continued to be under siege and, on the other, of the changes happening in our discipline. This was not a situation unique to Canada. Drastic changes in the university system in the name of efficiency, fiscal responsibility, and accountability and ethics had already been under way in Australia and the UK. Going by the personal accounts of colleagues there and the scholarly analyses of the impact of these changes, the effects had been ambivalent at best, and detrimental at worst. What we were witnessing, then, was in keeping with the ethos of globalization, an instance of the contingencies of global affairs.

We worried about the pressure from outside and inside the university for academics to perform in ways that met the goals of the newly intro-duced performance factors and strategic plans; to apply for grants, espe-cially large-scale ones; to join large collaborative teams and establish partnerships; to pursue research the results of which were immediately transparent and useful; and to engage in projects defined as innovative and interdisciplinary. All of these directives, we thought, offered signs of cer-tain kinds of potentiality, but at the same time were decidedly pre-emptive. By operating on the fallacy that the humanities, compared to the social and hard sciences, were lagging behind in their contribution to the Canadian polity (though never quite articulated as clearly, this was, in our view, the underlying premise), but, more importantly, by adopting the rhetoric of knowledge production, corporatization, and global citizenship, Canadian academe in general and the humanities in particular were caught in a web of paradoxical circumstances. Major changes were, at least in part, reinforc-ing some of the very systems of thought and knowledge gambits that many of us had been trying to dismantle.

We knew we were not alone in thinking along these terms. This was the year the Social Sciences and Humanities Research Council (SSHRC) had launched its Transformation process—"a nation-wide consultation to trans-form the Council so that it can better support researchers and ensure that Canadians benefit directly from their investment in research and scholarship" (SSHRC)[1]—and the entire professoriate was alert as to what impact that ini-tiative would have on the Canadian academy. SSHRC's transition from "Grant-ing Council" to "Knowledge Council" was of particular significance to Canadianists. Not only as academic citizens, but also as scholars for whom the politics that determine the making of culture in Canada are integral to our particular object of study, we understood this Transformation process to be intimately related to the epistemic frameworks within which CanLit is produced, disseminated, taught, and studied. The governmentality of knowledge production and the market mechanisms that influence as much how knowledge is regulated as what kinds of knowledge can circulate are embedded in the cultural grammar and materiality of CanLit.

In our view, that Transformation process, together with the unprecedented visibility of CanLit in the public sphere, marked an important juncture that called for large-scale critical reconsiderations of the pedagogical and curricular challenges facing Canadianists. This was especially urgent, we thought, at a moment when the multicultural idiom had become normative but was being challenged by the immediacy of diasporic and transnational politics in our daily lives. We realized, that evening at Alexis, that we could not afford to elide what that moment entailed. It called for a practice of what Donna Palmateer Pennee has defined as "literary citizenship": to instigate and take part in "communicative acts" that are responsive to the polity and the discipline, as well as to our production as subjects, that is, as citizens, scholars, and teachers, as men and women inhabiting particular locations.

We soon came to name the project we envisioned that night. "Trans-Canada" felt just right: a familiar sign, a highway most of us have travelled on at some point, yet another symbol of national unity—one, however, put into the service of a project designed to dislodge the notion from its familiar moorings. More significantly, the name was a direct homage to Roy Kiyooka, an artist and writer that both of us had an abiding interest in. Roy had edited Kiyooka's collected poetry, *Pacific Windows* (1997), and I was in the process of producing a corrected edition of his *Transcanada Letters* and editing *Pacific Rim Letters* (both 2005), all projects left unfinished at the time of his death in 1994. Kiyooka remained exemplary for us. His writings and his art, the instructive ways in which he performed his subjectivity, his practice of a pedagogy that disavowed coercion and comfort, his profound awareness of how the market place co-opted an artist's agency, his notion of academic citizenship that eschewed conformity and narrow concepts of specialization, and his inglish that spoke to his diasporic condition in a mode that resisted easy definitions—all of these aspects of Kiyooka, which had affected both of us over the years in different ways, were akin to the kind of critical attentiveness we wanted the TransCanada project to propose and enact.

Three things, we agreed, were equally crucial to materializing how we had imagined TransCanada to take shape. First, it would focus on CanLit, and it would do so in the contexts of citizenship and institutions. More specifically, as we put it in the call for papers for the first TransCanada conference, it was a project intended to create a forum that would foster "the study of Canadian literature as a field produced in the context of globalizing processes and critical methodologies, but also in that of institutional structures such as the Humanities, the cultural industries, curricula and anthologies" (*TransCanada*). Since the national, multicultural, and postcolonial idioms are affected by globalization in ways that make it imperative we confront how citizenship, in its different configurations, is controlled and performed today, it was important to make citizenship one of the operative terms in our proposed investigation of CanLit. Methodology was also central to our understanding of the thematics TransCanada was to explore. As we put it in our SSHRC conference grant application and explained in our different communications with the delegates, we wanted their contributions to directly address methodology, to take on method as constitutive rather than supplementary. The task, then, was to undertake a major rethinking of the assumptions that had governed the field of CanLit studies and to rejuvenate the field through a renewed sense of collective purpose. This, we believed, was essential both in dealing with the urgency of the moment to which the TransCanada project was responding and in bringing "to light the incommensurable aspects of the study of Canadian literature as praxis in Canada" (*TransCanada*).

Second, we wanted the project to be launched with a conference, but not a conference whose momentum would dissipate soon after it was over. Conferences as conventional venues in which we disseminate our research, network, and dialogue, no matter how productive, tend to be ephemeral. They may energize us, inform us, and make us think differently, but their effects rarely outlive their occasion. Even conferences that make history and become part of the CanLit archive—consider, for example, *Taking Stock: The Calgary Conference on the Canadian Novel* (Steele) and *Future Indicative: Literary Theory and Canadian Literature* (Moss)—often have a teleological structure that does not allow them to assess their own institutionalizing effects, be they intentional or beyond their control. In our effort to circumvent these limits, we conceived of TransCanada not as a single conference, nor as a series of three conferences (this number is more a matter of stamina than anything else), but as "a future-oriented project." This emphasis on futurity, we hoped, would allow the project to initiate a process that would be designed to generate its own momentum, thereby developing in a manner that could accommodate what transpired at the TransCanada conferences, what was happening elsewhere in the field in the interim between them, and all the other research and publications initiatives undertaken through the TransCanada project.

Third, the TransCanada mandate could be actualized only through collaboration, but not in the tightly administered sense of collaboration in currency these days. As we did with method, we encouraged the delegates to reflect on collaboration. Why did funding agencies and university research offices privilege it as the most desirable mode of research? Why were large collaborative clusters seen as being more effective in terms of research outcomes and more accountable to the community at large? Was collaboration, designed in clusters or otherwise, more suitable to the pursuit of interdisciplinary research as SSHRC seemed to suggest? What about the administrative challenges collaboration posed, the labour-intensive efforts it required? Could we think of collaboration in ways other than those designed by SSHRC? What difference would a sustained collaborative effort make to the study of CanLit? As we said in our description of the Trans-Canada conference's Research Cells, our goal was to see "a loose collective of scholars," students as well as faculty, from Canada as well as from elsewhere, coming together and networking in ways that would extend the dialogue initiated at the first conference to other venues: the future TransCanada conferences; the various TransCanada projects scholars would participate in; conferences and projects organized by others; and the work we are producing collaboratively as well individually. Though we had envisioned that "'collaborative' clusters" might "emerge from the Research Cells," a major part of the TransCanada conference's structure, we intended neither to make them happen at all costs nor to fully coordinate them if they did (*TransCanada*). Acting otherwise would run the risk of centralizing, if not homogenizing, the study of CanLit, thereby reproducing the same patterns and expectations we sought to resist and transform.

A quixotic plan? Perhaps. Still, the fact that the colleagues we invited to join us in this venture responded with a resounding "yes" confirmed our belief that the time was ripe for such an undertaking. David Chariandy, Jeff Derksen, Sophie McCall, and Kathy Mezei, the first members of the Trans-Canada conference's organizing committee, as well as Alessandra Capperdoni and Mark McCutcheon, doctoral students then, who joined the committee soon after, have played a seminal role in imagining this project along with us, giving clarity and direction to our original thinking, and, above all, making it happen. Together, we designed TransCanada as a provisional site, one enabling a collaborative endeavour through which we could begin to rethink the "disciplinary and institutional frameworks within which Canadian literature is produced, disseminated, studied and taught,"[2] and thus move toward the elsewhereness of CanLit.

Trans.Can.Lit

Initially presented as plenary talks at the inaugural event of the TransCanada project, the essays edited for this volume face head-on the issues the conference was intended to put forward. They place CanLit, the conditions that produce it, the idioms it privileges, and those it does not feel comfortable with under the lens. Provocative and eye-opening, they are marked by a keen awareness of how history, ideology, method, pedagogy, capital economies, cultural capital, institutional and social structures, community, citizenship, advocacy, racialization, indigeneity, diaspora, and globalization are all intricately related to CanLit and its complex, often tortuous, trajectories. CanLit is not the sole object of their focus, however. They display, too, great attentiveness to the politics of the critic's self-location, to the ways in which we are invariably implicated in what we take CanLit to be and in how we practise citizenship. Written by scholars and writers who have already helped shape the field of CanLit in significant ways, they split CanLit open. They reflect how daunting a project it is to "unmake" CanLit, despite its relatively short history, but also show that the undertaking of this project demands that we pursue different strategies and methods, ask new questions, and work collaboratively within and across the particular locations we inhabit. These essays are posited here as terms of action that we can deploy outside of the accustomed routes we have taken as scholars.

Guelph, 2007

ACKNOWLEDGEMENTS

First, we would like to thank all the colleagues and students who participated in and attended the "TransCanada: Literature, Institutions, Citizenship" conference in Vancouver, June 2005. We also thank the group of English graduate students at Simon Fraser University who, organized by Tara Lee, did an excellent job taking care of the logistics immediately before and during the conference. At the University of Guelph, Sandra Sabatini, research officer at the Office of the Dean, College of Arts, provided ongoing support in many ways. Andrea Bennett, Smaro's undergraduate summer assistant, took exceptional care of practical affairs and of many editorial issues concerning the production of this volume at the initial stages. Paul Danyluk, Smaro's graduate assistant, provided help in the final stage of the manuscript's preparation. From designing and maintaining the website to handling most of the correspondence, from organizing and carrying out the fundraising drive for subsidizing students to planning and taking care of the DanceCanada party, Mark McCutcheon, Smaro's graduate assistant for that year, performed masterfully in all his tasks. We thank Alessandra Capperdoni, David Chariandy, Jeff Derksen, Sophie McCall, and Kathy Mezei, members, along with Mark McCutcheon, of the conference's organizing committee, for responding to our invitation to join us in this venture with great enthusiasm. Without their support, creative thinking, and hard work, the TransCanada project would not have taken off. We thank our respective institutions for their generous financial support: at the University of Guelph, the Office of the Vice President Research, the Dean's Office and the Director of the School of English and Theatre Studies, College of Arts; at Simon Fraser University, the Office of the Vice President Academic (Conference Fund), the Office of the Dean of Arts, and the Humanities Institute. We are grateful to the many publishers, Canadian and non-Canadian, who responded to our call to donate books published by and/or about the participants in the conference; we used the revenue from these books, sold at the conference, to subsidize the travel expenses of all the students who participated in the event. (A list of these publishers was included in the conference program.) We would like to thank the Canada Council for assistance with our evening of literary reading, and we acknowledge the Aid to Research Workshops and Conferences grant we received from the Social Sciences and Humanities Research Council of Canada. Finally, Smaro would like to acknowledge the Canada Research Chair program that financed, in part, this event and that has made possible the publication of this volume. Our special thanks to Jacqueline Larson, acquisitions editor at Wilfrid Laurier University Press at the time, who demonstrated unflagging support for the publication of this volume, and to Rob Kohlmeier, managing editor of the Press, for his meticulous attention to all aspects of this volume's production.

SK and RM

DIANA BRYDON

METAMORPHOSES OF A DISCIPLINE
RETHINKING CANADIAN LITERATURE
WITHIN INSTITUTIONAL CONTEXTS

The Questions

Three questions underpin what follows:

1. How does change happen?
2. How are TransCanadian histories carried forward?
3. How do Canadian writers and literary critics negotiate these contradictory pulls?

In Canada, literary critics studying Canadian literature have posed these as identity and agency questions: Who are we? Where is here? What is to be done? Often, these questions assumed the context of the nation, in ways that privileged examining nationalism over the structures of the nation-state.[1] This essay explores the implications of working through a different framework. What if we were to think about Canadian literary studies within the contexts of literature, institutions, and citizenship? How would such a reorientation change the terms of engagement?[2]

I employ the word "we" with caution here, to refer to a community of scholars, mostly literary, who are interested in answering the questions posed above. In certain TransCanadian contexts, people from Ontario who employ that word "we" to refer to a pan-Canadian community are often viewed with suspicion, and with good reason. In employing the word, I am not trying to ignore differences within a particular community but rather to suggest ways in which people might want to get together to talk about a common purpose, employing their disagreements to generate productive debate. Because the community produced, maintained, and promoted through the institutions of Canadian literature is part of a larger, but shrinking, community of people devoted to the entangled disciplines and pleasures of literature, on the one hand, and to a differently constituted but overlapping constituency of people committed to the survival and the improvement of the Canadian nation-state, on the other, there will inevitably be contradictory impulses at play within such an address. It is not just, as Adam Carter notes, that "While nations are geographically bounded, national imaginings have often tended toward the geographically unbounded" (111), but also that nation-states continue to organize and govern social and political life with implications for the quality of life that make a difference.[3]

What is at stake in reframing "CanLit" (the informal shorthand for Canadian literature that names it as an established formation) as TransCanada? How is the object of investigation transformed and to what ends? What does it mean to explicitly think about the roles of citizens and institutions within the contexts of literary study? Within past divisions of disciplinary responsibility, these may have been seen as insufficiently literary concerns, distracting attention from the literary text and its author toward questions about knowledge production and reception.[4] I prefer to see it as an enlarging of range to resituate the literary and redefine what is meant by literature and its study. Those who care about literature (whether it be narrowly or more broadly defined) and about informed reading practices as taught through literary study need to ask how that reframing fits within larger institutional changes, when most disciplines are asking about their methods and mandates, when universities are shifting their financing and their functions, when science and all forms of knowledge production are being brought into question, and when states are reorganizing their priorities. In the midst of this upheaval, what is the role of university teachers and researchers? The university, traditionally an elite bastion of privilege, is currently in the throes of re-creating itself as a generator of patents and a promoter of competitively achieved "excellence" along business models.[5] Could this moment of uncertain transformation be seized to create an environment for a collectively creative imagining of alternative futures?[6]

In what follows, I develop a series of interconnected arguments in an exploratory fashion. I suggest that students of Canadian literature need to pay as much attention to the state as we have to the nation. Not only must we pay attention to institutions, but we must also value them for how they can enable literary work, even while recognizing the constraints that they impose and seeking to reform them to better match the needs of our profession.[7] The nation-state, which in Canada has a distinctive history that has shaped our culture and our values, is one of these institutions that should be neither dismissed nor underestimated. Attention to the interactions of institutions, citizenship, and literature should complement but not replace attention to other dimensions of literary study. At this historical moment, however, this particular conjunction has appeared as urgently requiring investigation.

Is Canadian Literature an Institution?

This question was raised at the TransCanada conference.[8] It goes to the heart of the uneasiness some participants felt in worrying that what were once sociological questions were now overwhelmingly more properly literary ones; yet it is possible to recognize that Canadian literature as a discipline grew out of institutional imperatives and exists within institutional contexts without reducing it entirely to its institutional dimensions. This section argues that the study of Canadian literature as an academic discipline grew out of the same area studies Cold War moment that produced Canadian studies (as Richard Cavell discusses elsewhere in this volume) but that it has now developed in its anglophone form as a subdiscipline of English Literary Studies, in its francophone form as a subdiscipline of French, and in its comparative study as part of comparative literature.[9] It is still working out its relation to Indigenous, diaspora, and postcolonial studies. Of these, Indigenous studies may pose the most radical challenge.[10] As Canadian literary studies merges with Canadian cultural studies, it becomes more interdisciplinary and arguably more anglophone, moving beyond the sphere of English into interaction with anthropology, sociology, and political studies. These disciplines operate in relation to established physical institutions, such as the university, research granting bodies, libraries, publishers, and academic societies. Canadian literature also exists in different institutional contexts outside the university. The writers and dramatists who produce the literature, the media that publicize it, and the readers and audiences who enjoy it also operate within their own institutional structures, both within and beyond the nation.[11] While individuals often assume a certain autonomy of action, paying little overt attention to the unwritten rules and regulations that legislate acceptable thinking or behaviour within these institutionalized contexts, these contexts influence action within the field. Rather than ignore these contexts, it can be useful to study them.

Literary studies, like Canadian literature, have always been fascinated by the identity question: what is Literature? To ask about the literary institution is to shift the terms of debate.[12] As Jeffrey Williams suggests, this question forces attention to "the institutional parameters and places demarcated by the rubric of literature." In short, "the question of literature is inseparable from our institutional practices and locations" (*Institution* 1). Since these institutional vectors are "constitutive and deeply formative of what we do" (3), we need to understand them and if necessary, change them to better suit what we want to do.

Williams employs Pierre Bourdieu's definition of *habitus*—as "the system of dispositions common to all products of the same conditionings" ("Structure" 59)—as "a way to characterize the institutional practices and conditions that actualize ideology" ("Life" 212). By this he means to draw attention to the "implacable way in which our institutional positions make us" (206). In investigating the limits and terms of the institutional *habitus* of English in the US, he develops an important argument against Edward Said's critique of professionalism, suggesting convincingly that our choice is not, as Said posed it, "between professionalism and anti-professionalism, but between different kinds of professionalism, and different ways to act within institutions" (218). This is an especially important reminder at a time when populist suspiciousness of elites is on the rise. The university itself is not an ivory tower but a form of public sphere, which participates within the national public sphere in ways that are institutionally determined but that also provide some space for agency and transformation. At the same time, Lawrence Buell is surely correct to note that "Criticism worthy of the name arises from commitments deeper than professionalism" (97). A commitment to language and literature may coexist with other commitments, to the environment (the topic of Buell's focus) or to social justice and equity. Literary study provides an especially wide scope for writers and readers to work through their engagements with the word and the world.

Michael Denning suggests that theories such as Williams's that stress ideological readings of institutional practices may be usefully supplemented by interpretations that employ the Gramscian notion of hegemony, which Denning sees as a theory of action as well as structure. Understanding hegemony begins "from the question of how social movements are organized among both the dominant and subordinate groups, of how social formations are led" (Denning 110). In this way, "a theory of hegemony provides the framework by which we may examine the historical articulations of class formations and commodity forms" (111). As a form of cultural practice,

Canadian literature became important to the national project at a certain point in time. The canon that emerged after the publication of Margaret Atwood's *Survival* identified a set of norms, values, and beliefs within a certain set of texts, which were then disseminated, taught, and studied within the formation that came to be called CanLit. What requires further study is the function of the myths that arose around this field, perhaps especially myths of Canadian innocence, deference, and goodwill.[13]

Like literature, "Canada" is an institutionally produced entity. With globalization, as institutional contexts change and come under scrutiny, literature, Canada and the notion of a national literature have all become problematized concepts. With the rise of new technologies, reading and entertainment are changing their functions, and literature no longer seems as important as it once did. With transnational mobilities of capital and people, nation-state functions are changing and the legitimacy of this institution is also being questioned. At such a moment, it becomes easier to see that the very concept of national literatures is the product of a particular time and place, and of a way of perceiving the world that may be losing its relevance or at least shifting its functions.

In this essay, then, I suggest that there is value in looking at Canadian literature as an institution in the looser sense of "designating an established practice or tradition" and in the more concrete sense of considering some of the ways in which it organizes and promotes its continuance through formally institutionalized structures (Williams, *Institution* 2–3). This looser sense includes Derek Attridge's observation that "To respond fully to a work that presents itself as literary one has to be embedded in the culture of which literature, and perhaps the literary form, is a part, and one has to deploy one's familiarity with the conventionalized routines of the literary institution. A great deal of patient labour is unavoidable if a responsible reading is to be achieved; but it represents only the foundation of such a reading" (86–87).[14] Furthermore, the literary text is "a set of coded signals which become a poem or a novel only in a specific reading, and within which the reader too comes into being (as a singular subject partly produced in the reading of the work)" (87). This latter process constitutes what I call in a later section of this essay, following Donna Pennee, literary citizenship, and it involves resistant as well as obedient responses if it is to prove effective.

Concrete literary institutions that contribute to the CanLit institution may be divided into three somewhat overlapping categories: government departments, agencies, and arms-length institutions that depend for their funding on the state; the market sector; and civil society non-profit organizations. While these deserve fuller attention, my interest here is in the more nebulous academic discipline that relies for its continuance on all of the above. My lifetime has seen the rise and re-formation of CanLit as an institution. Writers wrote in Canada before the rise of CanLit, and they continue to write here now, but the field and its institutional supports are shifting. Where once the nation and its literature were thought within the frame of international dynamics (implicitly if not always explicitly), it is now more common to understand these within postnational, transnational, and globalized contexts. When McClelland and Stewart issued the New Canadian Library paperback series, my parents bought the first run.[15] There were no courses in Canadian literature in the English department when I did my Honours degree in English Language and Literature at the University of Toronto in 1968–72. English as a replacement for religion; English as an education for citizenship: these were the implied but seldom-stated justifications for the discipline when I entered it.[16] They are under pressure now. Religion is reviving. Citizenship is fragmenting and multiplying. Literature is less hegemonic a formation than it once was.

Academic disciplines work, as we know, to "legitimate particular organizations of meaning" (Trouillot 8). It is helpful to compare the current crisis of English with that of anthropology. Michel-Rolph Trouillot argues that, in facing "dramatically new historical conditions of performance" (9), anthropology now needs to contest its historical formation. English and Canadian literary studies are involved in a similar process of rethinking beginnings. Anthropology was produced within a North Atlantic imaginary to fill what Trouillot terms "the savage slot" in an organization of knowledge production that is quickly becoming obsolete. To move forward, not just the slot but also "the symbolic order upon which it is premised" must now be questioned (23). Canadian literature finds itself in a similar position. Richard Cavell notes that Canadian studies is a product of the Cold War, but it is also a product of imperialism and formal negotiations among British, French, and Indigenous peoples over centuries.[17]

If anthropology occupied—and may still occupy—the savage slot within civilizational discourse of the colonial period, then literary studies, especially English, took the cultivated slot, the civilizational slot, the slot of Western "us" versus non-Western "them." How this worked in Canada is being studied, but more remains to be done, especially because Canadian literary studies complicates the pictures being drawn both of English and of postcolonial studies.[18]

The interplay between "civilization" and "culture" defines the scope of English studies in the twentieth century. Civilizational discourse dominated the first half of the century. Elsewhere in this volume, Daniel Coleman examines some of the ways that this discourse operated and continues to operate within an institutionalized Whiteness and discourses of civility in Canadian culture. With decolonization, culture replaced civilization as the coded term for the self-assumed superiority of the West. Out of the "culture wars" of the late twentieth century, civilization made a comeback, asserted in Samuel Huntington's "clash of civilizations" thesis and reaffirmed, for the Western triumphalist imagination, by 9/11 and its aftermath.[19] If the savage slot has been assigned to anthropology, then the "civilized slot," with all its ambiguities and hidden power dynamics, would appear to be the place assigned to English.

In such a system, English and anthropology emerged as secret sharers and English and sociology as rivals. Canadian literature is both complicit with this system and anomalous within it. Many of my colleagues in Canadian literature have been active in documenting and re-evaluating dimensions of this system. Part of the motivation behind the TransCanada conference was to share what we were learning and to think about how we could coordinate our efforts while generating new activity around them. From my own perspective as a postcolonial critic within the discipline who is also experimenting with work within a large interdisciplinary team, and as someone who is personally committed to the importance of maintaining a Canadian-based perspective in research on globalization and cultural studies, I find Canadian literary studies both enabling and constricting. I want to resist both commodified forms of nationalism *and* calls to postnationalism. I find that there is an increasingly imperfect fit between my own analyses of the problems faced by the humanities today and subsequent prescriptions for their solution, on the one hand, and those generated by colleagues working within the United States, on the other. My concern lies less with the dwindling cultural capital of my profession and more with the need to address the gaps between at least three intersecting discourses: a state-sponsored national boosterism in Canada, which currently promotes Canada as "model citizen for the twenty-first century" (Welsh 187), within which literature is often enlisted as an alibi (Iyer); a social justice critique of "the dark side of the nation" (Bannerji) and its cultural and institutional formations (Razack); and what Imre Szeman terms the "unspoken assumption" within some forms of Canadian literary criticism that "the writing produced in the nation must of necessity thematize the conditions of possibility of the nation itself"

(*Zones* 156). Such debates are further complicated by globalizing pressures, which have led some to theorize "literature as a globalized system" (Casanova, qtd. in Said, *Humanism* 128).

Global Contexts

To talk about literature in the contexts of institutions and citizenship leads to questioning some of the current terms through which globalizing processes are understood, especially Michael Ignatieff's "rights revolution" and Anthony Giddens's "runaway world." I distrust these terms because they keep current ideological frameworks intact. Equity-seeking groups such as women, First Nations, and anyone racialized within an assumed White normativity are cast in these narratives as themselves responsible for "our" runaway world through their "rights" demands. Exactly whose world is running away here? There are things I don't want to lose: literature (but I don't mind surrendering the capital L); the rational scepticism that characterizes academic inquiry at its best; a disinterested search for truth based on carefully sifting and testing the evidence available. Giddens is correct in noting that these values are threatened by the rise of various fundamentalisms, which themselves fear "the loosening hold of tradition, in institutions and in everyday life" (61); but he is only partly correct, I think, about the causes for these shifts. Ignatieff explicitly invokes a backlash frame, which I detect in subtler form in Giddens as well. Ignatieff states, "Let us acknowledge that the rights revolution must shoulder some share of the blame for family breakup and its consequences in our society" (*Rights* 106). In this view, any gains in equity exert a reactive cost. The politics of blame are used to blame the victims. Giddens asserts, "We shall never be able to become the masters of our own history, but we can and must find ways of bringing our runaway world to heel" (23). In the context he sets up, it is not unfettered capitalism or neoliberal globalization that create the runaway world, but women, the colonized, and other rights-seeking groups demanding changes to the status quo. Giddens and Ignatieff focus on social institutions, such as the family, and on citizens, for making their claims, but they implicitly see citizens as normatively male and White, rights-bearing individuals who own citizenship and only grudgingly share its perks. In contrast to such views, I find value in alternative histories of the legitimating values associated with the development of Canadian citizenship and in current proposals for expanding its agencies and its protections.

Citizenship

In what follows, then, I contest the view of the citizen implied by Giddens and Ignatieff, who privilege a rights discourse based on the individual and the social and cultural institutions of private life. Such a focus downplays the role of the state and distrusts or discounts the nation. I recognize citizenship as a foundational institution of democratic governance (Brodie 323) and take my working definition from Bryan Turner: citizenship is "that set of practices (juridical, political, economic, and cultural) which define a person as a competent member of society, and which as a consequence shape the flow of resources to persons and social groups" (2). Citizen activism, as it is being encouraged in Americanized, neo-liberal and even some social democracy movements associated with anti-globalization, can be diverted from participating in such institutionalized practices toward ineffective protests or band-aid solutions. Citizenship, although widely valorized as central to democracy, is not in itself an automatic good. It can be highjacked by populist movements with antisocial, anti-intellectual, and totalitarian agendas as easily as it may be turned toward progressive purposes.

On Canadian citizenship, my position is similar to that articulated by Caroline Andrew: it is important in Canada to think about citizenship as "multilayered" rather than exclusive (316). Using the vocabulary of interscalar relations, Andrew suggests that we can avoid thinking in terms of "a preestablished order of priority," moving instead to looking "at specific conditions, specific struggles, and specific sets of actors" (317). Against those who worry about what will hold the state together under such a shift, I am persuaded by Peter Russell's position, that "participation in a common political space" in which the terms of sharing can be negotiated and renegotiated will be a stronger glue than any fiction of a "common sense of civic identity" (283).[20] The shift from thinking through identity to conceptualizing the public sphere is not without its own challenges, but it holds potential for rethinking how Canadian literature operates within TransCanadian and global spheres.[21]

What are the roles for teachers and critics of Canadian literature in expanding those spaces? Clearly the classroom figures in the interscalar view of intersecting and multilayered modes of "citizenization" (Tully 9, qtd. in Russell 283). Cynthia Sugars's *Home-Work* elaborates some of these challenges and the strong institutional pressures working against innovative practice. In that collection, Donna Pennee argues that it can be helpful to "keep on the table for discussion how the *literary* and the *national* remain categories and modes of productivity and reproductivity" ("Literary" 76). She builds on the work of Smaro Kamboureli and Len Findlay, developing their idea of "critical citizenship" into an agenda for what she calls "literary citizenship." She suggests that "Literary studies organized under the rubric of the national create a space to ask civic questions of state policies and inherited notions of nationalism" (81). Globalization does not eliminate the need for such a space, but it may reorient some of the questions that need to be asked. As she concludes, "For the time being, there is no question of doing without the national; it is rather a matter of doing the national differently" (83). Doing the national differently will involve greater attention to institutions, citizenship, and the politics of the "trans," which through globalizing processes draws attention to the ways in which the nation is embedded in the global rather than stressing its distinctiveness. Possibly it may also involve paying more attention to what Michael Hardt and Antonio Negri term the "multitude" and Ian Angus "emergent publics."

From my reading in the explosion of citizenship literature over the last two decades, I am convinced that citizenship should not be disaggregated in analysis from the institutions that exercise regulative power, most especially the state (for a similar position, see Kurtz and Hankins), but also the university and other pre-existing public institutions, many of which, in Canada, depend on the state. Current enthusiasms for new social movements and the civil society sphere should not blind us to what can be accomplished through established institutions.[22] With Ian Angus, I agree that the role of the citizen in democracies is to "*judge* social, economic and political institutions, not pre-suppose their legitimacy" (10, emphasis in original), but I cannot share his faith in the value of shifting the emphasis of democracy from "institutional political practices" toward seeing it as "the core of a style of life" (19). Such a notion of citizenship, in de-emphasizing the role of the nation-state and its institutions, seems too close to trends identified by Lauren Berlant in the United States during the Reagan years, when "conservative ideology ... convinced a citizenry that the core context of politics should be the sphere of private life" (3). Ignatieff and Giddens share this view. As Berlant puts it, that ideology functions through the "story the official national culture industry tells in the contemporary United States" (13). Recent critical articles on biological, scientific, and cyborg citizenship also locate citizen agency within the private sphere of neo-liberalism, which operates "through the calculative choice of formally free actors" according to a market logic (Collier and Ong, "Global Assemblages" 13).[23] Canadians are being invited to assent to a local version of such trends through the emergence of a new brand of official CanLit—the "Globalit" story, promoted most memorably by Pico Iyer in *The Global Soul*, but available almost everywhere in media and publicity hype.[24] This view exists in uneasy tension with an older official CanLit story and supplements earlier versions of official Canadian multiculturalism.

The notion that private life is political licenses a turning away from formally constituted political institutions and a tendency to downplay the power that the state continues to wield. Academic writing that applauds citizen activism in newly authorized spheres, such as voluntarism and personal management of the self, tends to ignore the limits to agency built into these dynamics. In a world where everything has been politicized to the detriment of the genuinely political, Literature (with a capital L) remains a battleground as the traditional humanities disciplines divide between those who share the fears evoked by Giddens's "runaway world" and those seeking to understand what it means to say, with Arjun Appadurai, that "the globe has begun to spin in new ways" (*Modernity* 58).

Within such contexts, what does literary citizenship mean? I have suggested that it implies several things: the responsibilities of the literary scholar to her subject, her profession, her national and global situatedness, and her students, whom she introduces to these overlapping worlds. Insofar as the politics of citizenship entails "a struggle over ... the meaning and scope of membership of the community in which one lives" (Hall and Held 176, qtd. in Rosaldo 30), then the implications for what Renato Rosaldo calls "cultural citizenship"—that is, citizenship anchored "in the aspirations and perceptions of people who occupy subordinate social positions" (38)—are operative at both national and global levels in complicated ways.[25] Clearly cultural and literary citizenship need to be thought together on a range of scales. While global citizenship is now being considered something that both nations and individuals may aspire to, I think it unwise to pin hopes for social justice to action at the global level alone.

Metamorphoses

Neither literature nor citizenship, as I understand them, can be unconditionally valorized nor seen as exempt from current battles over power or from change itself. The trend within literary studies today is to valorize literature's extra-institutional qualities. Without wishing to deny these, I have suggested that critics also attend to the ways in which literary studies, but also literature itself, are formed institutionally. Defenders of literature, myself included, write as if it had the power, if not to create a better world, then at least to disturb complacent understandings and enable imaginings of alternatives. Surely this is the test we need to apply to Canadian literature today. Gayatri Spivak and Wai Chee Dimock invest their hopes for planetarity as a new mode of cosmopolitical consciousness in literature, described by Spivak "as what escapes the system" (Spivak *Death* 52) and by Dimock as a force "impossible to regulate or police" (174). For Derek Attridge, literature provides a way into understanding how "otherness enters, and changes, a cultural sphere" (19). Marina Warner draws attention to the "transformational power of storytelling itself" (210). These various attentions (which could be endlessly proliferated) indicate that literature still matters to many but that it depends for its power on its readers and their ability to act responsibly, in the double sense of responding to the call of the text and acting responsibly as a result (Attridge 131). While these are the roles performed by literary citizenship, they cannot accurately be predicted or generalized beyond their particular occasions.

Can these views of literature's anarchic force and social functions be reconciled with each other, and with the worlds currently authorized by the Canadian literary institution of which I am a part? The various canon wars, political correctness debates, and attacks on tenured radicals and postcolonial scholars, spilling over from the United States, draw attention to the struggle over control of the imagination that continues in the nation's public institutions and that in recent times has broadened out from attacks on literary study to embrace multiculturalism, postcolonialism, area studies, and secularism, perhaps especially in the United States, but the real danger here may be of an unwarranted Canadian complacency about our imagined immunity to the worst of these disputes.

As Ovid and Atwood note, metamorphoses can be frightening as well as enabling. Literature and its study are changing, and it will not be sufficient to retrench to the mandates of earlier times. Fear and the new utilitarianism are uniting to cement old Canadian colonialisms in their liberal forms into positions that can seem enlightened when compared with what is happening south of our border and elsewhere in the world; but truly dissident literary texts and their sharper analyses still find less scope for sparking discussion within dominant Canadian public spheres. While diaspora and globalization studies celebrate global flows, official Canadian discourse remains obsessed with social cohesion and integration, centre and margin, seeking to enforce a unified vision that might still contain what Smaro Kamboureli characterizes as "a history that bursts its seams" (*Making* 1). These are the two sides of globalization as we know it. Could they be brought into productive dialogue through embracing the politics and poetics of the "trans"?

TransCanada: The Politics and Poetics of the Trans

TransCanada: railroads and pipelines; communication and transportation; Pierre Berton, Harold Innis, Roy Kiyooka, Maria Campbell. The official story and its challengers. *The National Dream, Bias in Communications, Transcanada Letters,* the *Road Allowance People.* Implied in TransCanada, as conventionally employed, are the great themes of the nation-building narrative: transportation and communication; a movement from east to west, from sea to sea, from civilization to wilderness; a march of progress; a resistance to north/south pulls and to the ethos of the United States. Berton popularizes the state's capitalist venture as a triumph of the nation. Innis attends to the material contexts underpinning the national myth. Kiyooka reverses the directionality of that movement from Europe west, shifting the gaze from west to east. Campbell attends to the Road Allowance People, the Métis shunted to the side by the triumphal march of progress.

Is it already too late to focus on rethinking the integrationist assumptions behind the highway and railroad myths—the Trans-Canada Highway, the Trans-Canada Railway? Are new metaphors now energizing Canadian social and political imaginaries? Is Canada becoming transnational in ways that undermine the original impetus of the Trans-Canada, or has it always been so, with these so-called national links seamlessly congruent with global capitalism, given the privileging of goods over people in both? If the old Trans-Canadian imagination was already complicit with globalization, is there a place for a new TransCanada within current theorizations of planetarity, and if so, where might that be? These are genuine questions that Canadian creative texts are asking in a variety of ways and that literary critics need to continue investigating.[26]

In its call for papers and in published work by Roy Miki, the TransCanada project offers the Penelopean metaphor of "unravelling the nation."[27] I read this as a call to recognize that the creation of any imagined community is a continuous work in progress, involving making and unmaking, learning and unlearning, aiming not to fix boundaries but to encourage movements across them. If the role of the state is to consolidate, then the role of literature is to unravel those consolidations through the kinds of critique, questioning, and reimagining that enable new groupings to form that may be more responsive to the needs of the day. These processes need to be seen as complementary, but not in any simple way. I like to imagine government agencies such as the Department of Canadian Heritage and Metropolis networks[28] toiling on "integration," just as Penelope wove during the day, while writers unravel the integrationist texts of the nation, just as Penelope unravelled her creation at night. Might it be possible to imagine more productive forms of engagement between the nation's literary and governmental workers? I believe so, if the instrumentalist view of literature is abandoned and the time taken to respond to literary texts within the terms they set.[29] As I have suggested, multilayered forms of citizenship and asymmetrical modes of belonging, as theorized within Canadian political science, seem more congruent with current literary trends than do singular notions of the citizen and of national belonging. Shared value systems based on a willingness to enter into debate and an openness to change may provide stronger social glue than shared identities (Henderson and McEwan). Released from merely instrumental views of its functions, literature becomes more powerful. Both literature and the state need to be released from focussing on identity to contemplate what makes a good society.

In response to globalization, some have argued that we need new terms. I am suggesting that some of the traditional terms of Canadian identity and nationalism may need to be reconsidered. Hardt and Negri wish to move beyond terms such as representation, sovereignty, and citizenship, which they find too deeply imbricated in the politics of the nation-state (Brown and Szeman). I think that more may be gained by reclaiming and reshaping some of these old terms. In particular, most people still need the protections provided by the state, limited and fickle as those protections may be.[30] Richard Sandbrook summarizes Lou Pauly's contribution to *Civilizing Gobalization* as arguing that "national governments of industrial countries still possess the leeway to buffer their populations from harmful global trends—if they possess the political will to do so" (8). This is the position that I endorse: that political will can be strengthened through literary engagements and the kind of research and teaching that we perform in the university.[31]

Planetarity

In turning to planetarity at the end of this chapter, I gesture toward the need to rethink Canadian literature beyond older forms of nationalism and internationalism, and toward multiscaled visions of place—local, regional, national, and global—each imbricated within the other. Writers and critics are rethinking relations of place, space, and non-place in ways that complicate understandings of where and how the nation fits. They are not transcending nation but resituating it.

In her use of planetarity, Gayatri Spivak rethinks these relations within and beyond the disciplinary contexts of area studies and comparative literature. What I especially value in her work is the principled effort to think outside of given institutional constraints without imagining that one can do away with institutions entirely. Spivak's *Death of a Discipline* can be productively read beside Jeffrey Williams's edited collection *The Institution of Literature*, which as I have indicated earlier, documents the ways in which literary and academic institutions shape, acculturate, and "discipline" those for whom these structures are their *habitus*. Both Williams and Spivak argue against divorcing the literary from the political into separate forms of academic specialization that seem increasingly problematic in a world characterized by globalization's "complex connectivity" (Tomlinson 13). To identify the need for more inter- and cross-disciplinary dialogue, however, is easier than to determine how to take on such work, especially when some institutional frameworks seem to be out of synch with such projects.

In the sshrc-funded Major Collaborative Research Initiative on Globalization and Autonomy in which I work, for example, students are learning to work across disciplines and value what they learn, but they also worry that these skills may actually hurt them on the job market. Their fears seem well-founded. Few hiring practices are synchronized with emerging research models or with the recognition that globalization may be changing how meanings are made and knowledge produced. The model of interruption and complementarity that Spivak offers in *Death of a Discipline* is productive for thinking about doing interdisciplinary work from a perspective based in literary models of reading but does not address these practical problems. She finds in the chorus of classical Greek drama and the First Nations ghost dance images of interruption and alterity that counter the narratives produced by what she describes as "a time and place that has privatized the imagination and pitted it against the political" (37–38). Spivak offers various routes out of this dilemma: interruption, "turn and return" (46), "academic labour" (54), reconstellation (91), recasting women, not as a "special case" but as representing the human (70), "gender as a general critical instrument" (74), renewing a commitment to reading as learning "to dis-figure the undecidable figure into a responsible literality, again and again," and proposing "the planet to overwrite the globe" (72).[32] These tactics can all be thought productively, within the contingencies of different locations. Their value lies in resetting the terms of engagement.

Paul Gilroy takes planetarity in a different direction, locating it as a discourse centred on suffering, in which "suffering rather than autonomy and self-possession" lies at the heart of a reimagined public culture ("Where" 274). Within the contexts of the ethical turn, the so-called war on terror, and discussion of the role of torture in promoting democracy, such an approach may seem reasonable. However, my own research takes a different turn. I want to decouple Gilroy's linking of autonomy and self-possession to pose autonomy against "possessive individualism" as it has been analyzed by C. B. Macpherson and developed by others.[33] In this respect, I find Henry Giroux's emphasis on autonomy in his article "Education after Abu Ghraib" productive for thinking through global citizenship responsibilities. Giroux finds in the events of Abu Ghraib questions "about education as both the subject and object of a democratic society and how we might engage it differently" (793). He finds inspiration in Theodor Adorno's argument that "The only true force against the principle of Auschwitz would be human autonomy ... that is the force of reflection and self-determination" (Hohendahl 58, qtd. in Giroux 796). These processes can be activated through renewing citizenship in its various public participations, including renewing and making accountable nation-state institutions and encouraging the reading, writing, and discussion of literature. Spivak concludes that "In this era of global capital triumphant, to keep responsibility alive in the reading and teaching of the textual is at first sight impractical. It is, however, the right of the textual to be so responsible, responsive, answerable" (Death 101–102). For Canadian literary critics, that means reading our national literature in global contexts and in dialogue with Indigeneous concerns.[34] Canadians have much to learn from the texts emerging from the new South Africa, as it undergoes its own metamorphoses from an apartheid settler state to a multicultural democracy. TransCanada, as I wish to understand the term, can no longer invoke a "national dream" (Berton) but must find its way toward imagining a renewed federalism within a planetary imaginary.

RINALDO WALCOTT

AGAINST INSTITUTION
ESTABLISHED LAW,
CUSTOM, OR PURPOSE

Anecdote 1

Some time in the early 1970s, when still living in Barbardos, I received a number of books from Canada. I still remember two of those books. One was by Farley Mowat, and the other was by James Baldwin. The Baldwin made a bigger impression on me than the Mowat, for after all it was the height of Black Power in the Anglo-Caribbean. I recently tried to identify which Mowat book I received, but I could not figure it out. The Baldwin book was *Go Tell It on the Mountain*, I am sure of that. At the same time, I received the books I needed to prepare for that notoriously muscular experience called the Eleven Plus or Common Entrance Examination, which Austin Clarke writes so wittily about in *Growing Up Stupid under the Union Jack*. Some of the muscularity of the examination involved knowing the geography of Canada, especially that of the East Coast and the Grand Banks, better than Caribbean geography would ever be known by us. Such were the parameters of a still-colonial education in the aftermath of flag independence. I arrived in Canada knowing more about it than it would know about me. Canada would have been in me even if I had never arrived here. I might add, salted cod notwithstanding. The ingesting of Canadian salted cod, with its enduring colonial and racialized economic history, places Canada, at least metaphorically, within the domain of the Anglo-Caribbean.

Why begin with the above anecdote? In my trajectory as a scholar I have been obsessively concerned with the unruliness and non-foundationality of the Black Diaspora. I am particularly invested in Canada's Black Diaspora, but it was not always so. It was at first an interest, which continues, in African American and Caribbean subject formation that led to my concern with diaspora. The shift to Black Canada was one occasioned by the coming into a sense of citizenship in the eventful moment of the Yonge Street Riot of 1992 when the non-relationality between Blackness and something called Canadianness became evidently clear to me as a political subject.[1] In the eventful moment of that riot, much changed for me. I began to ask the questions that Black British scholars had been asking: Is it possible to be Black and British? What does it mean to be Black and British? I had to ask what and how to be Black and Canadian meant—even why this question was necessary. Asking these questions forced me to question the state narrative of multiculturalism, right alongside an encounter with outer-national Black affiliations and difference—even other national commitments.

Anecdote 2

I am trained as a sociologist in a faculty of education. My training immediately makes me sensitive and self-conscious about my academic location since many scholars in the academy have little respect for and/or interest in what happens in faculties of education (sometimes rightly so). I work in the department that I was trained in. When I applied for the job, the letter of invitation to the interview asked that I situate my scholarship within the discipline of sociology. I was at first shocked, but then I turned to W. E. B. Dubois. As one of North America's first sociologists, despite hardly making it into that disciplinary canon, Dubois offers a model and a method that are multidisciplinary and interdisciplinary, infused with what Jacques Derrida calls a cosmopolitical ethics. I modestly model my scholarship after him. It is a model that requires scholarship to articulate a politics of ethico-political concerns.

Why this anecdote? I am an interdisciplinary scholar, so much so that sometimes I honestly forget which discipline I am trained in. I am invested in and committed to an ethico-political project, which might produce new forms of human life (Wynter, "Pope"). I reproduce this anecdote because, while education desires to become a discipline to its own detriment, the disciplines in their insistence on "epistemological respectability" (Haver, "Of Mad" 352) refuse to leverage any opening to the discipline of education as having anything to contribute to education (outside of K to 12, that is). We must simultaneously refuse education's faulty desire to be a discipline and at the same time refuse and challenge the disciplinary tyranny of epistemological respectability and its resulting repressions. In this essay, I speak sideways to disciplinary respectability and explicitly against institutions, against the establishment of form and its manifold repressions. Thus I put out a call to all committed to ethico-political scholarship to act as if the "discipline has gone astray," as Diana Brydon put it in her TransCanada address.

The Argument

Let me return to where I concluded my first anecdote, on the question of multiculturalism as an institution in Canada. It seems that the TransCanada conference is poised to "memorialize the moment before obliteration," as Spivak says in another context of multiculturalism ("Harlem" 126), as a central and important category of Canadian literary studies. It appears that the moment of Canadian multiculturalism might be morphing into a transliterary moment of some substance, but I would suggest not with the attendant political imperatives of the multicultural historical past. I hope I misunderstand such a desire. I want to hold onto the idea of multiculturalism before I move to trans-anything, as a way to hold onto history, struggle, and the desire to resignify what the category of the human might and could mean. Along with Stuart Hall, I believe that "multiculturalism is now so discursively entangled that it can only be used 'under erasure.' Nevertheless, since we have no less implicated concepts to think this problem with, we have no alternative but to go on using and interrogating it" (Hall, "Conclusion" 209). Conceptually, multiculturalism is a major concession, as the liberal democratic nation-state does not extend citizenship in equal fashion to all its members. Such a concession opens up vast opportunities for rethinking the nation and for state struggles, and thus for rethinking liberal versions of citizenship and national belonging.

As part of the struggle to keep on using and interrogating multiculturalism, I like to invoke Himani Bannerji's term "popular multiculturalism" (*Dark* 5) or everyday multiculturalism, which are inextricably different from official multiculturalism. Recently, Dionne Brand in *What We All Long For* renders everyday multiculturalism visibly present among a group of twenty-somethings living in Toronto. Brand's rendition of multiculturalism is very different from the Aga Khan's recent investment in state multiculturalism in his diversity centre in Toronto. Multiculturalism in that venture becomes a form of Canada's global capital in the information society, to be consumed by others, especially Europeans. Everyday or popular multiculturalism requires us to think about the lives people make across differences and, importantly, connections that produce new modes of relationality and being.

This brings me to a curious phrase in "TransCanada: A Rationale" that the conference is not "triggered by anxiety over the loss of the margin" (*TransCanada*). The phrase produces an interesting sensation for me. What is the margin being lost? Whose margin is being lost? Margin in relation to what or from what? Who is anxious? I ask these questions as a prelude to another set of concerns. In over the more than thirty years that official multiculturalism in Canada has been critiqued by scholars on the Left, we have produced a body of research that points to its failure to produce a liberatory citizenry and its success at managing difference, especially racial difference. The time is ripe for a move away from official multiculturalism and a rethinking and reformulation of multiculturalism as ordinary and everyday.

Most recently, there appears to be a notion within the culture industries that Canada as a nation-state has achieved its multicultural moment of integration. Racial minority writers are published by large corporate outfits; visual artists, for example, Stan Douglas, are de-raced international stars; Atom Egoyan is Canada's singular international filmmaker with Armenian ethnic flavour; hip hop reigns supreme and Flow 93.5 now exists on your dial (if in Toronto); we could go on with examples. However, as Diana Brydon points out in her paper in this volume, "truly dissident literary texts and their sharper analyses still find less scope for sparking discussion within dominant Canadian public spheres." I am not suggesting that the writers and artists named above do not produce dissident texts—some of them do. The issue is that on the surface all looks well; arrival has been achieved. Thus talk of marginalization must seek different terms for a discussion to proceed. We need a theory of contradiction. We require institution without form, without laws, without rules.

Along with Spivak ("Harlem") and many others, I see a necessary and urgent need for a return to the collective. Any theory of contradiction must allow for a method to think the social and political categorization of our lives in overlapping and disjunctive ways. It is my contention that we must harken to the call of both Paul Gilroy (*Postcolonial Melancholia*) and Jacques Derrida (*Of Hospitality*), and turn to thinking and resuscitating notions of conviviality and hospitality respectively. Both notions offer us a way to work through the more stifling forms of identity politics without claiming that identity and its practices no longer matter. Such a return must twin class with racialization if we are to adequately imagine a genuine multicultural nation. Such a return to radical forms of conviviality and hospitality requires that we struggle against and, importantly, with nation-state discourses and practices of multiculturalism that produce what Spivak calls "mandatory culturalism" ("Harlem" 119) so that we might make of multiculturalism a different idea and thus practice.

In the context of racial profiling, debates about 9/11 security measures, immigration, and same-sex marriage have been rife in this country. All of these require talk of institution and institutions. To be against institution is then to be against the terms upon which the neo-liberal project legitimizes itself as a project that seeks to remake the human as a function of capitalist production. Within the context of knowledge production, our task then is to produce forms of pedagogical enquiry and engagements that lead towards what Diana Brydon, in her TransCanada conference address, rightly posed as "the conditions that could enable genuine dialogue to begin across currently privileged and eclipsed cultures." Brydon argues, "We need to pay attention to theory and the arts, even when at first sight they may seem to divert us from the urgent social issues of our day" ("Metamorphoses"). I think that this statement opens up a nuanced terrain that pushes literary studies into its worldiness. Thus I take up Brydon's challenge of literature's worldiness as possibly the only way that we might move towards remaking the human as a project of struggle that continues to refuse the dogmas of capital's advocates, which turn us all into units for commodity production and consumption.

As I wrote this paper, I spent time moving between Wayde Compton's amazingly performative poetics in *Performance Bond* and the War Party's album, *The Resistance*. The War Party is a First Nations rap group. I have tried to make sense of why I was repeatedly drawn to these two texts for thinking about these issues. The texts are brilliant in their artistry, but that is not why I kept returning to them. As I read and listened more carefully, the texts spoke to each other in their own ways, revealing a Canadian multicultural sensibility that shocked me to the core. Each of these texts is intended to do something political, social, and cultural, as S. Wynter puts it in "Rethinking 'Aesthetics.'" Take, for example, Compton's "Illegalese: Floodgate Dub" from *Performance Bond*. Its first line echoes histories: "if you arrive in the belly of a rusting imagination, there are grounds to outlaw you" (31). Then, Compton performs a poem/text that details the history of particular forms of crossing borders in search of a potential humane life, and the contradictory responses and forces that create the difficulties and the promise of such crossings. The epigraph to *Performance Bond* is taken from the Enforcement Section of Citizenship and Immigration Canada's legislation: "where a guarantor is necessary to ensure compliance, the Performance Bond form must be used" (Canada, "Detention"). In Compton's work, present touches past and identities cross each other as he poeticizes a cosmopolitical ethics that seeks to open a space for a different imagining of the nation. *Performance Bond* thus reminds us of the ways in which capitalism infiltrates and bonds us all to various non-human qualities masquerading as human existence, all the while framing the nation.

The War Party is of a similar but different order of cosmopolitical ethics. The first track on the album is a spoken word performance featuring Chuck D, formerly of Public Enemy. War Party's collaboration with Chuck D should not be read just as sharing the stage with a legendary rapper. At stake is a creole solidarity that reworks notions of indigeneity, belonging, and, ultimately, citizenship on the grounds of what I would propose is an ethical belonging. The rest of the album is a restating of First Nations resistance to the ongoing colonial conditions of Indigenous lives with a clear acknowledgement of living within a New World. The War Party is committed to an amelioration of the colonial condition that renders the new context new for all of us. What I mean by ethical belonging partially entails a reclaiming and rearticulation of subordinate and subaltern humanity as a site of strategic universalism, as Paul Gilroy suggests (*Against Race*). Such strategic universalism as espoused by subaltern artists must in fact be read as a form of resistance, which is a refusal to see the world only from the place of subordination or victimhood.

What Compton and the War Party produce is a cosmopolitical ethics and a pedagogy that requires us to engage the world beyond "divisive identitarianism and/or benign diversitarianism," as Spivak puts it ("Harlem" 136). Nation-state multiculturalism mandates such forms of diversitarianism. So why be against institutions? What's at stake? In my scholarly life, I refuse to engage in a practice that produces what William Haver calls "intellectual technicians devoted to the bureaucratic service of the concept" ("Another University" 26). The idea of the concept in the disciplines is the foundation of institution and thus the first repressive mechanism. Thus in this call to be unruly, to be non-foundational, to be rigorous in the politicality of the project of producing knowledge for a world of possibility and potentiality, interdisciplinarity must mean something more than the university's and the Social Science and Humanities Research Council's current institutional remaking of it as yet another marketing tool. In Haver's words, we must "make the political appear," not obscure it (27).

Conclusion: A Personal Note on the Problem of Institution

In standing up against institution, one must build institutions that allow for the promiscuity of concepts and their undoing. Thus I have brought together a group of colleagues to found *New Dawn: The Journal of Black Canadian Studies*, which pays tribute to the failed Dawn settlement of southern Ontario when many of the African Americans who had settled there returned to the US in the aftermath of the Civil War. *New Dawn* is an online open access journal dedicated to publishing scholarship that engages Black Canadian life and culture, and beyond. This imaginative project of cyber-vocality will work to produce forms of knowledge, both imaginary and empirical, about Black Canadians that might help to keep on with the necessary agenda of reimagining the human. This project is a strategic universalism indebted to making Black life and culture the source from which all human existence and experience might be rethought. This project is a refusal of CanLit in its institutional guise, and yet it depends on CanLit for its very sustenance. Remember: *contradiction*.

To conclude with the personal such as I began. Can CanLit read me? That is, Black faggot, dual citizen, sociologist, cultural critic? How would CanLit read me if it could? As exceptional? Who wants to be that? I take everything "trans" seriously, and therefore I understand that much is at stake when trans is invoked—the very foundation of the human becomes at stake, in my view. As Electronica artist Esthero put it in song and title, "We R in need of a musical reVoLuTIoN." We are in need of an academic revolution, because I am against knowledge production as merely industry and business. Lastly, I paraphrase from a different context and I ask, along with and following Jacques Derrida's direction in *Ethics, Institutions, and the Right to Philosophy*: what is our debt and/or duty to reanimating and remaking the institutions of knowledge production, citizenship, the postnation nation, and the desire for "a democracy yet to come"?

DANIEL COLEMAN

FROM CANADIAN TRANCE TO TRANSCANADA
WHITE CIVILITY TO WRY CIVILITY IN THE CANLIT PROJECT[1]

English Canadians are obsessed with maintaining a long-term trance that I call White[2] civility. This trance, like other quasi-mystical states, engages its members in the repetition of a mantra that affirms membership and meaning, a mantra that asserts that Canadians are more civilized than others on all levels—from large-scale international politics to everyday domestic arrangements. Canadians are more civilized than Americans *always*—whether in the recent decision not to join in the invasion of Iraq or in the eighteenth-century decision not to join the Revolutionary War. Canadians consider themselves more civilized than the terrorists of 9/11, just as they considered themselves more civilized than the members of Louis Riel's Northwest Council that used first diplomacy and then violence to resist the surveying of Red River lands in 1870. British North Americans thought themselves more civilized than the Beothuck they displaced in Newfoundland and too civilized to admit non-White immigrants such as the Sikhs of the *Komagata Maru*, Chinese railroad workers, or Black farmers from Oklahoma. Canadians think themselves more civilized than all other nations who don't have a multiculturalism policy, a Charter of Rights and Freedoms, or federal provisions for same-sex unions.[3] This is the Canadian trance—the ongoing mantra of our own civility. It is what allows us to imagine ourselves as a community, and we become extremely touchy when anyone troubles our self-hypnosis.

In a strategic interruption of this long-cherished, English Canadian trance over our own civility, Rinaldo Walcott titled his recent anthology

Rude: Contemporary Black Canadian Cultural Criticism:[4] in it, he compiled a series of essays that insist upon the long and rich history of Black litera- ture, arts, music, cultural politics, theory, and anti-racist activism in a Canada that has assumed White people and culture to constitute its "founding nations." In his introduction to the collection, Walcott writes that he has taken his title from Clement Virgo's film *Rude* (1994), which "opened up the space for thinking differently about Canada as a racialized space," and that the anthology works towards expanding this opening by means of "an engaged insubordination with respect to official narrative discourses of the nation-state of Canada" (7). Although the general project Walcott outlines here is common to the ongoing struggles for diversification that have done so much to expand and reorient the canons of Canadian culture,[5] his provocative use of Virgo's term "rude" goes to the heart of the blatantly obvi- ous and therefore usually unexamined assumptions of English Canadian civility that I argue underwrite the racialization of Canadian social spaces.

I am not dismissing civility as a worthwhile goal for Canadian society, nor do I think that the creation of Confederation, the Royal Proclamation of 1763, the rejection of slavery by Simcoe's Parliament in 1793, or, more recently, the establishment of public assistance for those who are sick, unem- ployed, disabled, or aging were all matters of a weekend's work. In most Canadian cities, people turn on the tap and have clean water to drink, water they did not haul or sterilize themselves. It is worth reminding ourselves that Canada's commitment to civil organization provides us not merely cause for warm and vague self-congratulation but the physical conditions of our daily existence. My teenaged years coincided with the revolution in Ethiopia, and I will never forget that early period when civil organization fell apart. Suddenly, even those of us who lived in the city had to boil our water for twenty minutes before it was safe to drink. The military leaders vied for power between themselves, and we could never be sure which side the men in fatigues were on when they stopped our school bus at checkpoints. An Ethiopian friend of mine spent seven years in prison without trial and with- out ever knowing what the charges were against him.[6] So I very much appre- ciated what I perceived to be Canadian civility and its commitment to peace, order, and good government when I arrived in Canada in 1979.

When I identify Canadians' obsession with their own civility as a trance, therefore, I am not engaging in snide dismissal. Rather, I wish to call atten- tion to the *structure* of Canadian civility itself and to the way in which it operates like a trance that insulates us from the realities in our midst. My cen- tral argument is that we need to move from a *Canadian trance* over a static and reified idea of civility, which has its foundations in White, British gentlemanliness, to a *TransCanadian*, dynamic, self-questioning concept of civility. We need letters from poet, artist, and cultural activist Roy Kiyooka's *Transcanada Letters*, the multiply cross-linked work from which this volume takes its name. We need TransCanada letters addressed, like his, not just from Montreal, Vancouver, and Halifax, but also from Kyoto and Sao Paulo; letters like his that address poetics, culture, politics, race, gender, painting, and performance, not in hermetically sealed units or isolated disciplines, but in relation to one another; letters that, by means of this cross-hatched, multiply vectored dialogue, generate what I call a wry or critical civility.

We need this more dynamic, self-questioning kind of civility because the static version, the heads-down-in-our-own-corner version, makes us blind to the exclusions and violences that take place in our midst. We too readily assume, for example, that everyone in Canada has equal access to clean drinking water until we are disabused of this assumption, as Canadians were by the evacuation in early November 2005 of over a quarter of the 1,900 Cree people from Kashechewan, Ontario, because of skin and intestinal ailments due to unsafe drinking water on the reserve ten kilometres upstream from James Bay. While most Canadians link unsafe water with the largely White-populated town of Walkerton, Ontario, where an in-depth inquiry was launched after high levels of E. coli in the water killed seven people and sent many others to hospital in May 2000, the drama of the Kashechwan airlift to Sudbury and Ottawa has caused the news media to investigate water conditions in other Native communities and to report that nearly 100 reserves across Canada have boil-water advisories, and one, the Kwicksutaineuk First Nation on an island off the BC coast, has had one in effect for nine years ("Kashechewan").

We too readily imagine, to give another example, that incarceration without trial happens in far-off places under chaotic regimes and fail to notice that a group of five Muslim men, known as the Secret Trial Five, have been detained in Toronto, Ottawa, and Montreal under the provisions of something called a Security Certificate, a document signed by the Minister of Public Safety that allows the Canadian Security Intelligence Service (CSIS) to imprison people suspected of being a threat to security without trial and without disclosing the specifics of the charges against them. Detainees were denied the presence of lawyers and translators at interrogations, and only after five years were two of the five given bail. According to the certificate legislation, the minister needed only "reasonable grounds"—grounds he or she was not obliged to reveal—to sign the security certificate. Under this measure, Mahammad Mahjoub has been in prison for seven years; Mahmoud Jaballah, six years; Hassan Almrei, six years in solitary confinement; Mohammed Harkat, five years; and Adil Charkaoui, four years. Mr. Charkaoui was taking a master's of education degree at the University of Montreal when he was arrested. All of these men are refugees from countries where lack of due legal process made them flee, ironically, to Canada and its fabled civility. At last, in February 2007, the Supreme Court struck down the security certificate system. In a unanimous 9–0 decision, the court ruled the certificates violate the Charter of Rights and Freedoms. The court, however, suspended the judgment from taking legal effect for a year, so that Parliament would have time to write a new law to replace it. Three of the detainees have since been released on bail (two of them, however, remain under house arrest), while the other two remain in prison (see "Canadian Security" and "Major Victory against Secret Trials"). The point is that all of these men were detained in Canada without trial and without access to due process. Like Native people who were given no appeal about their incarceration in residential schools or Japanese Canadians who were given no appeal about being removed to the internment camps, these five men were held as strangers within our nation's gates.

Now, from what I have written so far, some readers may be wondering what all this has to do with the current state of Canadian literary culture and scholarship. Everything: for it seems to me that literary scholarship is deeply invested in the project of civility. In fact, as writers, teachers, and cultural producers, we are engaged in the production and dissemination of Canadian understandings of the civil. We are not the only people involved in this work, but if we ask ourselves why we teach and write about Canadian literary culture, sooner or later we will come down to the project of civility. The historically inclined among us want our students and readers to understand the genealogies of the complex culture in which we live; those engaged with contemporary texts want our students and readers to understand the multiple layers and diversity of Canadian society; those focused on formalist concerns want our students and readers to understand how finding the precise image or literary figure can generate communicative power; and those of us who have not merely survived but who continue to relish the paraphrase want our students and readers to understand how the broad themes of literature comment on and critique the social structures in which we live. Canadian literary scholarship is deeply invested in the project of civility.[7]

What do I mean by "civility"? The meanings of the word civility in the *Oxford English Dictionary* extend from "a community of citizens collectively," "good polity; orderly state," and "conformity to the principles of social order" to "the state of being civilized; freedom from barbarity" and "polite or liberal education ... good breeding." Taken together, these various meanings indicate a concept of civility that combines *the temporal notion* of civilization as progress that was central to the idea of modernity and the colonial mission with *the moral-ethical concept* of a (relatively) peaceful public order—that is to say, the orderly regulation between individual liberty and collective equality that has been fundamental to the politics of the modern nation-state.[8] Throughout the evolution of the modern nation-state, the temporal concept of progress and the moral-ethical ideal of orderliness have been demonstrated by cultivated, polite behaviour (most commonly modelled on the figure of the bourgeois gentleman), which, in turn, has made these concepts fundamental to the production and education of the individual citizen. Education in civility shepherds people onto the path of progress because it names a future ideal as if it were a present norm. It projects an ideal of social interaction (all members of society should be freely included and accorded equal respect) as something to which individuals should aspire: if you wish to join the egalitarian progressive company, you must be willing to improve yourself, to become worthy of the respect that characterizes the civil group. In this way, civility operates as a mode of internal management: the subjects of the civil order discipline their conduct in order to participate in the civil realm, and they themselves gain or lose legitimacy in an internally striated civil society depending on the degrees to which they conform to its ideals.[9]

Combining as it does the temporal notion of progress with the moral-ethical concept of peaceful order, civility purveys the time-space metaphor of the race of civilizations. Departing from previous understandings of race as an eternally fixed and immutable destiny, liberal Canadians during the nation-building era of the late nineteenth and early twentieth centuries believed that all people had the potential to be civil, but some societies were farther ahead on the single timeline of civilization, while others were "backwards" or delayed. C. A. Magrath demonstrated this line of thinking in *Canada's Growth and Problems Affecting It* (1910) when he observed that many areas of southeastern Europe had been oppressed for centuries and therefore were "behind the march of civilization." Not through their own fault, but due to their having been denied familiarity with liberal democratic politics, people from such impoverished backgrounds "cannot understand the meaning of liberty, which to them is licence, [they] evidently have an intense hatred for the majesty of the law"; as a result, "we"—English Canadians—must be patient with "them," for "it will take many years under the British constitution with our free institutions to translate such people into good, intelligent citizens" (Magrath, qtd. in H. Palmer, "Strangers" 315). By means of this exemplary time-space metaphor, civility becomes, to borrow a phrase from Jennifer Henderson, a means by which "race has been attached not just to bodies but also to forms of conduct" (18). A prime instance of the way in which civility's time-space image of progress enforces certain codes for individual conduct can be seen in the way the idea of progress itself is deeply informed by a central value of Whiteness that Richard Dyer, in his study of the rhetorics of Whiteness in Euro-American culture, calls "spirit" or "enterprise." According to Dyer, enterprise is often presented as the sign of White spirit[10]—that is, as a valuation of energy, will, discovery, science, progress, the building of nations, the organization of labour, and especially leadership: "The idea of leadership," writes Dyer, "suggests both a narrative of human progress and the peculiar quality required to effect it. Thus White people [are understood naturally to] lead humanity forward because of their temperamental qualities of leadership: will power, far-sightedness, energy" (31). Of course, this dense interweaving of White enterprise and civility as progress insists, as Imre Szeman has discussed of European modernity in general, upon an isochronic temporality (i.e., a single timeline); it does not consider the possibilities of "allochrony," that different civilizations might operate on different temporal scales of progress, ingress, or regress (Szeman, "Belated").

European colonial expansion, as Stuart Hall explains in "The West and the Rest," was premised on this isochronic idea of progress. Hall observes that colonial-era Europeans tended to believe that "there was *one* path to civilization and social development, and that all societies could be ranked or placed early or late, lower or higher, on the same scale" ("West" 312). This idea of social evolution, however, introduced colonialism's troubling ambivalence, for while it confirmed the civility and modernity of White Europeans by contrast with the stages of primitiveness it posited among Europe's others, it also suggested that these others could be civilized, and that, indeed, the signs of European civility would be best demonstrated when those who were well advanced on the scale of modernity helped those who were less advanced to ascend the evolutionary ladder.[11] To put it differently, civility became more than something a person or culture simply *had*, it became something that a person or culture *did*—it became a primary instance of what Ruth Frankenberg in a different context has called a "white cultural practice" (194). The idea of civility as a (White) cultural practice made it not only a mode of internal management and self-definition, because it distinguished the civil from the uncivil, but also a mode of external management, because it gave civil subjects a mandate for managing the circumstances of those perceived as uncivil.

The ambivalence or contradiction of civility, then, can be seen as a central paradox of liberal modernity, for the civil sphere or stage of advancement in which all participants are guaranteed liberty and equality must be protected from those belated or primitive elements or identities, within and without, which may threaten, intentionally or not, that freedom and equality. As a result, the borders of civility must be policed in order to protect this vulnerable civil space of the advanced from those who, in the words of Johannes Fabian, can be denied as coeval, as inhabiting the same time (Mignolo, "Globalization" 35). As Henry Louis Gates Jr., Cornell West, and David Theo Goldberg have shown in their separate studies, in the very period of the Enlightenment, when concepts of democratic rule, egalitarianism, and individual liberty were emerging in Europe as social ideals, there also arose the most nefarious and complex system the world has ever seen for classifying and stratifying humans into a hierarchy of racial types. Goldberg summarizes the situation thus:

> So the irony of modernity, the liberal paradox comes down to this: As modernity commits itself progressively to idealized principles of liberty, equality, and fraternity, as it increasingly insists upon the moral irrelevance of race, there is a multiplication of racial identities and the sets of exclusions they prompt and rationalize, enable and sustain.... The more open to difference liberal modernity declares itself, the more dismissive of difference it becomes and the more closed it seeks to make the circle of acceptability. (6–7)

Thus, modern civility is, paradoxically, a limited or constrained universality that tends to proliferate and striate not only external but also internal differences.[12]

Civility, therefore, usually understands itself to have an inside and an outside, as well as a hierarchy from top to bottom, which is why the trance of Canadian civility operates usually by comparison with outsiders, as well as with what we might call internal outsiders, who are seen as less civil than we are. This means, as many Canadian scholars from John Porter, Himani Bannerji, and Eva Mackey to Richard Day and M. NourbeSe Philip have argued, that civility is a *bounded universal,* a *stratified liberalism.* In Canada, the sharp edges and striations of civility have been most consistently and explicitly drawn along the borders of race and ethnicity. This is not to suggest that they have not been drawn along other borders, such as religion, class, gender, and sexuality, but that they have had their most explicit expression in reference to race and ethnicity. I alluded earlier to *Strangers Within Our Gates,* a book published in 1909 by J. S. Woodsworth, which outlines a taxonomy of immigrants, produced in response to the mass influx of Eastern European immigrants who were being recruited to homestead the prairies in the late nineteenth and early twentieth centuries. Woodsworth organizes this collection of the latest in social science thinking that was being produced in Canada and the United States at the turn of the twentieth century into a series of chapters, each on a different immigrant group, which descend from British, Americans, Germans, and Scandinavians, who are most assimilable, to southern and eastern Europeans such as Italians, Ukrainians, and Baltic people who can be assimilated with some effort, to the cut off at the borders of Europe, where Turks, Persians, Asians, Blacks, and Aboriginals are understood to be completely unassimilable. Let us remember that Woodsworth was not a bigot or a snob. He was a Methodist minister and social activist who worked directly with the large population of Eastern European immigrants in Winnipeg at the beginning of the twentieth century, and he wrote his book as part of a campaign against British Canadian prejudice against them. He later went on to become a founding member of the Co-operative Commonwealth Federation and to broaden inclusive civil arrangements to make sure that senior citizens' pensions, free public education, and social welfare supports were available to all Canadians, regardless of race, caste, or creed. There were, however, limits to the inclusiveness he could imagine in 1909, and they were organized by gradations of Whiteness.

This is why I say the Canadian trance we have inherited is one of White civility. Woodsworth's advocacy on behalf of despised Eastern European immigrants manifests a central paradox of Canadian White civility, because his book suggests that Canada can prove its maturity—its preparedness to separate from its colonial British parent and step out into full manhood on the international stage—by bravely facing its responsibilities. This grown-up independence can be demonstrated by the courtesy and fair-mindedness White British Canadians show towards incoming immigrants who are the strangers within "our" gates. The way we know who "we" are is by our civil interactions with these "others." In this sense, the normative group establishes itself by means of its needy others, indeed, by proliferating and tabulating its disadvantaged others. White civility in Canada, accordingly, is structured paradoxically in relation to strangers who must be detained at the nation's gates—they are not full members, but remain always necessary as the beneficiaries of Canadian decency. These necessary strangers must remain perpetual others—not-quite, not-White "us," to adapt Homi Bhabha's formulation ("Of Mimicry" 131)—for "our" self-definition to remain intact. A survey of the function of Black or Indigenous characters in early literary works by Susanna Moodie, John Richardson, Oliver Goldsmith Jr., or William Kirby, as well as in more recent works such as W. O. Mitchell's *Who Has Seen the Wind,* Thomas Raddall's *Roger Sudden,* or even Margaret Laurence's *The Diviners*—where Black, Indigenous, or Métis figures are not central and fully rounded characters but usually ones whose function is to establish the roundedness, sensitivity, or civility of the British White character—demonstrates the tenacity of this paradox in Canadian self-representation. As Sherene Razack has recently pointed out in *Dark Threats and White Knights,* the current popularity of General Roméo Dallaire as a figure for Canada's traumatized but principled civility demonstrates not just how powerful is the Canadian desire to see figured our own civility, but also how the image of that civility is constructed by reference to the pain of others. Too often, the icons of White Canadian civility become meaningful by means of their relation to needy, non-White, peripheral others.

Whiteness—because of the French and English divide as well as the presence of many kinds of White ethnics—has never had the chance in Canada to remain undifferentiated, so it becomes important for us to understand why a second equally powerful concept in the Canadian idea of civility, Britishness, was and is so important to Canadians. Britishness is a remarkable category, for, as Linda Colley and Robert Crawford have shown, it is a pan-ethnic term, invented largely by eighteenth-century Lowland Scots to reconceptualize the formerly hostile groups of Anglo-Saxons and Celts that populated the British Isles into a coalitional identity that gave them access to the offices and spoils of empire. As the Canadian historian Donald Akenson argues, for New World settlers, "an integral and absolutely necessary aspect of the development of a sense of [colonial] identity was the creation of a 'British' culture in the new homeland, one that did not in fact exist in the old" (396). The Canadian version of this process of the invention of colonial Britishness is nowhere more visible than in the song "The Maple Leaf Forever," written by a Scot, Alexander Muir, which served as Canada's unofficial national anthem until "O Canada" nudged it aside in the 1960s. Remember Morag Gunn in Laurence's *The Diviners* belting it out in the Manawaka School, in marked contrast to the silence of Jules Tonnerre? In the song's popular images of cooperative pan-ethnic Britishness, of Wolfe planting Britannia's flag and of the thistle, shamrock, rose entwined, lies the kernel of the Canadian concept of White civility: "Britishness"—as a form of monarchical government, as a union of formerly hostile peoples, as a civilization—demonstrated that former enemies could set aside their differences, and, in a spirit of disinterested objectivity, work cooperatively together in a common enterprise. They could create an orderly society (some even called it a "race") that provided its members with freedom of conscience and access to economic opportunity regardless of differences of caste and creed.

The ideals derived from this concept of Britishness have long outlasted "The Maple Leaf Forever." As recently as 2003, the Africadian writer and critic George Elliott Clarke inscribed yet another elegy in the tradition of Canadian sorrows that we can trace back through Dennis Lee's *Civil Elegies* to George Grant's *Lament for a Nation* ("What Was Canada?"). Clarke notes that Grant's Tory tradition, despite its investment in White Britishness, was Canada's last and best resistance to becoming a branch plant of the American Empire. Whereas Grant blamed Pearson's Liberals for selling out to American capitalism, Clarke blames Mulroney's Conservatives and Chrétien's Liberals alike for selling Canadian social programs and public works down the tubes of the Free Trade Agreement, NAFTA, and the G8. Clarke is not naïve about the Anglophile assumptions that are fundamental to Canada's British connection, but he sees the values Grant ascribed to the Red Tory tradition as being Canada's last stand against the juggernaut of transnational capital. Thus the perennial need to define Canadian civility by contrast with that of the United States continues to fuel residual Britishness in Canadian thinking, long after the official campaigns to reinforce the "British connection" have faded away. One can see a different instance of how White Britishness remains central in Canadian literary culture in the titles of the two most famous anthologies of ethnic minority writing in Canada, Linda Hutcheon and Marion Richmond's *Other Solitudes: Canadian Multicultural Fictions* and Smaro Kamboureli's *Making a Difference: Canadian Multicultural Literature.* I have found these volumes very helpful in my own teaching, because they have allowed me to offer courses on diasporic, racialized, and ethnic writing in Canada, but the very need to name these anthologies "multicultural" and to inscribe them under the signs of otherness and difference, as my students regularly point out to me, indicates that there is a normative *Canadian*-Canadianness[13] still in place against which these terms signify, and that normative Canadianness is White and British.[14]

A third characteristic of the Canadian trance of civility is that it fears itself to be belated. The isochronic idea of civilization as being pursued along a single timeline puts immense pressure on the project of Canadian civility, for, as with all settler-invader societies, it makes Canadians feel belated—belated in comparison to the advanced sophistication of the metropolitan centres of Europe and the United States, but also belated, in a different register, in relation to First Nations people, having arrived after them in the New World and lacking the authenticity of being Indigenous. Describing settler cultures as "second worlds" in relation to these two opposite kinds of firsts, Alan Lawson has suggested that this split anxiety is constitutive of settler subjectivity, but my point here is that this sense of belatedness puts pressure on Canadian civility in two major ways: first, it makes Canadians overcompensate in their claims for their own civility in comparison to the metropolitan powers whose economic, cultural, and political clout places these powers at the forefront of the idea of progress, and second, it makes Canadians abandon their own history in pursuit of the cosmopolitan future.

This anxiety of belatedness manifests itself in early programmatic statements about the development of Canadian literature such as that by Edward Hartley Dewart, who said in 1864 that "If we cannot point to a past rich with historic names, we have the inspiring spectacle of a great country, in her youthful might, girding herself for a race for an honourable place among the nations of the world" (59). This foot race for the vanguard of modernity tends to abandon, even as it memorializes, history—particularly by consigning it, with Indigenous peoples, to the regretted but irrecoverable past. In 1884, for example, John E. Logan wrote that Canadian literary culture had "not amalgamated with the native and woven the woof of our refinement from the strong sinuous web of an Aboriginal tradition and religion. In our civilized arrogance we swept away that coarser fabric.... But we are here now and they are gone" (116). Too late, he says, even though he published this noble regret in 1884, months before the military expedition went west to meet the Métis at Batoche and the very culture that *had* done the amalgamation he called for was violently suppressed. We are always here now, and they are always gone. In case these examples make us think such pressures of belatedness are limited to nineteenth-century Canadianness, let me quickly refer to Donna Pennee's study of the rhetoric of vanguardism in the 1995 government document "Canada in the World," in which Canada is represented as a world leader in civility—in peace-keeping, in mediating international conflicts, and in welcoming displaced people (Pennee, "Looking Elsewhere"). The idea, once again, is that Canada leads the worldwide race for civility, but it takes a highly selected history, evacuated of images such as the torture and murder of sixteen-year-old Shidane Abukar Arone by members of the Canadian Airborne Regiment on a peacekeeping mission in Somalia in 1993, to make such a claim.[15]

Historical disavowal has a paradoxical complement, however, which is that the isochronic myth can make us in the present feel superior to those in the past, with the result that, on the rare occasions when we do admit the violences in our history, we tend to think that our admission in the present makes us more civil, more sophisticated, more generally enlightened than Canadians were in the past. We are not only more civilized than Americans or the strangers we keep at our gates, but we are also more civilized than our predecessors. In all cases, the trance of civility sedates us to the status quo, assuring us that we have already reached the ideals to which we so proudly aspire. In the process, we disavow the incivilities and violences in our midst: we adjust ourselves to Muslim men being held for years in prison without trial; to the fact that while Aboriginals represent only 4.4% of the total Canadian population, they make up 18% of the federal prison inmates and as high as 60% in some provinces' prisons (Diène 15); or to the fact that, although 62% of recent immigrants arriving in the last five years have higher education degrees compared to 23% in the general population, according to Statistics Canada in 2001, male immigrants with a university degree earned 55.8% less than their Canadian-born counterparts while immigrant women with degrees earned 56.6% less than their Canadian-born female counterparts (Galabuzi and Teelucksingh). The trance of Canadian civility, with its assumptions of Whiteness, Britishness, masculinity, and anxious belatedness, needs to be challenged, not just once but constantly, for what Malcolm X famously said about racism is true of all forms of discrimination: like Cadillac, there is a new model every year.

So what part can we as literary scholars and cultural producers play in transforming this Canadian trance into something less self-insulating, less self-congratulatory, into something more dynamic and inclusive, something more truly TransCanada? I would suggest that we need to shift out of the sedative politics[16] of White civility and into a mode that I call wry civility—that is, a reflexive mode of civility that works towards awareness of the contradictory, dynamic structures of civility itself in our ongoing commitment to building a more inclusive society. I derive the term "wry civility" from several sources, all of which emphasize the paradoxical structure of civility itself. Like Goldberg in his conception of the racialist paradox of liberal modernity outlined above, Étienne Balibar traces a paradox of exclusive egalitarianism to the heart of civility: if civil society exists when people of different identifications have equal access to and agency within a public sphere, Balibar points out, following Hegel, then they must allow their identification with that shared public entity (for example, the nation-state) to displace or subsume their other (regional, domestic, or tribal) identifications. Civility, in this sense, involves a violent marginalization of non-centralizing identifications (Balibar, "Three Concepts" 31–32). By calling for a "wry" civility, therefore, I wish to emphasize the importance of a dynamic, ever-renewed alertness to this fundamental paradox of the repressive violence that haunts the borders and stratifies the layers of civility.

I also use the term wry civility as a rhyming counterpart to Homi Bhabha's formulation of "sly civility" in his article by the same name. Bhabha takes his title from the transcript of a September 1818 sermon by Archdeacon Potts, published in the *Missionary Register* of the Church Missionary Society, in which Potts expresses frustration that when one tries to convince South Asian Indians of their "gross and unworthy misconceptions of the nature and will of God, or the monstrous follies of their fabulous theology, they will turn it off with a *sly civility* perhaps, or with a popular and careless proverb" (qtd. in Bhabha, "Sly Civility" 99; italics in original). Bhabha goes on to read the native's sly civility as a strategy of colonial resistance that sidesteps the desire of the colonial authority for confirmation of the legitimacy of its civilizing mission by a polite dismissal that frustrates the missionary's desire. Canadian settler subjects, however, inhabit a different position than either of Bhabha's figures, since they are neither unambiguously the agents of the civilizing mission nor its supposed beneficiaries—or, to put it otherwise, they are both subjects and objects of the colonial regime. As Lawson's "second world" designation suggests, they find themselves caught between the authority and authenticity represented by the First World of the colonial metropole and those of the First Nations whom they have displaced, which means that settler subjects are sometimes the practitioners of resistant sly civility in their own negotiations with metropolitan power and authority (whether British in the old empire or American-corporatist in the new one), and sometimes the recipients or targets of sly civility when First Nations resist and elude their attempts to legitimize White sovereignty. Given this ambiguous situation, I would suggest that wry civility offers a productive way to engage consciously with the contradictory complex represented by settler culture's White civility. Wry civility, configured in this way, represents the possibility of what Larissa Lai, in our roundtable conversations at the TransCanada conference, called "complicity without complacency." I do not believe that we can discard civility as a social ideal for the reasons I outlined at the beginning of this paper; yet we must remain always aware of its contradictory structure, for civility includes even as it excludes.

The kind of critical alertness I am calling for has significant parallels with what the political philosopher and psychoanalyst Cornelius Castoriadis has called "autonomy." Throughout his long career, but especially in a series of lectures and papers delivered in the 1980s and 1990s, Castoriadis elaborated upon the importance of social and individual autonomy, a term he rooted in its Greek etymology, *auto* (self) + *nomos* (law)—that is, the giving of oneself to one's own law. By contrast with heteronomy (being subjected to another's law), Castoriadis says autonomy is fundamental to the democratic project because it is "the capacity, of a society or of an individual, to act deliberately and explicitly in order to modify its law—that is to say, its form" (341). To engage in self-modification, autonomous individuals and societies must be capable of a "regime of reflectiveness ... in which one reflects and decides in common on what is going to be done, whether one is talking about the law or collective works. One also reflects in another sense. One can come back upon what one has said, thought, and decided so as to take it up again and make modifications" (194). In many ways, Castoriadis's concept of autonomy identifies precisely what I mean by a *wry* relation to civility, but for the following difference of emphasis: it seems to me that, despite Castoriadis's concerted effort to distinguish autonomy from the romantic fantasy of unfettered individual agency,[17] any public use of the term "autonomy," especially given mass culture's constant reproduction of the myth that individuals are agents of consumer choice, is too readily recuperated into the concept of the self-starting individual. By comparison, "wry civility" emphasizes in the word "wry" Castoriadis's critical reflexivity towards the existing social order, while, in the word "civility," it emphasizes the collective, rather than the individual, investment in the public, social realm. This wryness is not produced by individual genius but, in the Canadian context, by the structural fact that the project of civility in a settler society is fraught with contradictions, by the fact that the Second World, belated, in-between status of the settler disallows an easy, untroubled inhabitation of civility.

Let me give one example of how this structural situation can produce critical wryness in relation to Castoriadis's theory itself. Castoriadis insists that, historically speaking, moments of widespread critical consciousness that lead to true changes in the social order are extremely rare: "In almost all societies known to us," he writes, "it is impossible to put into question the proper world of the tribe. That is so, not because there is violence and repression but because such questioning is psychically and mentally inconceivable for individuals fabricated by the society in question" (339). He therefore identifies only two moments when self-questioning autonomy appeared in human history: in the Greek polity and in the development of the democratic movement in Europe after the thirteenth century. For Castoriadis, these two moments are "unprecedented in the history of being" (339). His translator and editor, David Ames Curtis, notes that critics have taken Castoriadis to task for the Eurocentrism of this claim, but Curtis defends his mentor by arguing that the desire to "flatten out history" and discount a Greek origin for the principle of autonomy loses sight of the fact that "politics as self-responsible conscious collective action to alter a society's institutions is also a Greek creation" (viii). Curtis insists, therefore, that it is because of the Greek formulation of autonomy that people in Western culture question the Eurocentrism of our political and cultural formulations at all, and that, in fact, the move to examine other cultures as a way to gain critical perspective on one's own culture is precisely an enactment of the Greek idea of autonomy (ix). It seems to me that Curtis's argument constitutes a classic instance of civility as a White cultural practice: Curtis reinscribes the civility of White European political tradition as that which sponsors and makes room for the (non-White) strangers at civility's gates.[18] His gesture towards other cultures and their differences turns out, in fact, to reinforce the primacy of Europe as the origin of the civil values of autonomy and democracy.

As it happens, however, I live half an hour's drive from the Six Nations of the Grand River, the largest Native reserve in Canada. I have Haudenosaunee students from Six Nations in my graduate and undergraduate classes, and these members of the Iroquoian Confederacy have prompted me to learn about a bursting forth of autonomy in pre-contact North America that Castoriadis, who was born in Greece and who lived most of his working life in France, could not or would not know about. I am referring to the *Kayánerénhkowa*, popularly referred to as the Iroquoian Great Law of Peace,[19] which is the system of democratic governance established in approximately 1450 by Deganawidah, the Lawgiver, among the five nations of what is now upper New York state, southern Ontario, and surrounding regions.[20] Very generally, the principles the Haudenosaunee people derived from Deganawidah provided the rationale for a consensus-model, united nations democracy, according to which the elder women of the five (and later, six) member tribes choose leaders to attend the council fires and discuss the governance of the confederacy. According to Haudenosaunee oral histories, Deganaw-idah came to the five nations when they were at constant war with each other and with powerful surrounding peoples. Deganawidah's institution of the three principles of righteousness, health, and power constituted a remarkable eruption of what Castoriadis would call critical autonomy, when the five nations of the Mohawks, Senecas, Onondagas, Oneidas, and Cayu-gas[21] "put into question the proper world of the tribe" and modified their laws and systems of governance to create a powerful confederacy, a system of representational government (each of the member nations has—the sys-tem is ongoing to this day—a certain number of representatives on coun-cil; see Wallace 36–37), and a complex mechanism of clan relations to provide a check against the divisions of the member nations and therefore protect against these nations rejecting or competing with one another—so, for example, there are Bear clan members in several of the nations, and these exogamous clans enforce a sense of family loyalty across the nations (Wal-lace 42–43; Alfred 102–03). My point here is not to develop an elaborate dis-cussion of the Six Nations' system of governance,[22] but to note how location in the settler-invader environs of Canada presents an allochronic alternative to Curtis's and Castoriadis's claim for an isochronic European origin for the principles of autonomy and democracy. From both First Nations and set-tler-subject, Second World perspectives, such exclusive claims contribute to the ongoing project to reproduce ignorance about the forms of civility devel-oped by Indigenous peoples independent of, or at least alongside of, Euro-pean histories of civilization.[23]

If Second World, settler-colonial locations generate what I am calling wry civility, then why does the Canadian trance of White civility persist? Why do Canadians hang on so tightly to the untroubled illusion of our own civility and not notice the violences at our borders and within our gates? I have already addressed the question of belatedness in settler culture and the way in which this anxiety of belatedness produces an overcompensating, history-denying tendency amongst Canadians to claim unblemished civil-ity and a moral high ground that cannot be fully realized in daily life. Another response to this question would attend to the structures of social privilege. If self-critical social awareness is generally rare, coming to that awareness, especially for those who occupy categories of privilege, is even more rare. For privilege is precisely the condition of not running into road blocks. As Ross Chambers puts it, the categories of privilege operate like a hand of cards; the more trump cards one carries—in Canada: Whiteness, Britishness, mas-culinity, heterosexuality, middle- or upper-class status, able-bodiedness, tenured professorship, and so on—the less chance one has of running into adversities that alert one to the obstacles people who do not hold these trump cards encounter. For people of privilege, it is tempting to settle into what Gayatri Spivak, thinking along similar lines to Sedgwick, has called "sanctioned ignorance" (Brydon, "Cross-Talk" 68). That ignorance, like all cultural forms, is not static; like racism, there is a new model every year.

The dynamism of sanctioned ignorance, of the self-regenerating power of the trance of White civility, has made me more convinced than ever of the importance of reading and writing about Canadian literary culture. Although I understand and appreciate the restlessness that makes people dismiss the ivory tower as preoccupied with otherworldly matters that are utterly irrelevant to the real world, the longer I work in the humanities the more I am convinced that what we do as writers, critics, teachers, and cultural producers is crucial to intervening in the Canadian trance of civility. Rather than making me less committed to the disciplines of close reading, historical research, archival reclamation, and the development of precise, attractive writing that are fundamental to literary and cultural studies, the persistent exclusions and violences in our civil society makes me more committed to them. As Diana Brydon has written, expanding from Spivak, we can destabilize and expose the many forms of sanctioned ignorance by working in and through the everyday moments of what Brydon calls "cross-talk" (recall Walcott's "rudeness"), by working in and through these moments of quotidian rupture, when conflict and anger break through the veneer of civility long enough to reveal the limits and incommensurabilities in what we as well as our students do and don't know. Reading carefully, paying close attention, not just to another person's voice in a given text but to the way in which that voice is embedded in cultural history, involves what Spivak calls "critical intimacy," a kind of cross-talk between the cultural location of the reader and the voice of the text, which has the potential to dislodge the sanctioned ignorance that repeatedly envelopes us all (Brydon, "Cross-Talk" 62–64). It is this kind of cross-talk, carried out between Castoriadis's and Curtis's location in Euro-American culture and that of Canadian critics in the Second World of settler culture, which is still working towards awareness of Indigenous knowledge and tradition,[24] that dislodges the sanctioned ignorance that theorizes autonomy and democracy as exclusively European ideas. For teachers of the Canadian literatures, it must not cease to startle those who have been teaching Kogawa's *Obasan* for the past twenty years that every year a new crop of students reports that they had never heard of the internment of Canadians of Japanese descent during the 1940s until taking this class.

Nor should it surprise us that students find that reading the intimate tensions and violences in *Obasan* or Beatrice Culleton Mosionier's *In Search of April Raintree* are much more powerful experiences than reading objective-sounding historical accounts about the internment or sociological reports on interracial sexual abuse. We don't have to become Arnoldians or Leavisites to see that the critical intimacy of reading imaginative texts has a remarkable power to intervene in the reproduction of sanctioned ignorance.

Of course, there is a good deal of reading that replicates rather than challenges sanctioned ignorance, and this is why Roy Kiyooka's multiregional, multinational, multiracial and -ethnic and -gendered, multidisciplinary TransCanada matters so much. Critical intimacy that produces a wry understanding of Canadian civility needs to recognize both the specificity of locations in Canada as Kiyooka did and the relation of these locations to the wider world. A wry approach to Canadian civility recognizes the need for what Donna Pennee has called "strategic nationalism" that does not wash out the specificity of local Canadian cultural histories, but that also recognizes the importance of reading Canadian literary culture in a transnational, comparative setting ("Literary"). As Leslie Monkman and Diana Brydon ("Introduction") have pointed out, there is a rich tradition that predates the rise to prominence of the kinds of postcolonialism associated with Said, Bhabha, and Spivak; this tradition, painstakingly charted by Canadian scholars such as John Matthews and W. H. New, advocated what Kiyooka might call Transcanada letters, a way of reading CanLit in a transnational, cross-colonial—and, with Six Nations in mind, an "inter-confederate"—context. It was a way of reading that realized, as I did when my family came to Canada periodically to visit relatives and friends during my childhood, that the Trans-Canada Highway connects very different regions, peoples, and cultures, and that it too can be read for its inclusions and exclusions.

For, you see, my father was from a town near Windsor, Ontario, and my mother from a farm community near Innisfail, Alberta. Every four or five years, when we came to visit the place my parents called home, we would drive the Trans-Canada. This trip meant, paradoxically, that I had seen both more and less of the country than most children my age who had grown up here. By the time I was eleven, I had played I-spy-with-my-little-eye on Highway 401, counted elk in Banff National Park, and witnessed grain fields devastated by hail on the prairies. I had learned, moreover, that the shortest distance between Ontario and Alberta is through Michigan, Indiana, Wisconsin, Minnesota, and North Dakota, and so the Trans-Canada included a good deal of the United States. For me, the geographical centre of Canada was the town of Steinbach, Manitoba. Because my parents were missionaries and many of their supporters and co-workers were from the Mennonite communities of southeastern Manitoba, this ethnic community marked the middle of Trans-Canada as far as I was concerned. Winnipeg was a mere gas station on the periphery of the thriving cultural centre of Steinbach. When I finally came to live in Canada in my late teens and went on a canoe trip with some university friends on the Churchill River system in northern Saskatchewan, I was surprised to see what the Trans-Canada missed: that Saskatchewan has more Canadian shield than it does undulating wheat lands, which had rolled by our car windows down in the southern part of the province; and that the Lac La Ronge First Nation had a thriving, internationally renowned industry in the production of wild rice on those clear northern lakes. A few years later, I played on the African soccer team in Regina just behind the Fine Arts building where Kiyooka used to teach in the 1950s and realized that many of my Ethiopian, Eritrean, Tanzanian, and Ugandan teammates had got there by means of the Trans-Canada. Whereas I had tried to discard my Ethiopian missionary childhood when I came to Canada, I began to realize that Canadian "civilization," Saskatchewan "culture," was composed of the concatenation of our non-charter-group histories. In one of his *Transcanada* letters, Kiyooka notes that when he was in Montreal, Europe had seemed very close, but now that he has moved back to Vancouver, "the Orient ... seems to be / a necessity therefore inevitable" (78). Wry civility rises from this kind of TransCanada awareness, with its constant back and forth, its incessant improvisation and exchange, and its state of being, like all roads across this country, always under construction.

PETER DICKINSON

SUBTITLING CANLIT
KEYWORDS

I n the spring of 2005, I followed with interest, and no little bemusement, a lively conversation on the Film Studies Association of Canada's listserv concerning the National Film Board (NFB) of Canada's failure to include either dubbed versions or English-language subtitles with their recent re-releases of the work of prominent Québécois filmmakers—including Denys Arcand, Anne-Claire Poirier, and Gilles Groulx—on DVD. Volleys were fired and indictments leveled concerning everything from the chronic under-funding of Canada's cultural institutions, to the sorry state of English-Canadian bilingualism, to the covert separatist agenda of the NFB since it moved its offices from Ottawa to Montreal back in 1956. Throughout, the tenor of this debate remained remarkably civil (as most do—unlike, say, the temperatures that occasionally rise and flare on the Canadian Association for Cultural Studies's listserv); indeed, civility prevailed even when, in one of the postings, someone offered a joke that was swiftly labelled "offensive" by another listserv member. This in turn resulted in an immediate and abject apology from the member who posted the joke, as well as an intervention from the listserv moderator, who hastened to shore up—to borrow and adapt slightly a term deployed by Daniel Coleman in his contribution to this volume—the electronic "trance" of Canadian civility by concluding that since only one "complaint" was received, and since an apology had been issued, no real harm had been done.

I offer this anecdote by way of introduction for a couple of reasons. First—and this is my only salvo against the self-critique of the CanLit critical establishment as it has been conceptualized by the editors of this collection and the organizers of the conference upon which the collection is based—it strikes me that, to borrow another of Coleman's metaphors, in the TransCanadian highway of institutional and representational politics we're mapping here in these pages, we've taken a noticeable detour around Quebec (Winfried Siemerling's and Lianne Moyes's contributions being notable exceptions). Second, and more pertinently in terms of what follows, I simply want to draw readers' attention to the fact that subtitles, whether in films or on the covers of dusty tomes of Canadian literary and cultural criticism, are not merely descriptive but also instrumentalist, capable of at once advancing a "civilizing mission" and an ideological critique of that mission. This is something that all of us attached to the TransCanada project are no doubt aware of, and would that we could all meet at subsequent Congresses of the Canadian Federation for the Humanities and Social Sciences at a newly amalgamated Society of Literature, Institutions, Citizenship. Until then, in this response essay, I want to zero in very briefly on not only two of the crucial keywords in Coleman's subtitle (civility and Whiteness), but also, latterly (and laterally) the words that make up the subtitle to the TransCanada conference (Literature, Institutions, Citizenship). Indeed, at the end of this essay I hope to use the issue of sexual citizenship, in particular, to circle back to questions raised by Coleman about the character and the limits of Canadian civility.

In arguing that we need to move from "a static and reified idea of civility, which has its foundations in White, British gentlemanliness, to a *Trans-Canadian*, dynamic, self-questioning concept of civility" (*White Civility* 3–4), what he terms "wry civility," Coleman has prescribed a much-needed therapeutic remedy for the trance-like condition that has bedeviled the CanLit and CanCult critical institutions; but that therapy, it seems to me, is still in search of a theory. Let me, then, propose three of my own keywords as a way of offering some suggestions in that regard (and, tangentially, as a way of intersecting with and responding to what Coleman has identified as the three primary characteristics of Canadian civility: Whiteness; Britishness; and belatedness). The three theoretical keywords I want to examine in more detail are *psychoanalysis*, *affect*, and *performativity*; the fact that their acronym spells "pap" may or may not be an indication of their usefulness as a discursive curative to the self-hypnotizing talk of Canadian civility.

Psychoanalysis, a discourse that at once seeks to describe and to pathologize repressed desire, can, I believe, prove useful in explaining how Whiteness emerges as the paradoxically (in)visible sign of Canadian civility's self-regulation—and, perhaps more to the point, how the racial other is dialectically deployed in service of this enterprise. I am thinking, in particular, of the notion of sublimation, especially as developed by Sigmund Freud in his unpacking of the sex and death drives (eros and thanatos) in *Civilization and Its Discontents*. There he demonstrates how sexual repression, when displaced onto or expended in "great works" or civilizing projects, actually becomes a constitutive and sustaining feature of Western cultural production; in this way, we can see how, in the post-Enlightenment literary canons of Europe and her settler colonies (Canada most assuredly included), the racialized body (broadly conceived) is positioned at once outside the law and, by this very act of negation, as that which preserves, sustains, and props up the law. There, as well, is where the discourse of civility overlaps with some of the more immobilizing (in the sense of not speaking for the other) aspects of identity politics. That is, White civility as it operates in Canadian literature, like Michel Foucault's take on Freud's theory of sexual repression, produces a field of infinitely classifiable and manageable subcategories—Asian Canadian literature, African Canadian literature, diasporic Canadian literature, Indigenous Canadian literature, queer Canadian literature, etc.—precisely in order to facilitate and rationalize its own proliferation and institutionalization as a site of epistemological control, discipline, and suppression (and I do not exempt myself from this process).

I'm not saying anything new here, yet, for all our *collective* awareness of these issues, and, indeed, our *selective* application, in our criticism, of psychoanalytical theories to the operations of sex and race in individual works of Canadian literature (from *Wacousta* to *Trou de mémoire*), where, I wonder, is our *Love and Death in the Canadian Novel* (John Moss's *Sex and Violence in the Canadian Novel* notwithstanding)? Where is our *Playing in the Dark*? As Coleman has stated, we like to congratulate ourselves here in Canada that we are more civil than our neighbours south of the border (especially where our famous multicultural tolerance is trumpeted as the necessary antidote to the simmering racial tensions of the US melting pot, a pot where, as Tony Kushner's Rabbi Chemelwitz would put it, nothing melts). There is something to be said, however, for the frankness and forthrightness with which Leslie Fiedler and Toni Morrison, in their separate analyses of Hawkeye and Chingachgook, Huck and Jim, Ishmael and Queequeg, confront the necessarily "miscegenated" (not to mention "homosocial") nature of American literature. Would that we could see more clearly the processes of miscegenation that underpin our own literary history, both generically in terms of its grafting of European gothic romance onto First Nations storytelling traditions and practices, and materially in terms of the often-ambiguous representation of White subjectivity at the heart of some of our most canonized works.

For this, however, I would argue that we need to move from Freud and theories of sublimation and repression to Julia Kristeva and theories of abjection. It seems to me that what we confront over and over again in Canadian literature is, to use Kristeva's terminology, a testing of the limits of "objectlessness": not a desire for coherence of meaning as a result of making that which is other homologous to oneself; but rather a straying "toward the place where meaning collapses" through an uncanny and fearful bracketing of the other as that which remains proximately unassimilable: "Not me. Not that. But not nothing, either. A 'something' that I do not recognize as a thing. A weight of meaninglessness, about which there is nothing insignificant, and which crushes me. On the edge of non-existence and hallucination, of a reality that, if I acknowledge it, annihilates me. There, abject and abjection are my safeguards. The primers of my culture" (Kristeva, *Powers* 1–2). Indeed, what we see repeatedly in Canadian literature is the White protagonist *not seeing* his or her own fearful other, the doubled self who cannot be shown and whose non-representability reflects to the protagonist an image of his or her own lack. Hence we see the repetition of narcissistic patterns of looking in much Canadian literature, the paranoid White hero or heroine, as with Mary Ann Doane's famous application of Kristeva's theories to the paranoid gothic woman's film of the 1940s, seeing everywhere the spectre of his or her own subjective annihilation, a collapsing of the self into non-self that is explicitly figured as a consequence of the estrangement of exile in a hostile and terrifying foreign land. In this regard, one might quote at length from *Roughing It in the Bush*, or trot out yet again familiar images of "haunted wildernesses" (Northey) and the "garrisons" (Frye) built to guard against them. In *Powers of Horror*, Kristeva poses the central question around abject identity in the same spatialized terms deployed by Frye in his famous conclusion to *The Literary History of Canada* (reprinted in *The Bush Garden*); as Kristeva puts it, "Instead of sounding himself as to his 'being,' he does so concerning his place: '*Where* am I' instead of '*Who* am I.' For the space that engrosses the deject, the excluded, is never *one*, nor *homogeneous*, nor *totalizable*, but essentially divisible, foldable, and catastrophic" (*Powers* 8).

Central to Kristeva's theory of abjection is the primary importance of the human body, and what she calls the "twisted braid of affects" that are consequent to and that animate the bodily sensorium (the smell of fear; the look of love; the touch of compassion; the taste of shame). It seems to me that a theory of affect can provide another avenue of inquiry into Coleman's second defining feature of Canadian civility, namely its "Britishness," especially where the characterization of Britishness as a de facto pan-ethnic Whiteness overlaps with aspects of group psychology to produce a static conception of the Canadian mentality (again, in Coleman's estimation, one distinct from its American counterpart) as reserved, restrained, and altogether lacking in emotional displays of attachment. In contrast to a behaviourist or psychoanalytical theory of drives (hunger, sex, death) as they hydraulically structure our unconscious, Silvan Tomkins, in his three-volume study *Affect, Imagery, Consciousness*, proposes an empirical and neurophysiological analysis of a core set of human emotions (joy, anger, shame) as they hardwire our conscious, expressive, and adaptive interactions and communications with others, and as attention to their consequences goes a distance toward correcting "Descartes' Error" (to quote Antonio Damasio), reconciling the mind/body split we have inherited from Enlightenment rationalism. Emotion, for Tompkins, carries with it motivational force and direction; emotion, in other words, and for better or worse, can effect change.

Canadian literature and culture have often been characterized as rather affect*less*, from Margaret Atwood's famously expressionless monotone and coldly clinical prose to the relative lack of fanfare with which we hand out our literary prizes. The recent glitz and festive theatrics of the Griffin Poetry Prize have been a notable and welcome exception, in this regard, with Scott Thompson waving a dildo in front of Atwood and Anne Michaels during the inaugural 2001 ceremonies, and Christian Bök exuberantly bounding up on stage and performing an excerpt from his award-winning *Eunoia* the very next year. I'd like to suggest that if we pay attention to two important aspects of a theory of affect, especially as they operate in the Canadian literature classroom, then we may be able to go a distance toward displacing the centrality of Britishness in Canadian literary culture and criticism. I am referring here to how affect is transmitted, and to its group dynamics.

Is there any academic who has not, to adapt Teresa Brennan, walked into a Canadian literature classroom—maybe on the first day—and "felt the atmosphere" (1)? What we are experiencing is in fact the transmission of affect, the reception of a physical impression or feeling that is social in origin (the gathering of a group of curious and excited third-year students who, in the minutes before class, start introducing themselves and discover their mutual love of and eagerness to learn more about the Confederation Poets), biological and physical in effect (the thrum of excitement that hits you, the instructor, as you enter the room, and that makes your pulse

quicken), and that results in an evaluative judgement that is either intro-
jected or projected ("Wow, these kids are hopping; looks like I've got a great
group this semester," or "Welcome, everyone, I can tell that we're going to
have a lot of fun together"). To provide another example, if, as I did in delivering the original oral version of this paper, I were to interrupt my dry academic prose and berate my lunchtime audience for clinking their coffee
cups too loudly and not according me the undivided attention that I deserve,
then I will have transmitted affect. That is, several members of my audience
will have no doubt received a physical shock or jolt ("Is he kidding?") that
perhaps momentarily made them squirm in their seats ("Maybe he's not
kidding"), and that likely resulted in a judgement ("What an asshole!").

Moreover, as both my examples demonstrate, theories of the transmission of affect overlap with analyses of group psychology in interesting ways,
especially where studies of the crowd and mob consciousness are concerned.
Again, we have only to look to our respective CanLit classrooms for evidence of this, all of us having experienced the weight of a collective emotional
response (whether positive or negative) to a particularly provocative work,
or to something controversial said in discussion about that work. My point
is that we can use the diversely constellated space of the CanLit classroom
to unpack the complicated affective history that accompanies the "British"
character of Canadian civility, drawing on the interactive dynamics of this
group (whose members bring different cultural codes relating to the display of emotion in different contexts) to peel back the layers of shame and
guilt, in particular, that accompany our colonial (and colonized) reserve
and restraint; further, we can use the positive energy of the classroom—
including, dare I say, a love of literature—not just to foster a hermeneutics
of suspicion towards the master narratives of Canadian cultural production and institutionalization, but also to create counter-narratives of repar-
ative possibility, and even revolutionary change, as Eve Sedgwick suggests in
Touching Feeling.

On this note of futurity, let me turn very briefly to theories of performativity, and in particular to their potential to speak to what Coleman has
identified as the "belated" nature of Canadian civility. In her very earliest work
on gender performativity, which drew more on Simone de Beauvoir and
Maurice Merleau-Ponty than it did on J. L. Austin, Judith Butler invited us
to consider gender "as *a corporeal style,* an 'act,' as it were, which is both
intentional and performative, where 'performative' itself carries the dou-
ble-meaning of 'dramatic' and 'non-referential'" ("Performative" 521–22).
Substitute "Canadian" for "gender" in this sentence, and we can begin to see

what Coleman considers to be the compensatory and dangerously presen-
tist poses we adopt in the performance of our settler-invader colony civility, where in a process of historical disavowal we rush to congratulate
ourselves on how cosmopolitan we have become and, indeed, have always
been. History, as Coleman throughout his essay makes clear, can never be far
from our considerations of the performance of Canadian civility. What Butler, again drawing on Merleau-Ponty, has identified as the body's "historical possibilities" (521) is a reminder that to the extent that gender, for example,
coheres as an identity, it does so through the "stylized repetition" of its performative acts *in* and *over* time (519).

Thinking, in this way, about the "social temporality" of performative
identities is key not only to understanding how certain of those identities
come to be constituted as normative and hegemonic (and others non-nor-
mative and minoritarian/oppositional), but also to how we might begin to
challenge and even dismantle the trance those identities cast through another
set of historical possibilities: "If the ground of gender identity is the stylized repetition of acts through time, and not a seemingly seamless identity,
then the possibilities of gender transformation are to be found in the arbi-
trary relation between such acts, in the possibility of a different sort of
repeating, in the breaking or subversive repetition of that style" (Butler,
"Performative" 520). I find in Coleman's call for a movement to "wry civility" a similar subversive repetition of the style or pose of Canadian White
civility, a "reflexive mode of civility that works towards awareness of the
contradictory, dynamic structures of civility itself in our ongoing commitment to building a more inclusive society," as Coleman defines it elsewhere
in this volume.

He derives his notion of wryness from the theories of Étienne Balibar,
Homi Bhabha, and Cornelius Castoriadis; but as a reflexive mode of critical inquiry, wryness is also of a piece with a long tradition of Canadian literary and cultural criticism, from Malcolm Ross to Linda Hutcheon, both
of whom have used the term "irony" to diagnose "our sense of identity"—
what Malcolm Ross, in the introduction to *Our Sense of Identity: A Book of
Canadian Essays*, calls a "Dynamic irony opening outwards against—and
through—a world of shut-ins. A hope, confronting both the anarchic and
the totalitarian" (xii). It is also symptomatic of the recurring phenomenon
of "postness" in left academic critiques of late modernity (whether post-
structuralist, postmodernist, postcolonial, post-Marxist, post-nationalist,
etc.): that is, these critiques are primarily self-critiques, meta-analyses of
the institutional politics of a discipline, a theory, an ideology, from within

that very institution (cf. Bill Readings's *The University in Ruins*, Gayatri Chakravorty Spivak's *Death of a Discipline*, and, dare I suggest in the Canadian context, Coleman's own recent book, *White Civility*). How many of us in the humanities, for example, have been to conferences throughout the course of our careers, and relating to our respective cross-disciplines, where we have been asked to "take stock" of what it is that we do, to prognosticate "future indications" of what the discipline holds, or worse still, to account for its wholesale "withering"?

Not that I am opposed to this kind of self-analysis and reflexive critical augury; indeed, I agree with Coleman when he writes, in the preceding chapter, that to the extent that "literary scholarship is deeply invested in the project of civility," and that, "as writers, teachers, and cultural producers, we are engaged in the production and dissemination of Canadian understandings of the civil," it is incumbent upon us to unpack critically those understandings. Following from Michael Hardt's analysis of the role that education plays for Hegel in the production of a civil society, especially as the educative process contributes to the abstraction of labour, we in the newly corporatized university do need to talk about our own complicity in the abstraction not just of our intellectual and affective labour, but also our wage labour, as per the new capital campaign recently launched by my university (where faculty have been encouraged to contribute—or "reinvest"—a portion of their biweekly salaries to dwindling student awards and bursary funds). At the same time, I worry that these conversations too often take place among ourselves, a closed and fairly circumscribed group of mostly privileged academics who use our institutional perches (and purchases) to affect a pose of wry detachment regarding a critical analysis of the Canadian social fabric, rather than a sincere engagement with some of the very real issues tearing at that fabric. With a few notable exceptions, we have never had a very robust tradition of public intellectualism in Canada (nor even a lively print or electronic culture in which to practice it); and we are definitely suspicious of being preached at. Nonetheless, we could do well to take a page from the evangelical fervour of our US neighbours on both sides of the political spectrum, and proselytize what it is that we do and what it is that we hope to accomplish by what we do.

Here, too, let me suggest that *in* our proselytizing we critics of Canadian White civility might borrow a page not just from our American neighbours, but also from recent critics of Black Canadian literature (fellow contributor Rinaldo Walcott chief among them), subverting our own subversive repetition of a performance of wryness or irony (which, let's face it, as a patron discourse cannot always count on everyone getting its critical "edge") with a strategic display of "rudeness." In this regard, let me conclude by offering a few final comments on the links between recent Canadian politics, stand-up comedy, and questions of sexual citizenship.

After narrowly surviving a confidence vote on his budget at the end of May 2004, and in the wake of the mudslinging and name-calling that attended Belinda Stronach's defection to the Liberals and the allegations of bribery and influence-peddling levelled by both sides of the Gurmant Grewal affair, Paul Martin rose in the House of Commons to plead for a return to a discourse of civility and cooperation among the federal parties as the government moved ahead in the coming weeks with a very full legislative agenda. A pity, I remember thinking, as Canadian politics had never been more exciting and fun—nor more nakedly honest in exposing, among other things, Stephen Harper's own ambitions for power. Who needed NHL hockey when there was this kind of political bloodsport to watch? And when there was Rick Mercer to weekly mine it for its comedic potential on the CBC?

As we geared up, only a week after the TransCanada Conference in late June 2004, for an eventually successful, but no less bruising, vote around same-sex marriage, I found myself longing for something a bit more in-your-face than the brand of gentle satire and self-deprecating, deadpan humour, the "wryness," practised by Mercer—who has, let's admit it, been holding his cards pretty close to his chest since his public outing in early 2003 in the pages of the *Globe and Mail* (Hampson), and, even more pertinently, since his not-so-secret wedding to long-time partner Gerald Lunz. Lost amid all the rhetoric around cherry-picking human rights and preserving religious freedoms is the very basic fact that, no matter where we stand on the issue (and I think that the Canadian government could have gone much further in reconceiving the legal parameters of all sorts of different affective bonds beyond the narrow and restrictive limits of conjugality), the debate around civil unions for gays and lesbians is less about preserving the "unity" of marriage than it is about whether or not to acknowledge the "civility" of queers.

Plus ça change. Fast forward to December 2005, as I put the finishing touches on my revisions to the original oral version of this essay. Not only is Rick Mercer's *Monday Night Report* now on Tuesdays, but we're also in the midst of another federal election campaign, with Stephen Harper promising to revisit the same-sex marriage law should the Conservatives be elected, putting its possible repeal to a free vote in parliament. We in the Canadian academy ignore such pronouncements at our peril. In foregrounding for our students abstract questions of sexual citizenship (what *civil* rights accrue to what *sexed* bodies in what *social* contexts?) through a material focus on representations of gender and the desiring body in selected works of Canadian literature, for example, in documenting and analyzing how one's individual—and intimate—experience of sex (as an act or as an identity) is subject to at times benign, and at times more violent, social administration and policing, we can make legible—performatively, affectively, psychoanalytically—larger structural asymmetries and power relations that continue to persist in our (un)civil society. Enter that saucy thong-wearing, rude dildo-waving, recently minted TV "wedding fairy" Scott Thompson—or, better yet, his alter-ego, Buddy Cole. Tart-tongued Buddy never had a civil word for anyone. He's someone who's unafraid of calling a homophobe a homophobe. He's also someone who could bitch-slap all of us out of our Canadian trance.

ORATORY ON ORATORY

Seeing Ourselves Through Story vs. Western Models

In the study of literature, Western instructors often pose the question, "What was the author thinking, doing, intending?" Salish thinkers and philosophers (orators) regard such questions as invasive, and do not grant themselves the right to ask them, much less answer, in the absence of the author. Such questions are meaningless in terms of the function of story in our society. The point of hearing (and now reading) story is to study it in and of itself, to examine the context in which it is told, to understand the obstacles to being that it presents, and then to see ourselves through the story, that is, transform ourselves in accordance with our agreement with and understanding of the story. The answer to the question governing the author's intent leads to the transformation of the author, not that of the listener or reader. We encourage growth and transformation in other humans, but we do not see it as our purpose to assist them in the process of maturation. The objective is mature, transformative governance.

This invasiveness marks the nature of the Diaspora. It is rooted in the Western notion that society can guess what is going on in someone's mind by what they write. In their successful global conquest, the mother countries, the Diaspora I am talking about here, collectively and individually, granted themselves the right to claim discovery, and then proceeded to define, delineate, and demarcate the cultural, intellectual, economic, spiritual, and physical being for the entire world. The institutions of this Diaspora usurped the authority of, and established exclusive dominion over, the standards for all sorts of things, including education and literary creation. This global positioning of privilege and dominion affects the Diaspora's attitude towards those outside its privileged location. Its right to speculate on what is in the mind, body, heart, and spirit of others is an unquestioned agreement. The citizens of this Diaspora practise this exclusive right based on the right of their state to arbitrarily determine the nature of their relations with all others, often without due consideration to those others. This has had disastrous results in the world. Disaster is the outcome of invasiveness, to wit, war and environmental destruction.

The structure of a building determines its style; the structure establishes the parameters of its foundation in a limiting way. The type of building constructed tends to be similar to others built before it. This, in turn, limits its function, its use, and its aesthetics. The owner of the building limits entry. Aristotelian definitions of drama and poetry were based on Greek aristocratic supremacy and exclusivity. They reflected Greek culture and Greek social norms. The structure of Aristotelian story reproduces the structure of Aristotle's society: hierarchical, patriarchal, and racist. The compliance by White male writers over centuries with Aristotelian definitions gave birth to a collection of writings that, designated the canon, governs our present. As Europe set about to establish colonial preponderance over the entire globe, it foisted this canon on the colonies. It erected structures globally to exclude and limit other types of participation.

Today the colonized are free to challenge this House of Lords.

Stó: lo Study Methodology

Study can be contemplative, reflective, dramatic, responsive, analytical, dynamic, collaborative, and inspiring. It is capable of sparking and moving people toward social transformation, dissolving inequities, eradicating dangerous assumptions, and altering oppressive conditions. It is also capable of rationalizing those same oppressive conditions and upholding inequity by ignoring underlying assumptions that may prove dangerous to position. Depending on the direction from which we choose to examine the subject and the position we hold as examiners, serious study can maintain or threaten the status quo. The motivation for our examination (gatekeeping or a desire for relationship) guides the process of examination. The objective of the examiner narrows or broadens the thoroughness of the examiner's search. If we are colonized, study can direct us toward freedom, and it can be liberating. If we are colonizers, it can direct us toward our humanity, and this too is liberating. If we fail to master study, to question the direction from which looking occurs, or to ponder the motive for seeing and studying, then study becomes reactive, reproductive, and colonial.

In a certain sense, fiction/myth, story, is real: it is historic and reflects life; it is conditioned by the desire to mirror a character's relationships with the world. Salish study looks for the obstacles to growth and transformation, both in the external and the internal worlds. Once an understanding is achieved, the mythmakers story it up in a way that they hope leads humans toward social maturity and growth. The assumption here is that growth and maturity are capable of inspiring intervention and will lead to the transformation of the dichotomous social arrangements in Canada.

For First Nations people, study is directed at that which is not seen, not known, at what is cherished and hidden. In the discovery of the unknown lies growth. At the bare minimum, consciousness of who we are ought to occur. This takes some humility and, of course, some witnesses who know you. Study, then, is a collective and collaborative process: collective not in the sense that one wants to come to a common position, but collective in that many participate, and collaborative in that we all wish to come to a good mind about what is cherished and hidden. The good mind ranges from clarity, consciousness, to the end goal of a good life. In order to see what is not known, personal agendas must be articulated and set aside. We engage witnesses to assist students in ensuring that we have truly set aside our agendas. The light must be bent in a direction that is not obvious, that is in the shadow.

In shadow land we experience the discomfort of the unknown. Healers are present to ensure that this discomfort is processed and pushed past, and that we don't make fear-based, discomfort-based decisions about the unknown. Each of us is called upon to open our eyes to see what we have not dared hitherto to look at. Study is about searching for what lies beneath the obvious, unmasking the journey of a phenomenon coming into being, and engaging ourselves in imagining its passing out of being.

Mythmakers, storiers, are present to bear witness, see, and understand the subject under study, and serve as adjuncts to the process, so that they may story up each round of discourse in a way that governs the new conduct required to grow from the new knowledge discovered. We assume that individuals have different viewpoints; in fact, the more variance in viewpoints, the better. There is no arguing or challenging someone's viewpoint. We are certain that there is a place for oppositional points of view, as all views are seen as an aspect of the whole. We are interested in clearly stating what we see and looking for the key to the unknown in the voices and words of others. We are listening—our imaginations fully engaged—to what is said, what is not said, and what is connected to what is not said. The words spoken by others direct the listener to imagine and think. Rememberers attend to the words spoken with care, so that the oratory can be repeated later. They commit to recalling without judgement every word spoken. The speakers use words sparingly with poetic force, vision, and poignancy, so the rememberers will have an easy time of recall. Once the first round of deliberations is up, we imagine the story that will encourage us to look again, to peel back each layer and gain deeper understanding.

The next round is to imagine what direction each of the pathways arising from each person's contribution leads. This is a query round, sometimes a round of mini-stories, to assist in our search. It is a round in which we attempt to look beyond ourselves, to gauge the future, and to reassess the masks we wear in the present. The moment we hear something we have not heard before, whether we believe it has value or not, we build on it as a way of arriving at understanding. We flesh out this new idea, and then we story that up.

Every deliberation leads to discovery, new relationships, new directions, and, of course, new story because we build on what we have not heard or said before. Once the new thought is understood, then the storiers, the mythmakers, the poets, and the dramatists conjure story in a way that will assist the whole in establishing a relationship to the new. They are expected to do so with freedom and choice in mind; the stories then must be lean narratives, narratives that enable the listener to contribute to the narrative and make choices about the direction he or she chooses to take in the light of this new phenomenon.

Orators are our knowledge bearers, teachers, scientists, environmentalists, agriculturists, aquaculturists, historians, and rememberers. For a people whose culture rests on becoming, not becoming is tragic. In order to blossom, we must be free to see, to study in a culturally appropriate manner. See is relentless, powerful or hampering, imprisoning or liberating. What we look at and what we do not look at is no accident. It is established by the place of the seers in the social fabric, the positions they hold and the journeys to their particular place. Position also shapes what is looked at and what is ignored. Culture abrogates personal responsibility for systemic being, or it calls us to question being and place and culture itself. It grants us a means by which to rationalize our position and place in relation to others, or it challenges us to question the arrangement and assignment of place. If we enjoy a position of privilege, we may engage ourselves in personalizing the journey of the story and resent the challenge to place. In seeing ourselves through story, we become part of the journey. Those who turn a blind eye to Canadian First Nations literature will not see the rock upon which the place and privilege of each member of the Diaspora rests.

When studying a subject, we first face our attitudes, our beliefs, and our agendas. We face the filters through which our specific cultural and personal origins affect clear and clean vision. Even though we may not be aware of our blinders, our masks, and our filters, we have them. These blinders, masks, and filters pervert the attention we pay or don't pay to the condition or being of others. Attention is a device driving us to implode—or explode or desire—transformation, or to exchange desire for the mundane and the old, driving us to plod along blind to the new and different in the world. We articulate the way in which we rationalize our place and identify how this colours our vision. It is not enough to articulate the masks through which we see. For see to be thorough, the seekers must engage their search in a conscious process of removing the masks and dropping the filters through which they are peering; we struggle to set them aside, to ensure that we are looking at the being and the phenomena free of our personal history. We believe that our attitudes, our beliefs, and our agendas are the ordinary, everyday masks we wear that facilitate the reproduction of social and cultural being in a static way. Stasis promotes decadence. The goal is to study something with transformation and growth in mind. These masks are not all that useful in establishing new relationships. Unless we bend the light in the direction of our attitudes, beliefs, and agendas, we will not be able to drop the mask, let go of our original vision, and expand it to "include" the vision of others in our scope of see. Oratory is braided to the processes of see, to study, to unmasking our attitudes; it requires the mythmakers to remove the filters that colour and taint vision. Our stories reflect all of these processes.

See has a methodology that is emotive, spiritual, intellectual, and physical. It can be affirming and mundane, as though it sought the repainting of the same picture, as though it were moved to repeat history, as though it were its own force holding the old social conditions and relations in place. In its possession of force, it may draw us to look again, to re-search, to play, to fiction ourselves in dreams of transformation or to escape the very force of looking. Intentions are masks constructed of experience; they hide cruel intent arising out of wounded and violated vulnerability, or surrender, or unrequited love. Force is a volcano waiting to explode. In the dichotomized world of Diaspora and chronic invasion, we are all equally capable of marching in these directions.

Story becomes a means of intervention preventing humans from re-traversing dangerous and dehumanizing paths. Oratory, then, is responsive. It challenges the state of being of the people who are being "storied up." It is transformative. It pulls up the sort of characters who can best "story" the subject, the obstacles, and the characters, which impede transformation and/or freedom.

The Object of Study

The object of study from a Salish perspective is ultimately the creation of oratory that will lead us onto a path of continuous growth and transformation, and that will enable us to engage all life in the type of spirit-to-spirit relationship that leads all parties to the good life. We did not have the concepts of law, order, and compliance that require systems of force to uphold them. Our concept of the good life was rooted in recognition of the perfect right to be for all beings. We do so from the emotional, spiritual, intellectual, and physical perspective that all beings enjoy a perfect right to be as they are. We believe that each being owns a sense of distance between itself and human beings, a survival right, and a value to the totality of life, even if we don't know what that value is.

Study is tempered by humans studying the space between the beings in the relationships humans engage. From the snow flea on a glacier to barracudas and sharks, the small beings and the invisible beings, all beings have a perfect right to be. We respect the barracuda, but we recognize that the charming smile of this predator is dangerous, and so we maintain a good distance from his territory, and we don't swim with sharks. Principles of fair exchange govern all of our relationships. We pick berries in such a way that the berries are assured of continued renewal, and we are cautious to leave some for the bears. We study from the perspective that, as the variable beings on earth, it is humans that need to transform and alter their conduct to engage in relationship with other beings and phenomena. Relationship engagement is disciplined by conjuring the least intrusive and invasive conduct possible, respecting the distance and reproductive rights of other beings, and ensuring the greatest freedom of beings to be as they are and always will be. This requires that we study the life of beings and phenomena in our world from their perspective, and not from the perspective of our needs.

The goal of study is to see a being or phenomenon in and of itself and for itself with the purpose of engaging it in a relationship that is mutually beneficial. First, we need to know *who we are* and the possible obstacles to understanding that our history may present. In the course of study, we deliberately engage people with different kinds of knowledge, points of view, and different understandings, people whose journeys are dissimilar to ours, who may have witnessed the phenomena under study from their own perspective. Should we discover discomfort during the process, we track back the source of discomfort from inside ourselves, inside our journey, our history, and face ourselves and our fears, face our discomfort and disconnect it from the subject under study. Then we story this up. We express the governing impact our history has on the way we see. We story up the blinders and the filters we inherit from our history. In this way, we develop an intimate appraisal of our emotional responses to history, to movement, to the dynamics and conduct of others in relation to ourselves. If we cannot let go of our history's impact, we abstain from the process. We imagine our desire, our capacity for transformation, and our place in the universe next to the being we try to relate to, guage its importance to us, measure our desire for relationship with it, and discuss it with our peers as story/oratory. We must study, and engage ourselves in the pursuit of study, in the interest of both ourselves and the subject of study. We are in varying degrees successful or not in this endeavour, but it is the goal of our study.

We know that standards, norms, and experiences can become obstacles to clear perception, and we take the time to clear the norms that reduce us to seeing through some kind of collective fog, filtered through old standards.

This Is the First Story That Needs to Be Told

On one hand, we recognize that humans have the capacity to be concatenate, to link with all beings and phenomena, to be conscious, to be aware of our personal motives, to be curious, to be open to the discovery of others, and to be creative, to make the links and connections happen in a mutually beneficial way. On the other hand, we recognize that humans are very much like viruses; given the opportunity, they will colonize another being, unless disciplined to travel in another direction toward relationship and away from conquest. Opportunism is an inherent part of our spirit. This opportunistic behaviour has both an upside and a downside. On the upside, opportunism creates a sense of doubt and desire that leads us to question ourselves and the world around us, calls us on our motivations, calls us to create new things from the world around us so that, when we feel uncomfortable, we can be inspired to track our discomfort and engage in personal and social transformation.

As variables in the grand scheme of creation, in our origin stories we enter the world as both fragile and resilient beings. Like viruses, we are difficult to contain. In fact, our resilience defies containment. Freedom is always on our agenda. Like viruses, we appear to have an edge on the animal beings. A wolf, for instance, cannot alter its being and become, say, a truck driver, a doctor, or a lawyer, while a doctor or a lawyer could in theory lead a wolf's life; he or she could live in very harsh circumstances, sleep under the stars with a minimum of protection from nature (like a fur coat), and sustain himself for some time on field mice, the primary diet of a wolf. This is not to say that wolves are not as intelligent, emotional, spiritual, character-driven, social, or complex as we are; it is just a fact that a wolf would not succeed at a contemporary law school, and it would be dangerous for a wolf to undertake to drive a truck. As variables that are fragile, and yet capable of great opportunistic destruction, we are called upon to pay attention to our relationship with others, to engage the world and all its beings in a responsive and responsible manner that is cognizant of the perfect right of other beings to be in relationship to us. We are not entitled to use the information gathered about the impossibility of the wolf becoming a lawyer to demean the wolf's being, or to give us the right to murder him. This is the exploitative work of invaders. This will not result in a future relationship with the wolf.

Conquest is neither the object of study nor the desire of relationship. We long ago relinquished invasion as a way of being. In so doing, we have come to see that if we see the story of a social formation as an inherently oppressive phenomenon, we are called upon to story up its oppressive features and the impact of these features on the myriad of characters from our world in the hope that our citizens will catalyze social transformation from within the story. This opportunism can sometimes drive us to sink into discomfort, pirate the things around us, retreat into blind denial, and entrench ourselves in the defeat of the business of personal growth in exchange for participation in conquest and colonization.

This Is the Business of Oratory

Even in the worst catastrophe, there is something unknown and cherished to be discovered. We are certain that all life and death contain something cherished that can be observed; if we listen, if we look for its internal dynamic, watch its behaviour, and commit to its being, we may discover it. Once we discover it, we can establish a relationship with it. Despite the distance maintained between the barracuda and ourselves, we still have a relationship with it. That relationship is one of cherishing the distance between predator and prey; in this way, the barracuda becomes a teacher, and the relationship is one of student and teacher. The space is deep green water. We determine the nature of relationship, and the mythmakers create oratory as story so that each person can conduct himself or herself in a complementary fashion. We can know that we are successful only if both the being and ourselves flourish, or if the phenomenon (e.g., colonialism) is transformed into something all agree is better than before.

This Is the Desire of Oratory

Salish people created the frameworks and language within which we may view the world in the way I'm outlining here to ensure the greatest absence of destruction, invasion, imposition, and obstruction in our engagement of the world, while still availing ourselves of the resources required for our specific continuance. These frameworks prevent us from becoming conquerors, and lead us away from systems of slavery and toward spirit-to-spirit relationships based on a profound understanding of ourselves. They did not lead us away from war, but we are sure they will in the end.

We set the unknown but cherished thing at the centre of a study circle. Each of the students is an expert gathered at the outer edges of the circle. Each person forms a wedge of vision observing the space directed toward discovery of the unknown. Each observer brings an angle of perception that, when rallied, engaged, and exchanged, brings vital observations, which will assist us in considering the internal dynamics that might govern the behaviour of the being in the least judgemental way possible. We do not believe we can fully understand the being/phenomena under study. We recognize that we are not able to walk inside the body/mind/heart/spirit of the being/phenomenon; we cannot know the thoughts/thinking, emotions/emotionality, and spirit/spirituality of the being or phenomenon. In our ordinary travels through the mundane tasks of life, we rarely look deeply at the world around us. In the course of study, we pay attention to ordinary beings and bend the light in the direction of the unseen, of the shadows inherent in any being. Inside shadow land lies the dynamics of hidden being. We can see its behaviour, guage its patterns, note the direction of its movement, and come to grips with it in relation to us. We can see its journey, and render it as story. We can study this journey and try to understand ourselves in relation to its story so that we can peacefully coexist.

We then story up the nature of safe engagement in mutually beneficial relations.

We attempt to story another being/phenomenon's behaviour and commit to its journey, its coming into being and going out of being, to this story. We then alter our conduct, our behaviour, to facilitate a common journey alongside of the being/phenomenon without interrupting its physical or cultural continuum, and we story that up. We commit ourselves to social structures, which lend themselves to creative, re-creative formation and transformation. This is how oratory is born. Oratory is a painting; it is about the freedom between beings and about cherishing the distance between them; it is about relationship, and as such it is about life. Oratory is comprised of the complex relations between disparate characters in their concatenation or their lack of it. It is the story of patterned events. Oratory is a human story in relation to the story of other beings, and so it is fiction, for it takes place in, while engaging, the imagination of ourselves in relation to all beings. Oratory informs the stories of our nations in relation to beings of all life.

The Study of Oratory Requires That We Peel Back the Layers

The process of study is based on story. Stories are about characters, and we believe that character is inherent and unalterable. Those who would alter character do so under threat of creating disastrous consequences; therefore we challenge conduct, not character. The conduct we challenge is, of course, the conduct of ourselves as humans. Under each pattern of conduct is a layer of history. We strive to protect the dignity, movement, and space of those under study. Thus we search and research the history of their conduct and deal with their history as influence. We attach conduct to the influence of history, inspiring the character to alter conduct if that conduct impedes relationship. This is our meaning of respect. We engage in the process without the expectation of agreement or amicability, without preset standards. This is the meaning of openness, which is a prerequisite to learning. No being is reduced to the conquered. No being is extorted by others or demeaned to a lesser place of being through humiliating practices. All phenomena are valid and acceptable, part of the picture, and it is in the creation of a whole picture, a totality, that the work of study begins as story, which becomes part of the body of our oratory. We do not leave the world of flora and fauna out of the process. The origin stories of the trees, the flora and fauna, and so forth are articulated during the process as needed.

We first see how the character moves, see how it conducts itself, how it marks its own sense of movement, its sense of time and being, its sense of territoriality, its organizational structure. We connect its conduct to its being, and then we connect its movement to its desire, its sense of time to its longevity, and its behaviour to its condition, history, and environment; and we story that up. Until we have a vast body of patterned movement and conduct observed through many sets of eyes, we make no deductions. *Raven-song* presents characters in the condition of patterned colonial movement. This is what oratory or a novel is all about to me. It is also one of the options accorded literary creation in the Euro-tradition. To include oratory as novel in the world of literature does not detract from western definitions.

This process of study is a collective process. It is not oriented toward collectivizing the thinking of those who participate in it. It requires many different sets of eyes, many different minds whose histories are known yet different, whose journeys have led them along adjunct but disparate paths, whose understandings and whose emotions/spirit/mind/body are determined to be travelling in the direction of relationship and good will. We gather people together who are the most capable of seeing and articulating what they see. Together, we paint a whole picture, as complete a picture as our collective can create. We engage one another through the images created by those sitting in the circle. The images must be sincerely and genuinely presented points of view—images, observations, and understandings, not biases. Should a bias arise, we are called upon to set it aside, and identify our ability to rise above our history and conditions and state our capacity for making, or not making, judgements based on some previous past.

The desire is to find the connections, to create the webs between the disparate points of view, images, and stories, and to ensure that the end of the journey is the spiralling down to a moment of peace and recognition. These connections are seen as the creation of windows of opportunity for seeing the future and for transformation. What the speakers/storiers do share is a common sense of direction and a common commitment to moving in the direction of discovering the unknown. We know that, if we examine something from one subjective angle (all human observation and thought are presumed to be subjective), then we will understand only an aspect of the being under study, and we are very likely to engage in huge errors, leap to absurd conclusions based on subjective assumptions, and so forth. This is a process that shows we have come to cherish what is new and struggling to be born.

Discourse Is Creative

This discourse of study engages the work of our creative imagination. The first round articulates the direction from which the viewer perceives. The second round engages with what is seen of the physical behaviour, the coming into being and the going out of being of the being/phenomenon. The third round articulates the being/phenomenon's interaction, its relations with other beings (water, flora, fauna, human, stars, night, day, etc.). Next comes the articulation of its characteristics—its personalities, quirks, oddities— and of its difference from the human condition. Then follows a discussion about what was cherished and hidden, but is now seen in the light of our different perspectives, from our separate, and now shared, observations. Where do we intersect and connect? How do we commune with this being/phenomenon? How do we interact in the least obtrusive way possible? This process requires a facilitator/teacher who has no personal stake in guiding the outcome, but rather is committed to the purity of process and maximizing the participation of each contributor.

We are successful in varying degrees, but we are all clear that that is the process to which we commit.

Conventions Governing Process

There are conventions governing the language of this process. Words are sacred, they are breath, breath is wind, and wind is power. Wind is earth's bellows transforming land, water, sea, and weather. Breath is human wind, our bellows urging us in the direction of transformation and relationship forming. In the end, life is lived through wind's breath. Hard truths require soft language—poetics; journeys are the language of story. The physical coming into being and going out of being is the language of drama; relationship is the language of poetic story. Everyone commits to remembering what others have said, which means brevity is critical. The story conjured is lean, the poetry as pure as the speaker can render it, and the drama short, open-ended scenes linked to the being/phenomenon. Relationship between listeners and the subjects of story becomes possible if the listeners can study the story, see themselves in the story, and transform themselves or their society. Some of the speakers' stories have to do with what lies underneath the past—storied observations presented—and enable the new storiers, the mythmakers, to deepen the story, broaden it, and find intersecting, connecting moments between human and the being/phenomenon.

We conjure the story in such a way that the best human conduct will show itself through it. How do we shape the story so listeners are inspired to consider conduct that will explicitly direct them to the specifics of transformation without narrowing or defining what may be learned? Without limiting the myriad of directions the transformation of all listeners might take? Every story is a guide fleshed out by the listeners in their consideration of future. Story impacts on the shape of the future the listener hears, and she or he completes the story from his or her own direction. The process of study must give listeners the option of determining the alteration of their personal conduct in an atmosphere of freedom. They must be free to make change in accordance with the limits of their character. At the same time, the direction of the whole nation must serve the longevity of relationship with the beings/phenomena generations into the future. If the story does not do this, then how do we story this up? The story calls upon listeners to lend their imagination and voice to it, contribute to its unfolding, and reshape their conduct based on their personal understanding of the relationship or the absence of relationship.

The story must re-present the obstacles to the future that are inherent in the story experienced by the listener. Its lean, poetic, dramatic, and narrative structure is deliberate. The circle of listeners provides the flesh of the narratives. Their villages carried history, story, romance, social being, cultural life, creativity, and growth and transformation from the village to the nation and back to the village. They did so in the language of the listeners. The more attitudes storied, the more perspectives presented, the more choices the listeners have. Thus I think it is funny when someone criticizes *Ravensong*, saying the character of Celia is insufficiently exploited; from the Salish perspective of oratory, this is a compliment.

The final step is to recognize a rememberer as guardian/keeper of the story. No elections are held, nor are appointments made or any agendas drawn up. This process is as fluid as the tide. We know when the story is born. The rememberer knows when she or he has committed to its telling. In the modern world, a book assumes the position of rememberer.

The end result is a powerful story, a long-lasting relationship, and characters that foster beauty, hope, heart, and song.

Students are responsible for identifying what they know of the subject of study before tackling the business of study. The instructor is responsible for facilitating the student's study. Thus study becomes a process of personal exploration of the truths within the layers of hidden being, peering past the obvious and ferreting out the unseen. Students pull on the threads that feed the story (Diaspora, sexism, racism, patriarchy, homophobia, etc.) and that constructed the cultural fabric. They seek the invisible threads that bind them to the characters in the story, and unravel these threads. Students travel on the story's journey to the centre where peace and recognition lie within them. When students have come to a place of peace with the journey, reconciled themselves to themselves, then and only then do they really know something. At that moment, they can remove their blinders, what keeps their feet on the ground, and see sacred black, eyes closed, light cut out, and their point of coming into being and the point of going out of being, and begin a new journey. We need to draw upon the tangled web of colonial being, thread by thread—watch as each thread unfurls, untangles, shows its soft underbelly, its vulnerability, its strength, its resilience, its defiance, its imposition, its stubbornness—rediscover Canada and First Nations people.

We desire to find the fullest, richest, and most interesting and mutually beneficial relationship possible in the least obtrusive and most congenial way possible, to engage the being/phenomenon—its history, its condition, and its conduct in relation to ourselves. This does not require that we shy from the obstacles in the path to relationship. Quite the contrary, obstacles need to be seen, and the hope of story is that the listeners will come together to clear the obstacles to future relationship. We imagine that this desire for relationship might be driven by our mutual right to be. We seek to satisfy our need for continuum as cultural and social beings alongside others—not under them or over them, but exactly like them, alongside them, different, known and cherished by them. This means that the current Diaspora and chronic invasion dynamic interrupting the relationships between us needs to be addressed. We have addressed this obstacle from our side of the table, but Canadians need to face themselves and commit to the transformation of the current relationship between us.

Desire is the hothouse motoring our opportunism and our doubt; it also motors our ability to be concatenate, to be creative, to be conscious, and to remain genuinely curious about all life. In our opportunistic self, humans look with a self-motivated affirmative purpose. That which does not serve our interests is not always attended to. Each human enjoys the capacity for transformation and seeks it on one level or another, or does not. In its unconscious opportunistic state, see's objective can be holy or perverse, and the seer has no way of knowing, without advice and counsel from the community, which direction the vision is guiding him or her. Humans bring intent with their vision. Intentions are sometimes dangerously reactionary. We may choose to see phenomena from the angle of perception we inherit. In our conscious state, we may seek that which is beyond our realm of perception, and this produces a visionary perception that can be transformative or reactive. Study is not about isolating parts; it is about seeing things in their separate movement and being, then connecting what we see to our own capacity for concatenation and the limits of the concatenate of the being under examination. At this time in history, Canadians are unable to face themselves, and so the concatenation between us will be limited. This does not mean that concatenation on a limited scale is not preferred to isolation; nor does it mean that examining parts cannot be interesting or that they are unworthy of study and recognition. But examining the parts—the thin wedges of being, of life, of society—is not the only way to study. Nor am I saying that Salish study formations are the only way to learn, the only way to achieve transformation, growth, or maturity. I am saying that we cannot arrive at whole understanding outside of a broadened and deepened framework. We cannot produce the results of study that will lead to the kind of story that will ensure our growth and transformation, lead to human maturity, to life, to freedom. The colonial system, which still rests squarely on our historic path, stultifies the possibility of concatenation between First Nations peoples and Canadians. The composition of an aggregate picture, a dynamic image of genuine being, and the imagining of the journey from separation to connection—these are the subjects of story and study that can produce freedom.

Instructors are not experts filling up passive empty heads. Students are as responsible for learning as their instructors are for facilitating this process. The student and instructor must be able to differentiate between what is clearly the responsibility of the student in the process of study and what is the responsibility of the instructor in the student's learning. Both must be able to see where teaching ends and internal learning begins. Students must be permitted to respond to education in their own voice. At the same time, critics, instructors, and institutions must respect that the picture First Nations authors advance is true, even if they don't see it that way, that it is half the colonial picture, that what you see may be true, but is not what we see. It may be the other half the picture. The moment we share a commonly constructed picture, a story, then we can begin to pull at the fabric holding the picture together, see its construction, and dismantle and recreate the design. Only then can we collectively recreate a community more human than before. This is the business of study in its totality for us.

From a Salish perspective, study ought to move us beyond the relentless reproduction of our cultural bias and remove the filters blinding our ability to see beyond this bias. In relinquishing the obstacles to new paths, we invite ourselves to this open field of fire we could be. Study requires characters that can challenge us to relinquish the mundane, the perverse, and the repetitive. We need to study stories whose characters and spaces will unlock our confinement and take us on a journey up to those planes of freedom. The spiritual objective of study is to transform the way we see, to broaden the field of vision, to inspire us to "turn around," to drink in the images both of the world and the imagination. When we speak to this process, this too is oratory. When we gather thoughts, examine the conditions of our story, re-present it as theory, and unveil the processes inherent in the journey of story—all this becomes the speaker's map to orating the future, and this too is oratory.

∾

Discourse, theory, cognizance, and the transference of knowledge are parts of a creative, oratorical, dramatic, process through which our narrative history and story—oratory—were crafted, understood, and transferred systemically, both locally and nationally. This is what has created the body of knowledge of the nation and shaped the oral tradition, which then the listeners use to govern themselves. Oratory has ensured continuous growth and transformation: a powerful sense of justice, a broad framework for seeing, and a method of study and representation. Holistic thinking and being are the result. *The study of Native literature, then, is a written and oratorical collaborative process of seeing the self and society through story, in which the instructor is the facilitator.*

STEPHEN SLEMON

TRANSCANADA, LITERATURE
NO DIRECTION HOME

I f there is an organizing principle to this gathering of trans-Canadianists, it must certainly be nothing less than a powerful dissatisfaction with the established methods of our discipline for engaging with the many and multifarious literatures in Canada, with the institutional frameworks we occupy and whose work it is to transmute those engagements into pedagogies and into public statements, and with the vast recalcitrance of the discipline of literary studies itself in understanding critical reading as a force for progressive social change. Since I am not really a "Canadianist," and since my dissatisfactions with Canadian literary criticism at this present moment are not, in the first instance, grounded in critical method, I therefore need to begin my comments in this position paper by saying to my fellow Trans-Canadianists—for you are my teachers—and especially to those new or emerging scholars in this discipline, who may still approach the profession of critical reading with hopefulness about its capacity to help generate greater equity in the future, that despite my personal distance from the TransCanada critical project, I share your rage. My comments here arise from a scholarly practice I persist in calling "postcolonial," despite and possibly in celebration of the fact that the critical field of "postcolonial critical studies," having summitted in the academy, is now on its downward climb. I hope from this postcolonial critical perspective to speak to the middle term in our triumverate of conference superordinates—literature, institutions, citizenship. My argument, in a nutshell, is that, despite all appearances, the mission of the panel for which this paper was originally written—namely, to speak after "the ends of literature" and before "the return of the citizen," simply about this one word, "institutions," and this in a hopeful and forward-looking way, is not actually a depressing and impossible assignment. I begin my argument with a meditation on the hidden logic behind the TransCanada conference's procedural structure, and what it might say about the problem of speaking hopefully about Canadian national institutions.

We often play a shell game when we speak of "institutions" in the human sciences. The definitional apparatus we apply to this general category skitters bewilderingly between meanings, and so the term "institutions" within university culture can refer to those associations or scholarly societies that provide national or international connection, and an avenue for research dissemination, to scholars in similar disciplines; or it can refer to the structural organization of those target-based research projects that position themselves between and across the established academic disciplines, as in the Institute for Globalization and the Human Condition at McMaster University; or the term can identify those foundations, both public and private, that provide specific training services, like the many "institutes" for ESL training in this country; or it can refer to the postsecondary academy or academy-complex itself. Nationally, the "institution" can designate structures that are obviously doing the work of distributive management—like the research granting councils, or the Canadian Radio-television and Telecommunications Commission, or whoever it is that administers the Junos. In the human sciences, "the institution" can also designate any individual unit that does the work of cohesive "institutionalism" within some administrative social massif—as when faculty councils reduce really exciting forms of intellectual and pedagogical pursuit into obedient curricular banality, for example, or when the honours English program or the ubiquitous Norton anthology work to channel students' curiosity-driven intellectual inquiry into disciplinarily sanctioned problem-solving at the expense of a more radical pedagogy based on problem-finding.

Beyond these mundane and dispersed instances of "institutionalization" loom those designations that pertain to organizations and complexes that visibly do the work of maintaining dominant cultural assumptions, like the Althusserian ISAS, the CBC News, or the homophobic Boy Scouts of Canada. And beyond these organizations for the manufacture of hegemony lurks a vast range of social practices, technical apparatuses, and dominant discursive assumptions that we tend to refer to as "institutions" because they operate along the lines of Foucault's "social instruments" for the actuation and implementation of "bio-political" power—"institutions" like individual medicine, the family, the parent–teacher conference, or the liberal subject itself. This skittering between housing shells in our disciplinary idea of "the institution" means that when we come to speak *in general* about this term, as we do in this panel, we always run the risk of seeming disorganized, or confused, or totalizing, and possibly even wilful. Paul Simon noticed this phenomenon, and wrote about it in his song "Gumboots":

> I said hey Señorita, that's astute.
> Why don't we get together
> and call ourselves an institute.

Put together, these several meanings of "the institution" sound menacing, and we can infer something of the reason for this by attending to the *location* we assign to institutions within our embedded disciplinary narratives.

My text for this argument—and I've chosen it because it is typical, not egregious—is this conference's own organizing logic and scheduling practice, where "the institution" appears as the middle, or second, or *antithetical* term within the tripartite structure of a logical argumentative *syllogism*. A syllogism, as you know, consists of a three-part argument—a thesis or main proposition, an antithesis or qualifying second term, and a synthesis or argumentative conclusion—and my general suggestion is that when "the institution" appears in narrative progression within our disciplinary thinking, as it does in our conference scheduling, it is almost always located in antithesis to some potentially emancipatory or ameliorative force. In the embedded logic of our conference's sequencing narrative, this panel on "institutions" occupied a middle position between an initiating "position paper" panel on "the ends of literature" in the first position, whose work it was to locate literature's potential for effecting a social dynamic, and a synthesizing "position paper" panel, in the third position, on "the return of the citizen," whose work it was to reconceptualize social citizenship in some tomorrow-oriented, politically transformative ways. My suggestion is that when we imagine "the institution" as a social force within our usual disciplinary practices, we do so in a way that positions "the institution" as structurally antithetical to something positive, and therefore as something coterminous with the idea of "the obstacle." Since most of the "institutions" we talk about in the human sciences are indeed doing the work of securing the social dominant, this habitual assumption is usually well founded.

But because we habitually envision institutions as obstacles, we commit ourselves a priori to thinking of ways of navigating around them, not to ways of working through them in the project of inflecting the social register. We foreclose on the possibility of institutional forces being redirected towards the emancipative work of social transformation. And we overlook the potential social force of syllogistic argument itself, which can actuate second-term forces or propositions, like the institution, not as obstacles to our desired social outcomes but as dialectic energizers of them. I want therefore to shift out of my own place of disciplinary comfort, which is to theorize, and instead to consider in a more pragmatic manner the possible *uses* of institutions to our mutual TransCanada aims. In taking this step, I draw strength from two of my intellectual mentors, only one of whom I am capable of embarrassing at this meeting.

My first mentor in this step, the unembarrassable one, is the Buddha, who according to the Vietnamese writer Thich Nhat Hahn refused to respond when the pedant Vatsigotra repeatedly demanded that he answer this question: "Is there really a self?" After Vatsigotra had exhausted himself and left, a disciple asked the Buddha why he didn't bother to answer. The Buddha told him: "Vatsigotra was looking for a theory, not a way to remove obstacles" (Hanh, 18). I take this performative moment to be an instructive one, for if much of our training in critical theory carries us to the practice of anti-institutional critique, the Buddha's interpretation of a certain kind of failure in critical energy implies that at least part of what obstructs us from effecting our desired social outcomes from our discipline may be our *idea* of the institution as obstacle, and not just the institutional apparatus itself. I read this moment as an exhortation to the practice of a generative dialectics.

My second mentor in this awkward venture—and this is the embarrassable one—is my colleague in postcolonial studies, Les Monkman, who occasioned my present argument through a conference paper he presented in Hyderabad in 2004. Monkman's claim—and he will not thank me for this savage simplification—was that a major obstacle to the advancement of a political postcolonialism in Canada was the *absence* of postcolonialists in the management of postsecondary institutions. To a large extent, Monkman argued, postcolonial critical thought is institutionally contingent in this country. But postcolonial teachers and researchers have trained themselves through the discipline itself to find ways to avoid institutional administration. Their positions and arguments may flourish in their own classrooms and in their research, but the institution will remain a structural obstacle to the generation of their political claims beyond this level of disciplinary insularity unless they administer the changes they seek. A postcolonial politics will not advance itself in the Canadian university, Monkman warned, simply through the voicing of a pure and unassociated theoretical critique, for no one outside the university will hear it, and no one inside is liable to care. The point is not simply to understand the institution, Monkman argued, but to change it. And that requires a form of institutional avowal.

The TransCanada conference was predicated on the argument that over the past two decades the "pressures of globalization" have changed Canada's "cultural geography" and "global politics," that a new "multicultural formation" has unravelled "the nation's coherence," and that Canadian literary studies are now at "a turning point," one "that necessitates complete rethinking of the disciplinary and institutional frameworks within which Canadian literature is produced, disseminated, studied and imagined" (Conference cfp). I believe very strongly in the general call for a reframing of our disciplinary practices, and I am completely at one with the genuine commitment of this conference to carry Canadian literary critical study forward to the project of social transformation. But I am not persuaded by the conference's predicative ruse. Over the past two decades the record of social reorganization around multicultural and Aboriginal claims in this country has proven genuinely undistinguished. Canada has not repositioned itself in global politics in particularly meaningful ways. The world has changed too little, not too much. The United Nations Millennium Project, which has the goal of reducing global poverty by half by the year 2015, reports that 22.5% of the world's citizens now subsist in conditions of "extreme poverty" (that is, they subsist on less than US $1 per day), that 17% of the world's population is severely undernourished, and that 121 million of the world's children are without schooling of any kind, a disproportionate number of them girls (United Nations, "Progress"). World Bank celebrations of poverty-level reductions in East and South Asia—down by half since the 1980s ("Global Poverty")—echo against a continuing postcolonial history of uneven global development, where poverty levels over the past two decades have stayed consistent in Latin America, Eastern Europe, and Central Asia, and extreme poverty levels in many countries in sub-Saharan Africa have actually gone up. The national situation is no more ameliorative than the global one. The Canadian Council on Social Development calculates that 16.2% of the Canadian population currently lives below the poverty line—a total that includes 23.5% of women over the age of 65, 42.5% of "visible minority children," 52.1% of Aboriginal children, and 55.8% of persons living in "female lone-parent" families. Each year these percentages *grow*. It is not, in my view, external change at either the national or the global level that is driving our sense of urgency at this conference about the project of disciplinary renewal. Nor is it a change that has happened within the Canadian literatures themselves—the resources we find now in literatures for multicultural, or postcolonial, or feminist or queer or Native social transformation, dispersed as they may seem at the level of enunciation and cultural provenance, differ quantitatively a little, but not qualitatively, from those that were there in the writing twenty years ago. What *is* changing now, however, is our collective sense of confidence in carrying our literary critical projects forward into social transformation. Our "turning point" is a disciplinarily insular one, and one of the implicit assumptions within the progressivist narrative I seek to challenge is that generative political effectiveness will come about through an inner redistribution of our objects, methods, and enabling theories for the practice of disciplinary criticism. My argument will be simply that disciplinary reformation, though necessary, will not be sufficient to our aims.

My evidence for this claim rests on the once-robust fortunes of the discipline of postcolonial critical studies, most of whose upwardly mobile practitioners are now employed elsewhere. It goes without saying that postcolonial critical studies found itself in desperate need of methodological renewal through the 1990s. The language of postcolonial theory was not a global language. Too many postcolonialists fitted too many postcolonies to the same conceptual straightjacket. Too many cross-national organizing principles displaced too many registers of internal national division, too many scholars sought anthological and other unities at the expense of radical difference, too many researchers conflated a postcolonial critical perspective with too many forms of minoritarian claim. And then there were the terminology wars. Administrators noticed this, and now hiring practices in English Departments are being refitted accordingly. Last year, Columbia University considered 200 applicants for a tenure-track position in postcolonial literary studies and rejected all of them. An applicant for a postcolonial job at a major research university in Canada was recently told: "We don't do postcolonial resistances anymore."

Postcolonial critical study is now in the process of disciplinary redistribution, and by far the most salient of its new formats is the emerging field of critical globalization studies—the new comet in the academic firmament. The reformation of postcolonial into globalization studies has reorganized debate within the discipline in some important ways: Jawaharlal Nehru's "underdevelopment theory," for example, now appears less often than it once did as an explanation for exploitative persistence; Hardt and Negri's enthusiastic meditation on "complex regimes" of "biopolitical production" now crops up quite frequently (*Empire*). But critical globalization studies, to the extent that they remain insular critical practice in the human sciences, have not sutured postsecondary disciplinary politics to the public sphere in new or transformational ways, and they have not accrued new interventionary powers in the fashioning of national or international social policy. In a telling critique of "the optics of globalization" from the perspective of "the research imagination," Arjun Appadurai explains why it is that a certain failure in democratization *continues* to attend research work in the human sciences, and why "globalization resists the possibility of just those forms of collaboration that might make it easier to understand" ("Grassroots" 4). "New knowledge" in the disciplines, Appadurai argues, has to meet established criteria within a stable "community of assessment" and must therefore be a product of "some sort of systematic procedure." Advances in disciplinary understanding, claims Appadurai, must be grounded in protocol, citational recognizability, and the principle of replication—they come about by "*re*-search," not by "search." The result is that "new knowledge" in the human sciences almost inevitably ends up being disciplinarily agonistic, parochial, inaccessible, and alienated. And so postcolonial studies give way to globalization studies in the academy, a new style of critical engagement comes forward to anneal the old, and new hires attend the disciplinary transformation. But research in the newly reformatted discipline, energized though it is from a sense of having distanced itself from a past political quietism, continues structurally to replicate precisely those disciplinary practices and protocols that maintain a distance between the critical field and the riotous, risky, messy, uneven, and generally unverifiable project of positive intellectual contribution to the work of social transformation. It is likely that by the time another academic generation has rolled through the discipline, the field of critical globalization studies, too, will have sped through its predictive undertheorizations and overgeneralizations, its own pitched campaign in the terminology wars, and settled into a similar state of political defeatism that now informs its disciplinary predecessor. A shift from postcolonialism to globalization may therefore have its uses to some forms of political critical practice within the academy, but at the level of genuine social transformation from disciplinary thinking outward, an insular shift within the discipline will not redress the originary disenchantment.

The progressivist logics of disciplinary reformation seek to package and displace our structural predicament—our contradictory location in the field of political work—into a discipline-specific fall-and-redemption narrative, and I take my own point of intervention into this progressivist narrative from another of my mentors, Homi K. Bhabha, who argues that "newness" is to be discovered *not* in the "progressivist division between past and present," not in a reification of the modern against the archaic, but *in medias res,* in "the foreign element that reveals the interstitial," in the "indeterminate temporality"of the structurally "in-between" ("Location" 227). Here is my thesis for this paper. The foundational first-term principles that brought us to this conference—postcolonial thought, feminist theory, Marxist, anti-racist, or queer critique—are *not* dated commitments within the practice of literary reading. Our political desire for third-term social outcomes for these disciplinary commitments—outcomes like genuine equity in a global cross-culturalism, representational inclusion at all levels of national articulation, a participatory role for everyone in public debate and decision-making—are not archaic forms. We cannot provide an answer to all of our anxieties about the generative political effectiveness of our disciplinary investments, for those anxieties are truly well founded. But we can seek some forms of contingent political effectiveness in locations *other* than the place of disciplinary reformation. And some of those locations will be at the disciplinary narrative's syllogistic second term. Not just obstacle, then, though still that; not just antithetical, but dialectical—my commitment in what follows is to attempt to understand at a pragmatic level what a thinking *through* "the institution" would look like if it were approached as a site of *necessary* incommensurabilty, engagement, compromise, and risk.

The Granting Councils

A claim made equally by a principled, student-centred professoriate in the Canadian university *and* by corporate university administration itself is that the primary function of the Canadian university is to teach, and the primary function of research in the university is to support that teaching. The reason the first group makes this claim is politically obvious: our postsecondary institutions should be devoted to the processes of intellectual empowerment and principled social engagement, not to the manufacture of resources for private profit taking. The reason the second group holds this position, however, *is* the profit-taking motive. The fact is that very little R & D in Canada receives public funding *outside* the postsecondary structure, and the reason for this is that what profit-taking industry requires most in this country is the "human capital" that R & D research produces through training, not specific research findings. For that, corporate Canada mostly draws on the international research community.

Researchers in the "human sciences" in Canada, however, have not attempted substantially to leverage the general principle of research-teaching continuity, grounded though it is in mixed university motives, towards greater disciplinary participation in national research funding. Fifty-nine percent of postsecondary students in this country are enrolled in Social Sciences and Humanities Research Council-funded programs, but SSHRC receives only 12% of the total funding allocated to the three main granting councils (CASA). This disparity, and the radical differences it produces between SSHRC and the other Councils in both success rates and funding levels, remains nationally normalized and disciplinarily aggrieved. For the most part, we have entrusted the voicing of this sense of grievance in the public sphere to SSHRC itself and to our university administrators. Not many in government, or indeed in the general public, have found good reason to be convinced. University administrators have found us a distraction. And SSHRC has advanced a distorted claim: its argument has been that research work in the Canadian human sciences comprises an end in itself, that applied and targeted research practice depends on foundational knowledge, and that research in the human sciences advances basic knowledge, and so it should be funded. We have internalized this argument in the disciplines, reified our critical research activities into intellectual practices of free-standing inquiry, and legitimized our research procedures and methods by placing them in opposition to other, especially earlier, critical practices within our own scholarly disciplines. Needless to say, there is nothing wrong with disciplinary thinking, but as public arguments our claims for why postsecondary intellectual training in the human sciences *needs* a research platform have generally been insular, and therefore weak.

The truly strong claim at hand is that research in most of the human sciences, and certainly in literary criticism, really matters, and should be funded, *not* because it pertains to a particular object or employs a particular method but because it has the capacity, when brought into alignment with a vigilant and forward-looking institutional pedagogy, to bring students to the heat of current research inquiry, where they learn, through the application of approaches and intellectual assumptions that may usefully fail in the production of positive research outcomes or "new knowledges," exactly how critical thinking advances and changes as it moves through new material. This argument, needless to say, can be made *only* by those whose professional work inhabits the teaching–research continuum, not by distant administrators, and not by the granting councils themselves. For the granting councils inhabit a structural anomaly. Research funding in Canada is a federal prerogative, but teaching a provincial one. In a meeting about SSHRC transformation at the University of Alberta in 2003, SSHRC President Marc Renault reported that he would have liked to advance further arguments about the centrality of human sciences research to postsecondary teaching practice but had been told this offended some political protocols and he should perhaps back off.

A dialectical engagement with the institutional framing of research funding for the human sciences, I suspect, would not acquiesce so easily to this structurally incommensurate ventriloquizing of our professional *raison d'être*, nor would it fail to notice the general practice of SSHRC, arrived at through the peer-review process (which means us), to afford most of the larger research grants in our discipline to methodologically conservative, and politically neutral, research projects. This engagement would foreground precisely what it is that students gain from their proximity to volatile, intellectually exciting, and politically committed research inquiry in the human sciences, it would enter into transformative discussion with the ever hardening research project norm in our discipline that trains participating students merely to put a competent research brick into a monumental and unmoving research wall, and it would noisily question the usefulness of those research institutes in Canadian postsecondary institutions that contribute nothing to university teaching. This dialectical engagement would embrace the commitment to speak beyond the university cantonment about the work of the human sciences. And it would seek good ways to bring our research methods and protocols, and not just our research findings, into line with our teaching practices. This last engagement would almost certainly prove the most substantial of all of these challenges, but it could also ground a form of disciplinary transformation that would begin to approach the public sphere.

Research Institutes

Research institutes appear within university culture when a specific research project cannot be mounted from within the individual disciplines. For the most part, such institutes draw on donor funding or corporate partnerships to energize their projects, and so it is unsurprising to find that the very few left or liberal research institutes seeking to contribute to public policy discussion in this country—the Parkland Institute at the University of Alberta, for example—are spectacularly outmuscled in Canada by an army of *derechista* institutes, both affiliated and "independent": the Frazer Institute, the C. D. Howe Institute, the Centre for Cultural Renewal ("we focus on the important connections ... between public policy ... and religious belief" ["Our Goal"]), or, at the University of Alberta, the recently proposed Institute for United States Policy Studies.[1] Because of this imbalance in institutional presence, we find reason to assume that the formal institutionalization of human sciences research within the university is generally the prerogative of interest groups for the social dominant, not for the forces of equitable social change. And so we continue our habitual practice of looking to the paradigm shift within the discipline, not to formalizations of the place between disciplines, when moments of disillusionment overtake us, hoping that some inner reformation in method or object will lead our discipline forward to the rivers of academic renewal.

Some in our ranks, however, have found a place for politically vigilant, socially transformative institutional work within the Canadian university, and my contention is simply that we might seek to learn from them. The Centre for Peace Studies at McMaster University seems to me an exemplary example of this kind of institutional engagement. Administratively it comprises representatives from arts, science, engineering, health sciences, and humanities. Pedagogically it mounts a foundational first-year course and then organizes student programming through courses in various departments—critical race studies, for example, or the history of modern Latin America, or peace-building through health initiatives. In programming the Centre mounts public lectures, organizes peace festivals, and runs essay-writing competitions for area high-school students, but it also co-sponsors, and seeks to learn from, the Mahila Shanti Sena ("Women's Peace Brigade") peace movement in Vaishali, Bihar, which among other things puts on an annual training camp in peace, democracy, and development for rural women. The impetus for the constitution of this Centre for Peace Studies, I am told, came from a university biologist (Singh).

One reason there could be real value in a dynamic, *initiatory* engagement with research institutionalization from literary scholars in this country pertains to the place of representations in the fashioning of both domestic and foreign social policy. Literary critics have long attempted to position their own cross-cultural approaches, which necessarily rest on representations, in dialogue with that vast range of social-sciences disciplinary practices that claim cross-culturally to *know* the condition, the assumptions, and the values of others, and we have consistently argued from within our discipline that the study of representations can help inform cross-cultural principles of mutuality and contribute to the development of a self-critique. What would it mean to carry this order of fractured and hesitant cross-cultural understanding out of postcolonial, diasporic, or multicultural critical theory, and into the framing of social policy in Canada and the world? My suspicion is that literary critics (like me) have tended to join research institution initiatives on social policy when someone else has conceptualized them, not through their own originating imagination and design. And so this question remains more or less unanswered.

Hiring

One of the major challenges now facing the discipline of literary critical practice in Canada—and this includes Canadianists—is not disciplinary reformation but disciplinary survival. Language departments in Canada are everywhere under pressure to drop literary and cultural engagements in lieu of language training. English programs are being morphed into training units for writing skills. At the global level, literature studies is being buried by the monolith of Media and Communications Studies, as has happened at the Mona campus of the University of the West Indies. And English Departments can just be cancelled and their professors made redundant, as they were in the late 1980s at the aptly named University of Darwin.

A seemingly rational response by scholars to such an obvious obstacle to their disciplinary vibrancy is to hunker down into research and teaching, and to seek continuation. We know the value of what we do, and we hope things will not change. This structural response can inflect the way we administer the particulars of institutional renewal in our discipline, however, and one instance of this pertains to our hiring practices. I have long been struck by the ways in which hiring habits within the discipline of literary studies rest on principles of recognition and comfort. Our tenure-track job advertisements have changed very little over the past four decades. We continue to fetishize undergraduate and graduate training in our own specific discipline at the expense of real experimentation and inquiry across disciplinary programs. We hope desperately to include third-world, Aboriginal, diasporic, and minority individuals of all kinds within our chromatically challenged disciplinary collectives, but we also want to set the critical and pedagogical agenda for them, assume our social issues are their issues, locate their critical edges, and know them by who they cite.

My closing suggestion for this position paper is that a discourse of continuance organizes our most fervent disciplinary hopes, and so our administration of disciplinary change becomes a shell game of its own. We manage our inclusions through a self-replicating principle of disciplinary citizenship, and in doing so we become complicit subjects of the institutions we abjure. But literary critical practice in Canada will not find its way forward into political effectiveness unless its organizing practitioners relinquish control of the transformational agenda and submit disciplinary management to the participatory unpredictability of radical inclusiveness. The true place of literary critical studies in Canada is open-gated and future-oriented. The highway runs through troublesome country, and there is no other direction home.

RICHARD CAVELL

WORLD FAMOUS ACROSS CANADA, OR TRANSNATIONAL LOCALITIES

The Position Paper (Unread)

"World famous ... all over Canada" was Mordecai Richler's snide jab at Canadian literary pretension and parochialism as he saw them in the 1960s (40), but the comment also highlights a critical crux that has plagued the literature especially since its post–World War II period of development, a crux that was energized by the centripetal pull towards the land, regionalism, and locality, and the centrifugal one towards the cosmopolitan, the international, and what we now call the global. One sees Northrop Frye fighting this one out time and time again: on the one hand, there's the "where is here?" syndrome, with its localized imperatives; on the other, the archetypal thrust into the crystalline realms of literariness ("Conclusion"). The fact that these realms were of a specific time and space (and race and class and gender) did not appear to bother Frye much, but they have bothered us and continue to do so more and more. Are the mantras around globalization simply a continuation of this critical crux, with the nation now taking the role of the local in this era of increasing inflation, or have we entered into a new critical context that is asking us to consider new questions? This, I take it, is one aspect of the interrogation that the TransCanada conference is positioned to effect, and I would like to explore it from a vantage that understands "Canadian literature" not as embodying a particular canon of texts but as an institutional (statist) and thus economic (cultural/industrial) phenomenon that came into being at a specific historical moment, investing it thereby as an object of material and cultural study rather than as a reflection (however displaced) of an ultimately undecidable nationalism and of a literature that refuses to be located—both tendencies compellingly exemplified by the title of the conference, in which Canada as place is de-signified and the author of the text to which the conference title alludes remains unnamed.

Canadian literature, for all intents and purposes, is a Cold War literature (Cavell, "Introduction"). It was conceptualized in the most important cultural document of Canada's Cold War, the 1951 Massey *Report* (Canada), and it was funded through the Canada Council by the death taxes imposed on the estate of Izaak Walton Killam. From this legacy emerged a system of cultural funding remarkable both for its immense generosity and for its statist interventions in what is often conceptualized as the culturally and socially isolated sphere of literary production. The goal was to create a cultural Maginot line (as Marshall McLuhan once put it) to protect Canada from the insidious effects of that immense entertainment machine to the south of us (Cavell, *McLuhan* 200); thus, while the US trained its sensibilities and its sights toward the Soviet Union in the ongoing battle against the communist threat, we looked south towards the real enemy (despite the fact that Canadians had created Superman and Metro-Goldwyn Mayer). The result of these regulatory interventions was a cultural isolationism, and it was achieved paradoxically by representing the cultural milieu as depoliticized, a scenario played out in one of the many untaught novels of Canadian literature, Earle Birney's *Down the Long Table* (1955), interestingly about the fate of a communist professor who abandons his political alliances in—of all places—Vancouver.

It was in this way that we entered into the complexities of the debate on internationalism, initially inspired by the attempts of Canadian authors such as A. J. M. Smith to get us on the Modernist bandwagon. Smith, in his 1943 introduction to *The Book of Canadian Poetry*, divided his subject into cosmopolitan and nativist strains, opting for the greater importance of the former in what the war had impressed on everyone as being a new international age. Ironically, this modernist sensibility was inadequate to the battles that would be waged in the cultural cold war, which would be dominated not by verbal icons but by "cultural industries and ideological state apparatuses" (Denning 4). McLuhan understood this very clearly; trained to profess Modernist poetry, he turned almost immediately to media, eventually publishing a book called *Culture Is Our Business* (1970), which featured T. S. Eliot in a boxing arena giving a lecture to an audience of 13,723 people in Min-

neapolis, Minnesota (44–45). Canadians were shocked by McLuhan's suggestion that culture was somehow in the world, and the University of Toronto
took the first opportunity to close McLuhan's centre for culture and technology, despite—*quelle horreur!*—an international protest (Marchand 273).

Frye, for his part, continued to elaborate Smith's antinomian world view,
whereby culture was either nativist or international, on the one hand telling
us that we had to focus our attention on the local while on the other hand
reminding us that all the action—indeed, literature itself—was on the uni-
versalist side. Frye's position was the old colonialism dressed up in the New
Critical language: we couldn't really have a literature because literature had
already been done in Britain. While elsewhere these debates were seeking
to move beyond the nation as the key concept focussing critical discourse,
in Canada, as a result of the Massey *Report*, attention remained firmly fixed
on the national project, though by understanding nation in the context of
"identity crisis" there was an implicit recognition that this term had ceased
to have the critical utility that it might once have had. Multiculturalism was
supposed to be an answer of sorts to this crisis (and not only in Canada, as
we sometimes think or like to believe); by valorizing something called difference, multiculturalism put a positive spin on the unending question of
national identity—the fact that we weren't a nation was a good thing because
we were really many nations. But the multiculturalist approach was characterized by claims to authenticity that merely reverted to the principle of the
nation-state, and the fallback position was the same one that subtended
Frye's work—White, British, and liberal was somehow never multicultural,
but, rather, just cultural. As Masao Miyoshi has commented, "multiculturalism has been paradoxically aloof to the establishment of a transidentity affiliation, and this indifference directly inverts itself into the aggressive rejection
of any involvement in the affairs of, for, and by the other" (45).

Another answer was to have been provided by postcoloniality, which
was in many ways the successor to area studies (Harootunian 170). The paradoxes of the term, especially as applied to Canada, have not made it a productive model, however, especially given its tendency to essentialize hybridity.
Anne McClintock's comment that postcolonial theory "'effects a re-center-
ing of global history around the single rubric of European time'" (qtd. in
Parry 122) is especially telling in the present context; once again we appear
to be back to Frye. A further problem with the postcolonial model is that it
tended to elide the nation in favour of subjectivities and "a politics of identity rooted in location" (Harootunian 154), perhaps as a response to the feeling that the idea of the nation was the only concept capable of anchoring what

was otherwise an immense globalized flux. This, I take it, is Imre Szeman's argument in *Zones of Instability*. Here globalization is clearly the villain, "whose chief *modus operandi* seems to be the erosion of particularity and uniqueness" (3); yet a problem emerges when Szeman turns from the literatures of the Caribbean and Nigeria to those of Canada, in that he is unable to locate in our literature the nationalist debates that have demonstrably energized these other literatures. In fact, "There is *nowhere* in Canadian fiction after World War II," he writes, "a national literature that aspires to write the nation into existence" (162); instead, he finds that this debate is located in Canadian *criticism*. This should surely tell us something about the phrase "Canadian literature," and it gives further sanction to the title of the Trans-Canada conference.

The fact remains that, after all of these attempts to theorize the nation in cultural terms and to theorize the culture in national terms, the national project is perceived by many to have failed. As no less an observer than Pierre Bourdieu remarked in the year 2000, "Canada … [has been] gradually dispossessed of any economic and cultural independence from the dominant power" (*Firing Back* 48); he repeated the comment again that year, stating that "*The effect of domination linked to integration within inequality* can be clearly seen in the fate of Canada (which could well be the fate of Europe if the latter moves toward a kind of customs union with the United States): due to the lowering of its traditional protective barriers, which has left it defenceless particularly in matters of culture, this country is undergoing virtual economic and cultural integration into the American empire" (90; emphasis in original). Whether we agree with this or not, we should find it sobering as the perception of one of the foremost cultural critics of the period under discussion.

Szeman seeks to reconcile the challenge to the nation posed by globalization through an argument that "the nation has to be seen as part of a dialectic that tries to preserve difference even as it destroys it" (*Zones* 165), although the inverse could as well be argued—that the nation has to be seen as part of a dialectic that seeks to exclude difference even as it seeks to speak a narrative of unity. This is not to suggest that the notion of nation should be abandoned critically or politically, but it does argue for a more nuanced account of nation, as well as for what Edward Said called a "contrapuntal" understanding of its relationship to such overarching forces as globalization (*Culture*). To quote Szeman again, "the nation is now part of the new problem of contemporary cultural revolution, a part of the problematic of globalization that one cannot avoid even if one shares Hardt and Negri's suspicions about the politics of actually existing nation-states" (*Zones* 207). In a sense, globalization has retrieved "nation" from the excesses of nationalism at the very moment of its supercession and reintroduced it within the domain of Benedict Anderson's "imagined community," although here the emphasis is on the materiality of the imaginary, as opposed to the virtuality of the communal. Both multiculturalism and postcoloniality were part of a Cold War narrative that sought to address "otherness" in terms of an "us" versus "them" narrative, a narrative that was transcribed within the Canadian context as "native" versus "cosmopolitan." A counter-narrative of "rooted cosmopolitanism" (213 ff) has been proposed recently by Kwame Anthony Appiah. As he writes in *The Ethics of Identity*, a "cosmopolitan should … be someone who thinks that the world is … our shared hometown, reproducing something very like the self-conscious oxymoron of the 'global village'" (217). In this regard, the abstraction of the "nation" is the guarantor of both the local (in its situatedness) and the global (in that nations represent an alliance of strangers). This is the "imaginedness" of Benedict Anderson's formulation, and, as Appiah notes, it is not less powerful as a concept for being imagined, as those of us who teach literature know full well (242). A similar dynamic is present in the allied notion of theory; as Meaghan Morris has noted, "theory is the work of extracting a cosmopolitan point from the most parochially constructed event" (*Too Soon* 6), and it is here that our interests as political subjects and students of literature come together.

As Bourdieu has pointed out, national cultures in the twentieth century are ineluctably the product of "an international tradition of artistic internationalism" (*Firing Back* 74). Frye's mistake was to argue one at the expense of the other. My argument is not that we deny the antinomian nature of the debate but that we understand it as a dynamic. As Denning has remarked, "Globalization … is … not something one can be for or against; it stands as an attempt to name the present, and its antinomies … are the sign of the unfinished nature of the present" (24). One aspect of this dynamic is the idea of the nation itself, which is far more fluid than its geographical locatedness might suggest, something we have seen time and again in the appropriation of the term—by lesbians and by gays, for example. As Bourdieu remarks, "People are used to thinking and waging struggles at the national level. The question is whether the new structures of transnational mobilization will succeed in bringing the traditional structures, which are national, along with them. What is certain is that this new social movement will have to rely on the state while changing the state" (*Firing Back* 43). It is within this interrogation, I suggest, that we are now to locate both

Canada and its literature, for it is precisely through the dynamic of the global village that we are able to assert the most transCanadian values of all.

The Abstract (As Published)

Canadian literature currently functions in an environment in which it is studied more at the international level (circa 7,000 researchers worldwide in more than 300 associations) and in which it achieves international fame precisely to the extent that it questions its own nationality (as when Yann Martel won the Man Booker prize). My position paper asks us to imagine what Canadian literature would look like if we sought to imagine it outside the fraught categories of "Canadian" and "literature"—both of them deeply exclusionary—and concurrently recognized it as an institutional (statist) and economic (cultural/industrial) phenomenon, investing it thus as a material cultural study rather than as a reflection (however displaced) of a non-existent nationalism and literariness.

The Gist of the Paper (As Performed)

Let's think about the structure of this conference. My paper is posted on a website, and so its production is both here and elsewhere. It is displaced temporally as well—I am performing its gist in a process of recuperation and retrieval.

How can we understand these complexities of dislocation, these coeval sets of temporalities? Rinaldo Walcott suggested in his paper that we need a theory of contradiction to do so. Perhaps we can recuperate that theory in poetry; perhaps, as scholars of literature, we can address the global imperatives outlined so compellingly in Diana Brydon's paper by speaking the language of poetry to these issues, which means speaking a language of ethics that is also a language of hospitality. Hospitality, Derrida reminds us, is not simply part of culture; it is culture itself (*On Cosmopolitanism*).

Morris L. Wosk, after whom this magnificent building in which I speak is named, sold stoves and refrigerators just down the street from us, on Hastings near Carrall; my grandmother bought her stove from Mr. Wosk himself, a Russian Jew who fled the pogroms of Europe, and his history should remind us that culture is about giving as well as about relinquishment.

My paper proposes that an engagement with globalization as a historical and situated phenomenon has the advantage of addressing our present political context while acknowledging a significant aspect of Canadian history—including literary history—which is that Canada is the product of not one but two empires, and thus that we were international before we were national.

One advantage of this encounter with globalization as colonization is that it repositions Aboriginality into a much more prominent position than it has thus far played in our understanding of Canada and citizenship. The first module in the third-year course I am teaching this fall on Global Issues in Canadian Studies begins in 1724 with Joseph-François Lafitau's encountering of the Iroquois (in *Customs of the American Indians*) and ends with the "Aboriginal" masks that Brian Jungen has crafted out of Nike basketball shoes. He calls these "prototypes for a new understanding," which puts it very well—not without irony, not without the possibility of transformation.

Adopting Appiah's notion of a "rooted cosmopolitanism" (213ff.), my paper further suggests that a dynamic engagement with the local and the cosmopolitan avoids the polarizing and ultimately self-serving debates that have characterized Canadian critical production over the last fifty years and projects our debates instead into the public sphere. We must stop talking to ourselves; we need to develop a public culture in Canada by becoming public intellectuals. The debate we encounter may be less certain than the one we hold in the academy, but, as Stephen Slemon suggests, there may be no other way to go home.

The Op-Ed Piece (Not Published): Is It Time for a TransCanadian Literature?

Is it time to start talking about a *Trans*Canadian literature?

A large group of scholars, students, writers and artists gathered last weekend in Vancouver to consider this question at the "TransCanada: Literature, Institutions, Citizenship" conference co-sponsored by Simon Fraser University and the University of Guelph.

Delegates from across Canada and beyond were motivated by a number of concerns. The first of these is the troubled legacy of nationalism. It's not just that nationalism can lead in directions that are deeply exclusionary—delegates were reminded of this every time they picked up a newspaper and read another piece on the same-sex marriage debate. It is also that nationalism is vying with globalization as the driving force in the agendas of the state, including cultural agendas. Canadian literature, for example, has been heavily marketed by DFAIT (Department of Foreign Affairs and International Trade) around the world, to the extent that there are now about 7,000

Canadianists studying our literature in more than 300 associations around the world, with the largest of these in the United States.

Globalization presented further concerns. How can we have a national literature when our authors are being urged to write for an international marketplace and especially for the lucrative prizes that are offered internationally? Canada, of course, has long stressed its multicultural attachments and multilingual realities, which are more and more evident in the classroom. How do we acknowledge these attachments without an easy acquiescence to global homogenization?

Finally, conference goers struggled with Canada's colonial legacies from Britain and France, and economic ties to the United States. How can we have a literature of our own when that literature is seen to be in thrall to Canada's past as a settler colony and to the present constraints of economic relations such as the North American Free Trade Agreement? What of the neo-colonial relationship to Aboriginal peoples? Canada celebrates First Nations culture now but not long ago tried to destroy it through such programs as the residential school system. How can we say we are "post" colonial under such circumstances? These are big questions, and, after four days of intense discussion, there were no easy answers—except that we need more meetings (the next one is scheduled for Guelph in 2007).

Nevertheless, a number of recommendations emerged. The first is that academics have to take these contexts into consideration in the classroom. It is no longer satisfactory to teach Thomas King's *Green Grass Running Water* without teaching the cultural history that lies behind it. A number of the graduate students present at the conference provided glimpses of these new approaches to research and teaching in Canadian literature, their papers moving easily across disciplines, from literature to architecture, from rave music to poetry.

Another recommendation was that the scholarly community share its concerns with a broader public through op-ed pieces such as this one, and perhaps even with a citizen's assembly of the sort that recently discussed BC's electoral procedures. As delegates agreed, the way literature represents Canada has as much to do with citizenship as the right to vote.

(Submitted to the *Globe and Mail*, June 30, 2005)

LILY CHO

DIASPORIC CITIZENSHIP
CONTRADICTIONS AND POSSIBILITIES
FOR CANADIAN LITERATURE

This essay arises out of my own perplexity with the place of a field such as Asian Canadian literature in Canadian literature. There are increasingly significant bodies of literature in Canada—significant in the number of texts and the ways in which these texts circulate in discussions of Canadian literature. These literatures are both "obviously" Canadian but also challenges to Canadian literature as a concept and canon. Black Canadian, Native Canadian, and Asian Canadian literatures, for example, are arguably, even unquestionably, Canadian; and yet, we cannot ignore the trenchant critiques of Canadianness embedded within these literatures. Of course, our answer to these critiques so far has been to understand Canadian literature and thus Canadianness as capacious enough for these critiques. That is, one could say that there is ample room in the national literary for critiques of the nation. However, the seeming capaciousness of the nation does not seem to me to solve the problem. It is not enough that the national literary graciously make space for the kinds of critiques of Canada and Canadian literature that emerge in literatures explicitly marked as Asian Canadian, Black Canadian, or Native Canadian. These explicit markings of difference call attention to a desire to be considered *both* within and without the nation. At the practical level, what does it mean to teach a course or do research in Asian Canadian literature, as opposed to Canadian literature with an emphasis on Asian Canadian? What does it mean to argue for a separate course on Black Canadian literature or to publish as a Native Canadianist? These questions seem simple enough in some ways. Being an Asian Canadianist does not exclude one from being a Canadianist; but a Canadianist is not necessarily an Asian Canadianist and, for that matter, an Asian Canadianist is not necessarily a Canadianist. These are not simply questions of inclusion or exclusion. They are questions that point to the unresolved relation between minority and majority literatures in Canada and, as I will argue later, between the competing demands of citizenship and the desires of diaspora.

We are at a particular historical moment in terms of the study of Canadian literature where Canadian literature as a field is marked, on the one hand, by a recent emergence from institutional precariousness and, on the other hand, by the increasing visibility of minority literatures whose claims to specificity can be seen as threatening the coherence of the field. As Cynthia Sugars notes in her introduction to *Home-Work*, the study of Canadian literature is not only relatively new, but also marked by a perception of the "subordinate status of Canadian literary study" (2). Noting that graduate and undergraduate curricula in Canadian literature were not institutionalized until the 1960s, "and even then ... on a somewhat ad hoc basis" (3), Sugars asks, "to what extent is Canadian literature, now that it has been secured as an independent field of study, in danger of being rendered obsolete, and is this cause for concern?" (10). Sugars suggests that this "problematic is perhaps comparable to the dangers associated with the deconstruction of the unified subject for women and colonized subjects more generally" (10). This connection between the dangers posed by the deconstruction of a unified subject and that of a unified national literary culture highlights the problematic role that the rise of minority literatures in Canada plays, given Canadian literature's relatively recent institutional stability. Even though it seems alarmist to speak of Canadian literature as nearing anything like obsolescence given the plethora of celebrations of CanLit in contemporary culture, the very headiness of these celebrations hints at some anxiety about the coherence of a national literary culture.

My questions are not driven by the wearying questions of Canadian unity, nor do I wish to return to that other question that so often attends the problem of unity: whither bilingualism and multiculturalism? Rather, I am concerned with the problem of the relation between minority and majority cultures in Canada. I will unfold the problem of this relation by exploring the ways in which the subject of diaspora does not map easily onto the subject of citizenship. Within the spaces created by the "unfitness" of the diasporic subject and the citizen, I situate minority literatures in Canada as contested sites of the uneasiness of diasporic citizenship.

Untangling Literature and Citizenship

I want to start by addressing the entangled relationships between literature, nation, and citizenship. One recent articulation of this entanglement occurs in Michael Posner's recent *Globe and Mail* article on Noah Richler's *Literary Atlas of Canada* for the CBC program *Ideas*. Responding to Posner's questions, Richler draws attention to his own understanding of the ambivalence of Canadian nationalism and the modern nation-state as an absurd idea: "[Canadians] know that better than most. We have absurd borders. We don't call ourselves patriots. And every day we are forced to entertain how irrational it is, or how it might fall apart. We love it, but what is it? What does it mean to be a modern citizen?" (R2). Richler's observations highlight the complicated and naturalized relations between the nation, the literary, and the notion of citizenship. Tellingly, for Richler, the question of what it means to be a modern citizen follows directly from what constitutes the modern (in this case, Canadian) nation. However, the question of citizenship can follow directly from the question of nation only when we assume the nation as the site of citizenship.

The nation is not necessarily the natural site of citizenship. Recent work on citizenship in fields such as sociology, political theory, and globalization studies unfolds the possibilities for uncoupling the notion of citizenship from the nation. In "The Repositioning of Citizenship," Saskia Sassen questions the collapse of the nation and citizen, and argues for an "unbundling" of this package while still retaining the nation as a reference point for thinking about citizenship (62). Distinguishing between denationalized and postnational citizenship, Sassen proposes a "pluralization" of citizenship that may "explode the boundaries" (56) of its legal status.[1] Echoing the language of human rights, Keith Faulks argues that the obligations of citizenship demand an understanding of how the concept moves beyond the state. He suggests that "it is becoming clear that the idea of the nation is increasingly a barrier rather than a supporting pillar of citizenship" (42). Untangling the notion of the citizen from that of the nation reveals the ways in which the nation has bounded citizenship not only geographically but also in terms of understandings of community and identity.

While there may be compelling possibilities to explore in thinking of citizenship either in denationalized or postnational terms, the national literary continues to connect citizenship and literature almost as tightly as the nation has been connected with citizenship. The relationship between citizenship and literature has its clearest articulation most recently in Donna

Palmateer Pennee's "Literary Citizenship: Culture (Un)Bounded, Culture (Re)Distributed," where she argues that "national literary studies, understood as a process, provide for a kind of literary citizenship as a form of cultural and civic participation and cultural and civic legitimation in the social imaginary" (81). Risking both a kind of optimism and a belief in our work as critics, Pennee then suggests that there is a possibility that the "statement—that national literary studies are exclusionary—may be operating at its historical limit" (82). I want to hang on to Pennee's risk even as I am less optimistic about the historical limits of the exclusionary practices of the national literary; but I also want to situate her claims within the context of the untangling of citizenship from the nation.

For Pennee, the nation is the indispensable site of citizenship. She closes her essay with a clear call for retaining the space of the nation in thinking about literary citizenship: "For the time being, there is no question of doing without the national; it is rather a matter of doing the national differently. For diasporas do not come from nor do they travel through and exist in thin air, nor do citizenships. They *are* grounded even if not always landed" ("Literary" 83). In this grounding of diasporas and citizenships, the relationship between minority and majority literature emerges as a threat to the national literary: "Minoritized literatures remind us that nations are made, not born, and are thus open to refashioning. Majoritized literatures, if studied historically and comparatively, also remind us that nations are made, not born. It does not follow, however, that the nation is a category to be dispensed with" (78). Pennee's emphasis on the constructedness of Canada belies an elision of the processes of naturalization that insist on the innate relation between citizenship, literature, and nation. Untangling these relationships leaves us open to the question of the *differential* relations between communities and histories in Canada. It may be that both minoritized and majoritized literatures remind us that nations are made, not born, but they do so in crucially uneven ways. This unevenness puts into question the evenness of the relationships between literature, citizenship, and nation. As Sassen notes, the promise of equal citizenship has been betrayed again and again. She observes the "growing tension between the legal form and the normative project towards enhanced inclusion, as various minorities and disadvantaged sectors gain visibility in their claim-making. Critical here is the failure in most countries to achieve 'equal' citizenship—that is, not just a formal status but an enabling condition" (43). The question then is not whither the nation, but how it is that we can fully embrace the differential forms of citizenship that the nation engenders.

The challenge to the integrity of Canadian literature posed by minority literatures, the threat of its fragmentation, increases the pressure to institutionalize and therefore contain them. A problem then arises around resources and the ways in which we understand Canadian literature. Whether or not Asian Canadian or Native Canadian literature qualifies as CanLit is not the critical question. Decades of liberal multiculturalism assert that they do. Rather, we must grapple with why it is that the marking of something like Native Canadian literature matters, why it actually is not "obviously" CanLit; why these differences must be registered, and why the problem with registering these differences isn't just one of inclusion or potential ghettoization. Minority literatures in Canada demand an engagement with long histories of dislocation both within and beyond the nation. Moreover, minority literatures in Canada insist on an engagement with histories of dislocation that are differentially related. As the work of Asian Canadian texts such as *Diamond Grill* and *Disappearing Moon Cafe* affirm, the story of Asians in Canada must be told in relation to, and with an understanding of the differential relation with, First Nations communities in Canada. Complicating a personal history that involves Chinese, Swedish, Scottish, and Irish crossings and mixings, *Diamond Grill* also depicts interactions between Japanese, First Nations, Doukhobor, Jewish, and Chinese communities. Similarly, Sky Lee's novel centres on a relationship between a Native woman, Kelora, and an Asian man, Wong Gwei Chang, who came to Canada to collect the bones of Chinese labourers who died building the railway. The "secret" of this marriage and Wong Gwei Chang's abandonment of Kelora become the unravelling centre of the Wong family several generations later. These are not relationships that can be easily celebrated in terms of minority relations. As Tseen-ling Khoo argues, "the particular colonial oppressions and legacies of Canada's indigenous groups are situations for which Asian-Canadians can express sympathy and some forms of solidarity but [which they] cannot claim to share" (177). Both Wah's and Lee's texts suggest that these are deeply complicated and vexed relationships; but it is precisely this messy, discomfiting space that we need to explore in our criticism.

Minority Literatures, Majority Relations in Diaspora

I have been referring to fields such as Asian Canadian, Native Canadian, and Black Canadian literatures as minority literatures partly as a way of naming their relation to each other and partly to mark their difference from what I, in accordance with Pennee, have been referring to as majoritized literature in Canada. In its general usage, minority discourse calls for an understanding of minority communities as defined relationally through and within each other. Wary of the reification of binaries inherent in the minority–majority axis, Avtar Brah suggests that "the discourse then becomes an alibi for pathologized representations of [minority] groups" (188). Because of "the genealogy of signifying practices centred around the idea of 'minority,' the continuing use of the term is less likely to undermine than reiterate this nexus of meanings" (188). Despite her skepticism, Brah builds on the concept of minority discourse to develop her understanding of diaspora as "embedded within a multi-axial understanding of power; one that problematizes the notion of 'majority/minority'" (189). My use of the idea of minority literatures builds on Brah's enmeshing of the minor with the diasporic.

Diasporic formations are thus not simply static, unitary objects. They are the subjects of relations in and between diasporas. For Brah, "the *concept* of diaspora concerns the historically variable forms of *relationality* within and between diasporic formations. It is about relations of power that similarize and differentiate between and across changing diasporic constellations" (183). If, as Pennee notes, diasporas do not emerge from thin air, then we must also understand them as formations that do not exist in singularities but are defined through their relation with other diasporas and with majority cultures whose claims to autochthony attempt to elide histories of difference.

My understanding of minority literatures throughout this essay is thus deeply connected to race. Minority marks a relation defined by racialization and experienced as diaspora. That is, Asian Canadian literature, for example, relates as a minor literature to Canadian literature not because it is less important, valuable, and illuminating, but because it cannot be divorced from the long histories of racialization that mark Asian Canadian communities as being in the minority in relation to a dominant culture. In this experience of racialization, Asian Canadian communities are marked both by a fierce sense of belonging to this country, of having helped to build it, and by histories of dislocation that sustain a sense of belonging that exceeds the nation-state.

In that histories of dislocation and racialization define my understanding of minority literatures in Canada, I thus want to differentiate diasporic communities from those that are defined as immigrant or transnational. We like to think of ourselves as a "nation of immigrants," and part of the recent triumphalism surrounding Canadian literature emerges out of a certain kind of satisfaction regarding the diversity of our writers. In her influential 2002 Killam lecture, Martha Piper points to the Canadian representation in the 2002 Booker Prize competition with justifiable national pride, noting that Yann Martel was born in Spain, Carol Shields was born in Chicago, and Rohinton Mistry was born in Bombay. For Piper, "Each [of these writers'] writing draws from and reaches out to the world—interpreting life events from a perspective that is both Canadian and multicultural" (n.p). Piper's identification of Canadian literature as increasingly diverse in its roots celebrates that diversity even as it flattens out the differences between the major and the minor, the diasporic and the immigrant. Chicago, Bombay, and Spain are not equivalent spaces of departure. Not all elsewheres are equal. The differences cannot be collapsed between the multiple-passport carrying transnational subject and the diasporic subject whose agonized relationship to home engenders a perpetual sense of not quite having left and not quite having arrived.

Without a sense of the relations between minority and majority literatures and the histories of dislocation and racialization, the celebration of different birthplaces as a means of recognizing the diversity of Canadian literature also risks losing sight entirely of Native literatures. Native communities continue to live through legacies of dislocation that can be too easily elided in the rush to recognize diversity as something that comes from elsewhere. In "*Sui generis* and Treaty Citizenship," James Sakej Henderson argues that the romantic conception of Canada as a nation of immigrants problematically collapses diversity with immigration: "Within this romantic narrative, the diversity and richness of each ethnic group is a constitutional value to be protected, preserved, and enhanced. Nevertheless, this model avoids and effectively denies the *sui generis* and treaty relationships of Aboriginal peoples with the British sovereign" (417). At the level of the academic institution, a number of critics have noted the ways in which diversity and multiculturalism have consistently pushed out indigenous concerns and criticism. As Craig Womack caustically observes, "Departments often look for someone to do multicultural literature rather than Native literature; teach an Amy Tan novel now and then, throw in a little Ralph Ellison, a native author once in a while … reducing literary studies to little more than an English department version of the melting pot" (8). Similarly, Shari Huhndorf notes that "in US institutions, the vantage point from which I write … even ethnic studies programs dedicated to interrogating social power and racial inequalities have, for the most part, ignored or neglected Native America"

("Indigeneity" 29). While Womack and Huhndorf refer to experiences in the United States, their observations remain crucially pertinent for Canadian literature. If I began my essay with perplexity about the situating of Asian Canadian literature within Canadian literature, the situating of Native literatures in Canada within and against majoritized Canadian literature further aggravates the uneasiness of simply containing minor literatures under the umbrella of CanLit.

It is within a commitment to the uneasiness of these relations that I want to differentiate the transnational from the diasporic. Not all dislocations are transnational. As Jonathan and Daniel Boyarin note in *Powers of Diaspora*, "focusing on diasporic spread across national borders, we unwittingly reinforce the prejudice toward thinking of those borders as the 'real' power divides, the ones that really count" (*Powers* 23). The Boyarins refer less to the withering of the nation-state than to the urgency of understanding other kinds of borders that mark diasporic communities and dislocations. They propose that

> thinking of diasporas within states may ... give us new ways of thinking through cultural dynamics of groups such as Native Americans—dynamics that may well include hitherto overlooked instances of the persistence of specific identities. Thus, although the Delaware Indian populations of the East Coast lost their corporate local identity at a relatively early stage in the history of European–Indian encounters, at present there are still individuals born and still living in the west of the Mississippi who identify as Delaware Indians. (*Powers* 23)

For the Boyarins, the power of diaspora enables an understanding of the survival of specific cultural identities despite the often violent dislocations of peoples from their communities. Thinking of Aboriginal communities within the rubric of diaspora provides a glimpse into the possibilities of relations between different histories of dislocation. Not all elsewheres are equal, and not all dislocations are the same. It is on the land from which Native communities have been expelled that Chinese labourers have come to work; it is one thing to be displaced from one's homeland by colonialism and another to arrive to work as a coolie. Part of the commitment of thinking along the lines of Brah's "multi-axial" approach is to think through the relations between diasporas as well as those between majoritized and minoritized communities.

Diasporic Citizenship

I want to propose diasporic citizenship as a rubric for thinking through what I understand to be the contradictions and possibilities of Canadian literature. In its most prominent usage to date, Michel Laguerre's notion of diasporic citizenship articulates the ways in which Haitian communities within the US have built a civil society that could not thrive within Haiti itself. However, I want to use the idea of diasporic citizenship in a slightly different register from that of Laguerre.[2] The current use of diasporic citizenship in the social sciences understands the diasporic as an extension of citizenship practices that tend to be located at the level of the nation-state. While this usage offers a number of possibilities for thinking about transnational forms of identity and belonging, I want to emphasize the inherent dissonance between the terms "diasporic" and "citizenship." I do not see diaspora as a different kind of "container" for citizenship. The idea of diasporic citizenship seems to offer the shimmering possibility of something new, something that might supplant the nation as a site of citizenship and might take into account the underside of transnational mobility, those not accounted for in the idea of Aihwa Ong's "flexible citizenship."[3] I am deeply unconvinced by this shimmering possibility. A new phrase will not necessarily get us out of old problems. Instead, I want to pursue in my exploration of diasporic citizenship precisely its "unfitness." "Diaspora" and "citizenship" do not fit easily together. The former emerges through collectivities; the latter has been grounded in notions of individual autonomy. The former exists uneasily alongside the nation; the latter emerges within the nation. The subject of diaspora and the subject of citizenship do not map onto one another. This uneasiness and dissonance could be very productive for thinking through the differential histories of dislocation in Canadian literature. I want to explore this dissonance in two ways: first, through the push and pull of history and memory; and second, through the problematic legacy of citizenship itself.

The problematic legacy of the concept of citizenship begs the question of its recuperation. As a number of scholars have already noted, modern citizenship emerges through the legacy of the French and US revolutions and has, from its inception, been constituted on forms of exclusion. Attempting to think through the contradictions of modern citizenship, John Hoffman ultimately has to err on the side of exclusion, arguing that "an inclusive view of citizenship, which refuses to make distinctions, will be inclusive only in name. In reality it will merely replicate the repressive hierarchy of divided societies" (150). While Hoffman's argument seems reasonable when applied to the idea of extending citizenship to children or animals (the immediate context of his argument), it cannot help but echo the kinds of rationalizations that were once, and in some places still are, used to deny groups such as women or Aboriginal peoples the rights of citizenship.

Hoffman's insistence on the necessity of exclusion as a principle signals the legacy of exclusion that remains unresolved by the language of universalism. Véronica Schild notes that the tripartite vision of social citizenship developed by T. H. Marshall, which has been so influential in post–World War II examinations of citizenship, remains fundamentally flawed both in its belief that the rights of citizenship would level class difference and in its gender bias (279–80). Building on Schild's assessment of the failures of the Marshallian concept of social citizenship, Isabel Altamarino-Jiménez argues that "marginal groups achieved liberal citizenship rights (if at all) later and in different sequences ... The compatibility of the various citizenship rights has been historically constructed and contingent rather than inclusive and evolutionary" (351). Examining the prehistory of modern citizenship, Susan Maslan argues that modern citizenship attempts to resolve a foundational divide between the "human" and the "citizen" upon which the early modern models of citizenship depend:

> If we think that "human" and "citizen" are or *should be* corresponding and harmoniously continuous categories it is because we think in the wake of the 1789 Declaration. In the early modern political imagination, to be a citizen meant to cease to be human. This is the legacy that the Declaration tries to overcome and that it conceals ... and so the new Republic turned to—or better yet, invented—the language of universalism to repress and resolve the tensions it can neither dissipate nor acknowledge. (372)

Maslan's argument breaks the familiar Greek to Roman to French to American narrative of citizenship's progression as a concept. Her examination of premodern citizenship in relation to the legacy of the French Revolution, the event most closely connected to modern conceptions of citizenship, thus reveals a deeply uneasy relationship between the universal claims of citizenship and the exclusions of its practice. As Giorgio Agamben notes, the discontinuity of the human and the citizen "is implicit, after all, in the ambiguity of the very title of the 1789 *Déclaration de droits de l'homme et du citoyen*, in which it is unclear whether the two terms are to name two distinct realities or whether they are to form, instead, a hendiadys in which the first term is actually always already contained in the second" (*Means* 19,0).

For Agamben, it is thus the refugee who illuminates the failure of the language of universalism to disguise the break between the human and the citizen: "If the refugee represents such a disquieting element in the order of the nation-state, this is so primarily because, by breaking the identity between the human and the citizen and that between nativity and nationality, it brings the originary fiction of sovereignty into crisis" (*Means* 20,1). While the refugee reveals the break between the human and the citizen, Aboriginal peoples contest the possibilities of citizenship for fully achieving constitutional rights. Within the specific context of Canadian citizenship, James Sakej Henderson argues that the offer of Canadian citizenship to Aboriginal peoples in Canada "subverts the constitutional rights of Aboriginal peoples for the interests of the dominant immigrant groups.... Its purpose (deliberate or inadvertent) is to restrict the constitutional rights of Aboriginal peoples of Canada and make them formally equal to other Canadian citizens" (416). In the context of citizenship, too often equality functions as a silencing act rather than an act recognizing historical differences. Given its problematic legacy, I invoke the idea of citizenship here with deep uneasiness.

I want to examine the conditions of citizenship that we have inherited and the ways in which these conditions signal the inexorability of our choice *for* citizenship. Despite any uneasiness that we might have about the idea of citizenship, despite the ways in which we might point to its legacies of exclusion and even violence, we cannot, given the choice, choose not to be citizens. To do so would be to render ourselves refugees—a state that Agamben identifies as one that illuminates the limit of citizenship. Instead of guaranteeing one's rights, what the 1789 Declaration would term the Rights of Man, the loss of citizenship thus endangers the guarantee of rights. The only claim that can return the refugee to the relative safety and security of a social existence lies in a claim for citizenship. Agamben observes that, "even in the best of cases, the status of refugee has always been considered a temporary condition that ought to lead either to naturalization or repatriation" (*Means* 19,0). Despite the long-term existence of millions of refugees, "illegal" migrants and other stateless persons, statelessness continues to be understood as a form of transience. We must all always either be citizens of somewhere or be on our way to such a condition. Citizenship is indispensable. We can seek to transform the institution of citizenship; indeed, following from the work of Henderson and others, we must continue to struggle for forms of citizenship that might better encompass the vision of a society in which we hope to thrive; but we must still choose to enter into this process of transformation, choosing within the contingencies of a situation, at least in part, not of our own making, of a legacy that is not entirely our own.

In my reflection on this choice, I am moved by David Scott's reading of C. L. R. James's *Black Jacobins*, and in particular by Scott's exploration of the choices made by Toussaint L'Ouverture. In what is often considered the beginning of the end of the revolution, Toussaint, threatened by an insurrection led by Moïse in the north, has him shot at Port-de-Paix on November 24, 1801. Unlike Toussaint, who sought to appease the former colonizers, Moïse supported an alliance with the Blacks and Mulattoes against the French and the Creole populations. Moïse also wanted to break up the old plantations and redistribute the land whereas Toussaint wanted to keep them intact. For James, the execution of Moïse was inexcusable but, as Scott notes in his reading of the *Black Jacobins*, James also insists that "it is not self-hatred that motivates [Toussaint] but the working out of a detached and single-mindedly held principle" (*Conscripts* 205): "What Toussaint ... is committed to is a humanist hope for a civic compact conceived on the basis of racial harmony. His hope is to transcend the old animosities and prejudices ... and to join the old divisions together in making an enlightened Republic guided by the abstract principles of liberty, equality, and fraternity" (*Conscripts* 205). Scott's reading highlights the tragedy of Toussaint's enlightenment. It is tragic not because Toussaint sought to appease his former oppressors or because he makes the wrong choice at the wrong time, but because his choices are contingent upon conditions that expose the incommensurability of principle and praxis. The choices that Toussaint makes reveal the impossibility of those choices. They also point to the necessity of making a choice at all, of the necessity of risking contingency.

In Canada, we choose to live with the particular legacies of our postcolonial era, but we do not have to understand those choices as unproblematic, and in fact we must understand them as choices in the first place. I do not want to diminish the specificity of Toussaint's situation, nor do I want to suggest that there is a direct parallel between the choices that Toussaint faces in the midst of a revolutionary moment and the ones that we make from our situations of relative safety and security. Clearly, in Canada, our choices will not result in the executions of our compatriots; they will not condemn us to our own deaths. There are real differences between Toussaint's choice to build a postcolonial society on a vision of liberty, equality, and fraternity, and our own choices for civility, even if our visions of civility share so much with those of Toussaint. Toussaint's choices reveal the fragility of principle and the necessity of contingency. In this sense, choosing to be in favour of civil society, of the obligations of citizenship, reveals the fragility of those principles of civility upon which we must base our choices, and the necessary contingencies of those choices. We cannot have citizenship without its troubled legacy—without the potential anti-humanism, anti-feminism, and elitism of its origins. And we cannot dispense with citizenship.

It would be a mistake to dispense with citizenship, but perhaps we can, on some level, consider being *against* citizenship. Borrowing from the closing meditations of Laura Kipnis's polemic *Against Love*, I suggest that we might be against citizenship in that we approach it—something that on so many levels seems, even in its indispensability, so unassailably right and good—with skepticism even as we embrace it:

> Maybe no one can be against love, but it's still possible to flirt with the idea. Or, as Adam Philips asks in his own later essay on the virtues of flirtation, "What does commitment leave out of the picture that we might want?" Note that "against" is one of the few words … that can mean both itself and its opposite. It flirts with paradox.… As with "against." To be against means to be *opposed*: resistant or defiant. It also means *next to*: beside or near. Which leaves the problem of a phrase like "up against" which is indeterminate, bivalent.… (Kipnis 201)

Maybe we can hold something close even as we fight for a little critical distance. Riven with paradox, citizenship invites more than simple opposition or unquestioning fidelity. As a way of denoting the complications of embracing citizenship, I suggest we consider diasporic citizenship as a mode for understanding the contradictions and possibilities of Canadian literature. I understand diasporic citizenship as a way of registering the profound unease with the idea of citizenship and as a way of recalling the anguishes attendant upon the project of citizen-making. If, returning to Pennee, literatures, be they minoritized or majoritized, remind us that nations are made, not born, then diasporic citizenship can function as a perpetual reminder of the losses that enable citizenship to flourish.

Not unlike the modern nation, citizenship demands particular forms of amnesia. In order for there to be equality among citizens, there has to be some forgetting of difference. In Canada, this injunction to forget emerges with particular force in the case of Aboriginal peoples. In 1947, Canada passed its first Citizenship Act. Prior to January 1, 1947, there were no Canadian citizens, only British subjects living in Canada. As James Sakej Henderson recognizes,

the call of federal citizenship to Aboriginal peoples transforms the sacred homeland of Aboriginal nations (with their *sui generis* Aboriginal orders and their
treaty confederation with the British sovereign) into another version of Euro-
Canadian self-congratulation and individualism. In favouring colonial over constitutional models, the invitation asks Aboriginal peoples to comply with colonial
narratives posing as modernity, instead of asking Canadians and their institutions to comply with constitutional supremacy and shared sovereignties of
treaties. (416)

Canadian citizenship thus exacts a forgetting of forms of civility that pre-
cede the imposition of European forms of citizenship. Harnessing the language of fraternity and liberty, Queen Elizabeth II's "gentle invitation"
(Henderson 415) suggests that we need not lose our connection to pasts that
do not necessarily belong to Canada, that Canadian citizenship will demonstrate true fraternity in forms of mutual cultural tolerance. At the same time,
the losses incurred in the name of equality demand a form of remembering that exceeds that of citizenship.

In the hope of retaining the obligation to memory, I want to put diaspora up against citizenship. Diasporic communities are formed through the
processes of memory, which bind vertically through generations and hori-
zontally across individuals. Diasporic subjectivities emerge not simply from
the fact of geographical displacement, but also from the ways in which forgotten or suppressed pasts continue to shape the present. Paul Gilroy's notion
of "living memory" powerfully calls attention to the ways in which diasporic
pasts live on in secret or forgotten gestures, habits, and desires (*Black Atlantic*).
And so we carry anger that is not our own. We have cravings for tastes we
cannot name. Writing of his sudden desire for *lo bok*, Chinese turnip, Fred
Wah guides us into the geography of longing. He writes in *Diamond Grill* of
"a craving for some Chinese food taste that I haven't been able to pin down.
An absence that gnaws at sensation and memory. An undefined taste, not in
the mouth but down some blind alley of the mind" (67). He finds this lost
taste, the fulfillment of this craving, in a Chinese market. He sees a pile of
turnips and has to ask a woman in the market how to use the vegetable.
Journeying down this "blind alley of the mind," Wah finds a form of community out of a craving and through a stranger. Deeply connected to memory, diaspora calls us to what David Scott, citing Kamau Braithwaite, describes
as "an obscure miracle of connection" (*Refashioning* 106).

These obscure, miraculous connections remain grounded in cultural
identities defined within difference and resistance to forms of domination
such as colonialism and imperialism. Diaspora is not a state of continual

ethnic insularity, but rather what Jonathan and Daniel Boyarin understand as "a synthesis ... that will allow for stubborn hanging-on to ethnic, cultural specificity but in a context of a deeply felt and enacted human solidarity" ("Diaspora" 108). Diaspora's commitment to difference is also entangled in forms of resistance. As Brent Hayes Edwards observes in his genealogy of the uses of the term "diaspora,"

> the crystallization of these figurative allusions [to the Old Testament tales of Exodus and the idea of the "scattering" of peoples] into a theoretical discourse of diaspora, explicitly in dialogue with the long-standing Jewish traditions behind the term, responds to a set of historiographic needs particular to the late 1950s and early 1960s, especially in the work of historians George Shepperson and Joseph Harris. Although it is often overlooked, the necessity of this conceptual turn is first developed in a work in the growing field of African history, and specifically around the issue of African resistance to colonialism. (49)

As Edwards recognizes, although it is often forgotten, contemporary uses of diaspora emerge from an engagement with the politics of postcolonialism and resistance to oppression. Despite the increasingly broad uses of the term, it is crucial that we recall the genealogy of its emergence in contemporary critical thinking not because origins matter, although they often do, but because the dialogues between Jewish traditions and Black anti-colonial intellectual work provide for us a vital and incredibly rich resource for futures that we have yet to imagine.

In the spirit of a commitment to these futures yet to come, I want to risk optimism forged out of a deep sense of irreparable loss. Reading over *The Black Jacobins*, I could not help but be moved by Toussaint's consistent reference to his fellow revolutionaries under the title "Citizen." He claimed the language of citizenship in the fullness of its promise. The Atlantic may separate Haiti from France, but Toussaint's understanding of citizenship crosses that ocean and moves well beyond the boundaries of national borders and into the realm of revolution, of freedom, equality, and fraternity. Writing to the "Citizen Directors" in France in 1797, Toussaint passionately reaffirms the impossibility of re-establishing slavery in the colony, declaring that "the same hand which has broken our chains will not enslave us anew" (qtd. in James 196). As James notes, these ideas were uncomplicatedly real for Toussaint in a way that they could not be for the Frenchmen in Europe:

> For even these masters of the spoken and written word, owing to the class complications of their society, too often had to pause, to hesitate, to qualify. Toussaint could defend the freedom of the blacks without reservation, and this gave

his declaration a strength and a single-mindedness rare in the great documents of the time. The French bourgeoisie could not understand it. Rivers of blood were to flow before they understood that, elevated as was his tone, Tousssaint had written neither bombast nor rhetoric but the simple and sober truth. (198)

Toussaint's truth lies in a belief in the promises of citizenship and the 1789 Declaration made real in Haiti in ways that it could never be made in France. The shattering of these beliefs stands not only as an enormous betrayal of citizenship and the right to be human, but also as an enormous loss. We cannot return to the single-mindedness and strength of Toussaint's commitment to the principles of citizenship. Colonialism has not ended, and the vicious exploitation of the global underclass has not abated. We cannot reclaim this language and the strength of Toussaint's commitment because we inhabit a present whose futures are shaped by these losses; and yet, we cannot simply cut our losses, so to speak. Citizenship remains with us and we with it.

Diasporas function as a perpetual reminder of the losses that enable citizenship. Diasporic citizenship is then not a new, shiny, improved version of citizenship that might be seen as the underside of cosmopolitan citizenship. Nor can it address the failures of the nation-state to safeguard against the violation of the right to be human. Nor is diasporic citizenship a panacea for the contradiction inherent in the conception of modern citizenship itself. For me, at least in this context, it is something much smaller. As I have been arguing, the profound dissonance between these terms, diaspora and citizenship, enables a dialectical tension between them. The disparity between the subject of diaspora and the subject of citizenship opens up a recognition of the contingencies surrounding our choice for citizenship. Diaspora allows us to be up against citizenship, to embrace it even as we hold it at some distance, to recognize it as both disabling and enabling. To return to where I began, the situating of minority literatures within Canadian literature as a field, it is my hope that diasporic citizenship might allow us to think through the entanglements of a national literary that remains committed to long histories of dislocation even as it exists within the contradictions of citizenship. I understand minority literatures such as Asian Canadian, Black Canadian, and Native literatures as existing in an uneasy lockstep with Canadian literature in much the same way that the subject of diaspora and the subject of citizenship might co-exist in uneasy but nonetheless unavoidable relation. Engaging in what Huhndorf calls the "rituals of citizenship"[4] reveals an ongoing occupation of diasporic identities as an elaborate act of national forgetting. Being against citizenship, being both intimate and in opposition to it, requires more than a rejection of ritual. It requires an exploration of those messy spaces where the subject of citizenship and the subject of diaspora do not overlap, where they pull and sometimes tear away from each other. The work of diasporic citizenship is thus the work of dwelling in this dissonance between diaspora and citizenship in order to enable memory to tear away at the coherence of national forgettings.

LIANNE MOYES

ACTS OF CITIZENSHIP
ERIN MOURÉ'S *O CIDADÁN* AND THE LIMITS OF WORLDLINESS[1]

Literature, Institutions, Citizenship

Citizenship is most immediately understood in terms of the national institutions and discourses that produce the relation between a subject and the polity, and in terms of the constitutional and legislative apparati through which this relation is regulated; yet the institutions currently in place are far from equal to the task of protecting rights or ensuring participation, whether of citizens or non-citizens. Serious inconsistencies, oversights, and injustices in the state regulation of citizenship leave subjects variously stateless, barred from certain states, moving constantly, existing without asylum or without hope of immigrating, living unauthorized within a state, living authorized but without equality, and risking their lives, often losing their lives, in the attempt to land. Change, in such contexts, comes about not just through laws, acts, and charters, but also through agitation, civil disobedience, and other modes of radical intervention. Indeed, change of the kind that would address the exclusions and shortcomings listed above is unimaginable within the terms of citizenship as they currently stand. We need a different set of terms, a different set of discourses, practices, and institutions through which citizenship might be lived and embodied, indeed, "materialized" (Butler, *Bodies* 1–3).

Literature is arguably one of the sites where such alternatives might be explored. I do not want to exaggerate what can be claimed for literature in the project of reconceptualizing and reworking citizenship; I take seriously the words of Lisa Robertson from one of the epigraphs of Erin Mouré's *O Cidadán*, "When pushed to the wall, art is too slow" (n.p.).[2] At the same time, I want to suggest that literature helps in making legible the inconsistencies, oversights, and injustices of state-regulated citizenship, and in developing forms of critical cultural knowledge about the relation between subject and state (Pennee, "Literary" 77–79). Literature has a lot to tell us—through its enunciative postures, its mapping of social space, and its mobilization of affect, for example—about the production of citizens. Itself a cultural practice of citizenship and a site for the iteration and regulation of "the public relation" (Mouré, *O Cididán* 63), literature frequently reinforces the prevailing terms of citizenship; yet literature is also eminently susceptible to dissident imaginaries forging relations among subjects that exceed the conventions of citizenship and the state–citizen bond. As a site for the iteration and regulation of citizenship, literature can reinvest the public relation and challenge the practices and discourses through which citizenship is made intelligible and thereby legitimized.

Intelligibility

Erin Mouré's 2002 collection of poems, *O Cidadán*, is of particular interest because it resists the codes that routinely produce the subjects we call "citizens" and regulate the institutions of citizenship. Perhaps the most obvious instance of the text's resistance to prevailing codes of intelligibility is the word "*cidadán*" of the title. The title is unfamiliar, gives pause, unless one reads Galego,[3] the language of Galicia, the place in northwest Spain from which Mouré's paternal ancestors emigrated. In confronting readers with a language they may have not seen before, the title foregrounds the problematics of intelligibility. The point of the title is not "unintelligibility," however. After all, "*cidadán*" is reminiscent of "citadin"[4] or "citizen." To cite the text's preamble, it is "A word we recognize though we know not its language. It can't be found in French, Spanish, Portuguese dictionaries" (n.p.). An unfamiliar language marks a possibility as well as a limit, a possibility for an alternative "citizen." Unorthodox layout, typography, and grammar, and shifting discursive frames function in similar ways throughout the collection, exposing the regulatory mechanisms of discourses of citizenship and questioning what Judith Butler calls "the very terms of [their] symbolic legitimacy and intelligibility" (*Bodies* 3). Opening the space of the page to charts, catalogues, footnotes, citations, cut-outs, paste-ups, erasures, demarcations, fissures, fractions, vectors, and other indicators, the text presents itself as a workbook for diagramming relations: words, borders, bodies, and spaces are reorganized in the direction of alternative public relations. The project of *O Cidadán* is explicit: "Making new formulations, new reticulations possible. And new localizations. (Because *new readings* are made possible)" (115). Mouré's text is difficult but it is possible to make some sense of it, and therein lies hope for producing a citizen who would be intelligible and legitimate otherwise.

O Cidadán is not so much a collection of poems about citizenship as a field of conceptual inquiry into the epistemological limits of discourses and practices of citizenship. One of the text's strategies for pushing these limits is its work with what might be called a "prosthetics of citizenship." A prosthesis is a "foreign" part whose addition allows a subject (or a nation, text, or border) to function. The word "*cidadán*" is such a device. As the preamble explains, "*cidadán*" "seems inflected 'masculine'" (n.p.), yet it is adopted by the woman writing subject: "In this book, I decided, I will step into it just by a move in discourse. I, a woman: o cidadán. As if 'citizen' in our time can only be dislodged when spoken from a 'minor' tongue, one historically persistent despite external and internal pressures, and by a woman who bears—as a lesbian in a civic frame—a policed sexuality" (n.p.). Through "a move in discourse," Mouré's text locates the border between feminine and masculine within the term *cidadán*. In so doing, the text denies the "transcendent value" (n.p.) of the generic (masculine) and the heterosexual regime—as well as that of the English language. When Mouré's writing subject asks, "Is the *Cidadán* a prosthetic gesture (across 'languages')?" and then goes on to speculate, "The citizen is just an enactment across prosthetic boundaries?" (7), she reminds readers that there is nothing natural about the citizen, the boundaries of gender, or the boundaries of the nation. The boundaries are prosthetic in the sense that their addition attempts to "secure" the nation (Balibar, "Borders" 221) or give contours to the self. The *cidadán* is prosthetic in the sense that her addition to the conventional formulation of "citizen" allows readers to imagine a citizen constituted through her body, her sexuality, and her relations to several languages.

The translation of "citizen" into *cidadán*, a word from a language that is not the official language of any state, destabilizes the idea of citizenship as a natural tie to a nation-state. It also locates the border between foreign and familiar within the citizen. These gestures of "intersecting" the citizen (n.p.) help us, in Balibar's terms, to imagine the citizen "as a border" ("Borders" 217; Mouré, *O Cidadán* 86). Given that a national border is one of the institutions of citizenship, one of the places where citizenship is materialized and policed, the concept of the citizen as border is suggestive. When the border between languages (French, English, Spanish, Portuguese, Galego), between national identifications, between inside and outside, and between feminine and masculine lies within the citizen—traverses the citizen—it is more difficult to constitute citizenship as a line of demarcation between those who belong and those who do not, between those whose lives matter to the state and those whose lives do not.

Resistance

The decision of Mouré's writing subject to inhabit a word, a masculine form from which she might otherwise be excluded, and to write about it so as not simply to disappear within the generic, is worthy of pause. This "move in discourse" is an embodied practice of resistance, that is, a gesture of materializing the citizen as a woman and a lesbian, subjects who have frequently been abjected from the ranks of the enfranchised and who do not necessarily experience citizenship as an enabling condition. It also recognizes with Franz Fanon, to whom the text makes explicit reference, that "Human struggle is always sited in human bodies. Not in bodies as signifiers, but in bodies as lived apparatuses" (*O Cidadán* 51). Although the practices and institutions of citizenship have roots in revolutionary struggle, citizenship is not routinely posed as a question of struggle. Rather, it is taken to be a "status," conferred by a state and entailing rights and responsibilities. This seemingly innocuous formulation turns a practice into a static condition, makes of citizenship a state decision, alienates the citizen from the decision-making process, and requires compliance in exchange for sometimes dubious rights.

What if citizenship were taken, claimed, rather than granted? What if it were understood as a practice of resistance rather than a status? For Saskia Sassen, the possibility of new forms of citizenship emerges from precisely such a practice, that is, from "the enactment of a large array of particular interests—from protests against police brutality and globalization to sexuality preference politics and house-squatting by anarchists" (43–44). Sassen cites the latter struggles, carried out at a local level, often in global cities, as instances of disadvantaged subjects acquiring "presence in a broader political process that escapes the boundaries of the formal polity" (62). *O Cidadán* is another such instance: a cultural practice of citizenship as resistance. I read Mouré's text as radically continuous with the work of intellectuals such as Sassen and with the forms of protest she cites. *O Cidadán*'s modes of resistance are discursive and conceptual, and are therefore all the more necessary in the production of new forms of citizenship.

Soil's Sovereignty

The relation of citizen to nation-state is a key site of interrogation and negotiation in *O Cidadán*: "It is citizenship's *acts* I dream of, acts not constrained or dilated by *nation*, especially as *nation-state* and its 19th c. model of sovereignty" (42). In this model of sovereignty, communal ties among subjects are weakened in the interests of building what Zygmunt Bauman calls "manmade collective identities" (696). Nationalism makes its "bid for exclusive rights to a territory" on the basis of the homogeneity of such collectivities, a homogeneity achieved by "drawing the boundary between the *natives* and the *aliens*, between the prospective nation and its enemies" (683). Such boundary-drawing continues long after the constitution of the state. One has only to think of the various instances of citizens being branded aliens or being deported.[5] National identity, Bauman suggests, is inextricably bound up with "the invocation of soil and blood" and with expressions of patriotic allegiance (696) to "home and native land." The title of Mouré's collection is itself a nexus of associations related to the nation-state, including a reference to the national anthem, "O Canada." But the poems of *O Cidadán* are a song to a citizen rather than to a state. They remind us that pledges and anthems are not the self-willed acts they appear to be. Pledges and anthems are performatives; they not only *constitute* the attachment about which they speak but also are vulnerable to subversive repetition.

For the writing subject of *O Cidadán*, citizenship is not a question of national identity or of patriotism but one of acts and especially of border crossings:

> Is citizenship, really, the willingness to "defend" a territory? or an ideal? or is it *an acting across a surface....*
> Citizenship as enactment = => to cross a border. What hides behind the old model of sovereignty is, alas, often not defence of locale or of dignity but of local "political" interests (which means: economic and its corollary—exclusion). (94)

Crossing a border, in Mouré's poems, is most often an act of resistance to the economies of exclusion through which nations and citizens are constituted. As well as extending citizenship beyond the limits of the nation, crossing a border exposes the border as an "effect, an apparent stabilization in 'matter' of what is actually a materializing process not matter itself" (*O Cidadán* 98; Butler, *Bodies* 9). Drawing upon Butler's understanding of signification as a "regulated process of repetitions" (Mouré, *O Cidadán* 98; *Gender Trouble* 145) and of agency as "located in the possibility of variation on that repetition," Mouré's writing subject wonders if citizenship isn't "*that agency*" (*O Cidadán* 98). She finds an example of such agency in the work of De Sousa Mendes, Portuguese consul-general in 1940 Bordeaux, who "issued 30,000 visas to refugees, admitting them to Portugal in direct defiance of instructions" (98). His "borderwork," his citizenship across borders, intervenes in the materializing process and makes the borders strategically porous. Such an intervention is dependent upon the border guard who, as the border's prosthesis, makes a decision—an ethical decision—to resist. An individual's decision to act does not constitute social change, but it does alter the local terrain upon which change might be enacted.

Moving between languages is another way in which *O Cidadán* challenges "soil's sovereignty" (63). Just as a map generates the boundaries and the relations it pretends to represent, the gathering of languages within the space of the page reconfigures public space. The result is a disarticulation of language and territory, a move "To *conduct* a leakage out of originary language, out of the monolingualism in one's own language that would keep boundaries pure" (103). Such multilingualism is not conventionally sanctioned by the nation-state, a fact that is evident, for example, in the "French fright (spring '99) at signing a charter to protect regional European languages. Fear for its 'language of the republic'" (78). In the case of nations such as Canada and Spain, the "bid for exclusive rights to a territory" (Bauman 683) has to take into account more than one language. Galicia's relationship to Spain, like Quebec's relationship to Canada, is one of contested nationalisms, and both Galicia and Quebec have had to struggle to sustain their languages.[6] The poems of *O Cidadán* honour this struggle for "the right to speak a language" as well as for "the right to have [some]one listen"(78). As the writing subject makes clear, living and writing in Quebec allow her to "bear a strange tongue,"[7] to "be foreign," and at the same time to "be, paradoxically but sensibly, a part of the body politic" (82). Stated in slightly different terms, terms that might apply to Galicia as well as to Quebec, "To enable a language (returning) is also to allow intrusions, and to enable intrusions or their possibility as *part of* the cultural order" (75). Such a vision of Galician or Québécois culture—or, indeed, of Spanish or Canadian culture—as able to accommodate intrusions is quite different from the "dream of origins" (135) that subtends ethnic nationalism. The writing subject can imagine "Quebec citizenship" without ethnic nationalism—that is, *"without the Québec of Michaud raising its head again"* (135).

Civilian Love

The act of citizenship that enables a border official to destabilize a border or a collectivity "to enable intrusions" (75) might be called "civilian love," a term I draw from the title of Mouré's 1992 collection *Sheepish Beauty, Civilian Love*.[8] Civilian love is, in my reading, a practice that allows a citizen to imagine as integral to the social not only those she is with, those she knows, but also those who are not present, those she does not know. In French, Mouré's writing subject points out, there is a term for the latter: "l'autrui" (72). The writing subject calls for the same relationship of care between subjects who are intimate as between subjects who may never meet. Through the word "l'autrui," *O Cidadán* explores citizenship as an ethical practice of "being among," an ethics that allows for the "elsewhere" and irreconcilable difference of "others." "Being among" is also understood within the text as "a kind of reading," in the sense that "not everyone is 'now present' *sur place* in this 'among,' just as people in a book are not present" (72). Such acts of citizenship—the leap of imagination that is reading or that is "being among"—constitute civilian love.

In *O Cidadán*, there is a transposition of the project of "civilian love" from the sphere of the city to that of the globe. Read through the lens of Mouré's 2002 collection, "civilian love" is a way of redefining citizenship so that its acts extend beyond national borders and take into account (recognize as legitimate) those subjects who are without papers, who are stateless. To think citizenship beyond the paradigms of the nation is to think, potentially, of *world* citizenship. By the latter, I do not mean a "status" granted by some supranational body or a position of cosmopolitan entitlement taken up by those who consider themselves at home anywhere in the world. I am thinking, rather, of a practice of resistance, a collective struggle toward human rights and social justice. "Civilian love" also needs to be distinguished from "White civility," that is, the nineteenth-century British codes of gentlemanly conduct which, as Daniel Coleman argues in the essay in this volume, continue to permeate Canada's sense of itself and its "good works." Investing imaginatively in civility, Coleman suggests, means overlooking the differential privilege that structures Canadian "civil society" and informs the decisions made at its borders. The "wry civility" Coleman finds in the work of the TransCanada project can also be found in the critical and enunciative postures of Mouré's writing subject. In *O Cidadán*, "civilian love" is far from discreet:[9] it is the embodied desire of one girl for another (34), the disobedience of border guards and other functionaries who make their "own inviolable seam permeable" (42), and the critique of state policy that informs a line such as "The ambassador of blankets-covering-the-drowned (immigrants by water)" (124)—a vivid example of the ways in which state-sanctioned borderwork in the form of diplomacy or immigration law fails to enact the decency or basic care for human life on which civil society prides itself.

Cosmopolitanism and the Affect of Citizenship

As I suggested above, to think citizenship beyond the paradigms of the nation is to think, potentially, of world citizenship—and of cosmopolitanism. Mouré's *O Cidadán*, in its dream of citizenship's acts "not constrained or dilated by *nation*" (42) and in its search for "'idioms ... that resist the bloody idiocies of identities indicated by blood, soil, self'" (63), engages with practices and discourses of cosmopolitanism. Cosmopolitanism is often set against nationalism and understood as freedom from ties to a specific territory, language, people, or culture. According to Amanda Anderson, the term has been used historically to denote "cultivated detachment from restrictive forms of identity" (266). A cosmopolitan has also been understood, Martha Nussbaum suggests, as a "person whose allegiance is to the worldwide community of human beings" (4). This seeming tension within the affect of cosmopolitanism between detachment and attachment needs to be read in the light of Anderson's observation that "cosmopolitanism is a flexible term, whose forms of detachment and multiple affiliation can be variously articulated and variously motivated" (267). This flexibility makes the term easy to harness to dominant interests. Mouré's writing subject demonstrates both Nussbaum's ties to a worldwide community and Anderson's detachment from restrictive forms of identity. However, her text throws the concept of "allegiance" into question in favour of citizens' acts; the approach to restrictive forms of identity is not so much one of detachment as one of embodied resistance. After all, the writing subject's identification as a woman and a lesbian perturbs the assumed gender neutrality and heterosexuality of "the worldwide community of human beings" (Nussbaum 4) or of "universal humanity" (Anderson 267).

Bruce Robbins, in *Cosmopolitics: Thinking and Feeling beyond the Nation*, argues that "instead of an ideal of detachment, actually existing cosmopolitanism is a reality of (re)attachment, multiple attachment, or attachment at a distance" (3). *O Cidadán* might be read in terms of such attachments. The specificity of Mouré's text, however, lies in its inquiry into the relationship between body, affect, and politics. When Mouré's writing subject describes the citizen as "a bundle of affect, affectability" (7) in the first page of the collection, her meanings include, for example, "ties of adoration elsewhere" (7), "a seal or bond with this world" (9), "cravings" for a woman lover (9), "the 'between-us' which we must touch with care" (19), "a tie between 'melancholy gender' (Butler) and the 'citizen'" (49), "How the body invests what is outside its rim" (87), and how "a polity needs bodies in order to cathect itself" (97). Affect, Mouré's text suggests, is a connection among bodies, among "cared selves" (9). It also locates bodies within social relations and mobilizes bodies through specific forms of political organization. As Clare Hemmings points out, affect is often taken to be "autonomous and outside social signification" (549).[10] Citing Fanon's and Audre Lorde's descriptions of "*other people's* affective response to their blackness" (561), Hemmings shows that affect is not outside social signification or radical in itself, but, rather, frequently reinforces prevailing social meanings. At the same time, she observes, subjects whose racialized and sexualized bodies bear the burden of (negative) affect also know the ways their bodies mean for themselves and for alternative collectivities: "the social world is always crosscut with fissures that have a social and political history that *signifies otherwise*" (558; 564). The affect of citizenship, in *O Cidadán*, is invested precisely in that which *signifies otherwise*. A woman's desire for another woman is legible in the pages of Mouré's text in the form of "a girl's ardorous invitation to a girl to inhabit/intersect her spaces" (34). Lines of political affiliation among women writers and intellectuals create a "public space" between nations, where the writing subject and her lover are "both signs" (9). Mouré's writing subject imagines "harbouring ... 'l'autre homme' without insisting he 'make sense' according to [*her*] structures" (51).

Global Designs

Given the derivation of "cosmopolitanism" from the Greek words for "world" and "citizen," one might hope that the term would have something to say about world citizenship as I outlined it above. However, any project that asks cosmopolitanism to speak to questions of human rights and global social justice has to cope with what Timothy Brennan calls the term's "unacknowledged historical accretions" (*At Home* 25). The term's connotations

in the English language, Brennan points out, are positive: "'free from provincial prejudices,' 'not limited to one part of the world,' 'sophisticated, urbane,
worldly'" (*At Home* 19).[11] At the same time, he reminds us, the term was used
in the nineteenth and early twentieth centuries as a "code word in Eastern
Europe for the Jew, where rootlessness was a condemnation and a proof of
nonbelonging precisely *there*"; and it was used by Joseph Stalin to denigrate
the "Jew-as-foreigner, interloper ... [and] 'intellectual'" (21). Brennan's point,
to which he returns in his essay "Cosmo-Theory," is that cosmopolitanism is
"a fundamentally ambivalent phenomenon," one that "is *local* while deny-
ing its local character" (660).

Also local, suggests Walter Mignolo, are the global designs of Christianity, colonialism, and globalization to which cosmopolitanism has been har-
nessed ("Many" 721–22). Mignolo finds in cosmopolitanism projects that aim
to manage the world, as well as projects that aim to emancipate the world;
in some cases, these projects are one and the same. Both have their weak-
nesses: managerial projects "are driven by a will to control and homoge-
nize," and emancipatory projects fail to imagine the agency and enunciation
of those to "be emancipated" ("Many" 723). What is needed, Mignolo insists,
is neither "benevolent recognition" nor "humanitarian pleas for inclusion"
(724), but "critical cosmopolitanism," that is, "the transformation of the
hegemonic imaginary from the perspective of people in subaltern positions" (736–37). Among the practices of critical cosmopolitanism advocated
by Mignolo is "border thinking," which he characterizes as a dialogue among
cosmopolitans, initiated by those who have had to live with the global
designs of others (744). Although Mignolo offers little sense of how such a
conversation comes about or of differences among those in "subaltern positions," his idea effectively reconceptualizes cosmopolitanism from the perspective of coloniality. At the same time, Mignolo's gesture has to be read
in the light of anti-colonial discourse, where cosmopolitanism has decidedly negative connotations. Fanon, for example, explicitly rejects the term
because of its investment in the practices of the colonial power at the expense
of the local (98).

"Why dredge up this tainted and problematic word?" (285), we might
ask with Amanda Anderson. If the term has currency at the turn of the
twenty-first century, that currency is a function of its ambivalence, its "flexibility." Cosmopolitanism holds the promise of harmonious coexistence
among world citizens in spite of uneven relations and, at the same time, the
promise of a meaningful "counter" to the homogeneity or seamlessness
sometimes associated with globalization. It cannot deliver on both of these

promises—that is, it cannot both conjure seamlessness and reveal the work of the threads, the strain on the fabric, the overlaps, the junctions, the frayed edges (Mouré, *Sheepish* 50–59). Or perhaps it can; and perhaps the contradictions of cosmopolitanism will prove helpful in making arguments that require both universality (of rights, etc.) and differentiation (of location, etc.). In any case, Anderson's answer, through Robbins, is "dredge it up so we know our hands are always dirty" (285). My interest in cosmopolitanism lies not so much in rehabilitating it as in understanding its contradictions and thereby better understanding the complicities, as well as the critical potential I find in Mouré's text. Although the term occurs only once in the poems of *O Cidadán*, the engagement with "worldliness" (9) and with acts of citizens across borders invites inquiry into the text's own attempts "to think and feel beyond the nation."

Not to Deny Borders

O Cidadán dramatizes the contradictions Ella Shohat identifies in "a world where transnational corporations make sure that 'we're all connected,' but where at the same time borders and passports are under surveillance as a reminder that some have more 'connections' than others" (215). On the one hand, Mouré's text seems to take for granted access to travel, ease of border-crossing, and the possibility of transcending national ties, all of which have been associated with the privilege of the cosmopolitan subject (Cheah, "Given Culture" 296–97, 302; Massey 24–26). The *cidadán* is presented, for example, as "a product always of migrations or emigrative qualities," as "a seal or bond with this world, nothing to do with country or origin" (9) and as "one who carries a passport, for she has already been somewhere else" (94). "Soil," a number of poems suggest, has no necessary sovereignty over the citizen, in the sense that she is not rooted in it; she is mobile and can develop ties beyond the nation (39, 63, 94). On the other hand, Mouré's text is attentive to the local and to the limits on mobility and border-crossing. The footnote, for example, evoking "the Fujian women jailed by Canada for exercising their 'right to depart' (which does not include the right to arrive somewhere)" (124) reminds readers that, for women without a passport, having "already been somewhere else" is no guarantee of arriving. There is a flip side, the text suggests, to the seemingly positive "rootlessness" of cosmopolitanism.[12]

Border-crossing, I argued earlier, is one of the ways in which *O Cidadán* figures the acts of citizenship. Mouré's poems alter the ways borders are imagined and regulated. They suggest that borders, insofar as they gain their appearance of stability through a regulated process of repetitions, might be materialized differently. The poems of *O Cidadán* do not, however, call for a borderless world: "But not to deny borders. For they mark a disruptive and unruly edge. And in auguring an outside, they constitute the inside" (112). A borderless world is precisely the illusion sustained by the world of global capitalism that Shohat describes; it is also the illusion sustained by discourses of cosmopolitan privilege. What is needed is a *making visible* of borders and of the lives at stake at borders. A project of thinking citizenship beyond the limits of the nation—a project that might be construed as cosmopolitan—must not come at the expense of those without the mobility or the documents necessary to cross borders. In *O Cidadán*, the dream of "citizenship's *acts* ... not constrained or dilated by *nation*" (42) is accompanied by the question, "how to articulate this without invoking transcendent 'citizens' as if Platonic 'ideas'?" (42). By way of an answer, the writing subject cites the act of a Swiss border guard who, in 1938, "altered 3600 passports to permit Austrian Jews entry to his country" (42). Mouré's text is attentive to the historical and material contingencies of border-crossing and is at pains to ground or localize its exploration of transnational citizenship.

Whereas the citizen of the world, the cosmopolitan, is not typically encumbered by the local, Mouré's *cidadán* is localized by "ties of affect" (7), by her body (47), by the memory of the landscape in which she was born (65), by the places from which she writes, and by the texts that traverse her own. But affect, body, memory, language, and intertextuality are never simply "local"; they connect the *cidadán* to a lover in Yorkshire, to a family history of migration, and to a network of writers and intellectuals throughout Europe and the Americas. If the "connections" the writing subject makes are sometimes by Internet and sometimes between airports, they are also connections forged through critical reading practices and efforts at "transnational literacy" (Spivak, *Outside* 269–70). The writing subject makes a link, for example, between Madeleine Albright, who prevented the UN from intervening to stop the deaths of 800,000 people in Rwanda, the Vichy government, which overlooked the deportation of Jews from France in 1942, and a US student who does not attribute humanity to the people of Spain (106). This reading of local instances of the failure to recognize the humanity of others, often of those one does not know, foregrounds the imbrication of local and global, and makes it difficult to sustain an opposition between nationalism and cosmopolitanism.[13]

Worldliness

Mouré's text prefers the term "worldliness" to that of "cosmopolitanism." Indeed, the poems of *O Cidadán* enact the kind of "worldliness" introduced by Edward Said in *The World, the Text, and the Critic* (35); that is, they enact a practice of reading and thinking that, as Brennan points out, is mobile, wide-reaching, and capable of broad connections, but never loses "its sense of immediate correspondence to a conjunctural politics" (*At Home* 122). It is not, however, Said's worldliness that is cited throughout Mouré's text but Jean-Luc Nancy's: "the human being ... becomes worldly in the sense that it blurs the boundaries of the various territories and home soils that lie within it" (*O Cidadán* 69; Nancy 157–58). Nancy's philosophical intervention into the relation between politics and aesthetics provides some of the conceptual work through which Mouré's writing subject reimagines nation, citizen, and border. *O Cidadán* reformulates the nation, for example, as a seam or fold within the subject, a seam or fold that renders the subject radically continuous with other subjects, with "autrui": "What if 'nation' ceased to be pure given and were instead a nexus of differential topolities in the subject, who is formed partly by the coextensivity of subjects-around-her?" (39). With its combination of "topos" (a place) and "polity" (a form of political organization), the term "topolities" constructs the nation as a series of localized instances of civic practice and civilian love. What Mouré's text brings to Nancy's worldliness is precisely the "correspondences with conjunctural politics" that Brennan finds in Said. In contrast to the anti-nationalist strain in some cosmopolitanisms, Mouré's text opens spaces for politics at the level of the nation.[14] The text, in its "worldliness," can imagine Quebec as a state in formation and can accommodate "Quebec citizenship" (135). It can also imagine Canada and Spain as "borderlands" (94). In other words, the text includes the nation-state in the project of "the political as *sense to come*," as long as "state" is understood as a "multiplicity and plurilocality of relations ... Zones that can overlap" (63).

Worldliness, in *O Cidadán*, works on several registers, generating both sites for acts of citizenship within and against the nation-state, and transnational links among sites, struggles, and histories. These transnational links are especially important for Mouré's writing subject insofar as they generate circuits for the interventions and radical questioning of institutions and categories that are less possible within the framework of the nation-state. Cheah's objection that such networks cannot be counted on to produce social change, a change he locates at the level of national movements, is worth considering here: "global loyalty," he argues, "is thin, an ideal vision largely confined to activists and intellectuals" ("Given Culture" 312). Yet transnational connections have been crucial to writers and intellectuals, especially to women writers and intellectuals—albeit those with some access to global mobility—throughout the twentieth century. Because national institutions and narratives so frequently forget the struggles and interventions of women, fail to recognize lesbians, and short-circuit women's culture, women writers and intellectuals have often affiliated otherwise. It is in this light we might read a line such as *O Cidadán*'s "To dream a heterogeneity of borders, to speak a sororal idiom without that myth of forebears" (132). "Sororal idiom," with its connotations of "sisterhood" and "global feminism,"[15] is a risky term that raises questions about who is speaking and where the conversation takes place; yet Mouré's text is willing to take the risk. In tying "a sororal idiom" to "a heterogeneity of borders," the text suggests that there are differentiations within the words "sororal" and "idiom." The use of "sororal" is not unlike the writing subject's gesture of inhabiting the term "*O Cidadán*." In the latter case, the writing subject chooses the masculine as the default, and, in the former, she chooses the feminine.[16] In my reading, "sororal idiom" includes the voices of men as well as those of women.

Beyond Inclusion

In spite of the preference in *O Cidadán* for the term "worldliness," the word "cosmopolitanism" does arise in a reference to Julia Kristeva's *Strangers to Ourselves*, a text that can be read as a theory of cosmopolitanism. Unlike Brennan, Mignolo, or Cheah, who are interested in the political undertones of cosmopolitanism and its colonial legacy, Kristeva is interested in the figure of the foreigner or stranger and its integration within the social. "Cosmopolitanism" surfaces in Mouré's text in a footnote that includes a citation from Kristeva: "'The banquet of hospitality is the cosmopolitanism of a moment, the brotherhood of guests who soothe and forget their differences, the banquet is outside of time. It imagines itself eternal in the intoxication of those who are nevertheless aware of its temporary frailty'" (*O Cidadán* 131; Kristeva, *Strangers* 11).[17] Several poems in *O Cidadán* (105, 116) reference Kristeva's argument that the stranger—at the root of both "guest" and "host"—is uncannily "within us" (*Strangers* 191). In Kristeva's terms, "If I am a foreigner, there are no foreigners" (*Strangers* 192). This sense of "difference within" surfaces in Mouré's text in her assertion that "To make one's own inviolable seam permeable: this act a citizen's act" (42) and her desire

"That my thinking ... may be 'French' thinking, even in English" (75). Mouré's writing subject locates herself in Quebec without claiming it as her home or positioning herself in exile: "To be a stranger ... here," she explains, breaking into French, "is to faire partie de tout ce qui comporte le civis" (82).[18] Of course, inclusion in a collectivity, however cosmopolitan it takes itself to be, does not ensure justice for all citizens.

Mouré's text has certain continuities with Kristeva's in the sense that its acts of citizenship are frequently the acts of citizens who make themselves vulnerable, who expose the borders within themselves, and who let others cross borders. At the same time, Mouré's text exposes some of the limitations in Kristeva's world view. The poems of *O Cidadán* draw attention to subjects who fall outside formulae, such as "we are all foreigners" (Kristeva, *Strangers* 192). Among these subjects are citizens subjected to deportation, genocide, or torture (Mouré, *O Cidadán* 106), and immigrants who drown, are jailed (124), or are found dead (n.p.) at borders. It is not that histories of uneven global relations do not surface in Kristeva's text. The difficulty, Brennan points out, is that when Kristeva "unearths the cosmopolitan temper in its colonialist mode," she is unable to see that "her ethical preference for cultural 'concord' might actually *be* the form in which imperialism expresses itself" (*At Home* 146). This difficulty might also be read through Mignolo's comments on the problematics of inclusion. Inclusion, he suggests, is contingent upon an agency that, although it presents itself as impartial, outside, is "already within the frame from which it is possible to think 'inclusion'" ("Many" 736). Mignolo offers the example of Immanuel Kant's cosmopolitanism, which "presupposes that it could only be thought out from one particular geopolitical location: that of the heart of Europe, of the most civilized nations" ("Many" 735). The same might be said of Kristeva's cosmopolitanism. Mouré's worldliness, in contrast, is pieced together from Montreal, Vigo, and Yorkshire—with Yorkshire described in *O Cidadán* as "a pediment of unease" (7). *O Cidadán* cites numerous French thinkers and theorists influenced by French thought, but it is not centred in France in the way that Kristeva's text is. Perhaps most importantly, Mouré's text exposes the limits of "cultural 'concord.'"

Limits

I have been preoccupied in this essay with the contradictions of cosmopolitanism and with the possibilities of worldliness, as well as with the implications of all of these for citizenship. The term "worldliness" is somewhat less freighted with metropolitan privilege than is "cosmopolitanism" and more accommodating of heterodox locations and positions; but worldliness, in *O Cidadán*, has its limits. Some are limits of the text, and some are limits the text makes legible. Trying to differentiate these two—the limits of the text from the limits it makes legible—is not easy. Indeed, it has been my experience that to take a position on this question is to stop reading Mouré's text, to write with the uneasy feeling that if I began reading again, my position would change. The "sense of place" in Mouré's poems is "extraverted" (Massey 28), yet the languages it employs are those of Europe and its colonies in the Americas. The text's intellectual affiliations are largely with post-Enlightenment philosophy and the social and political thought of Europeans, North Americans, Australians, and South Americans with strong ties to Europe. Read in this light, the anti-colonial theory of Fanon, who was born in Martinique, trained in psychiatry in France, and participated in Algeria's struggle for independence, stands out. It reminds us that Quebec, too, can be read as a site of anti-colonial revolution, however "quiet," and that Europe, North America, and Australia are far from homogeneous spaces of privilege. Spain, for example, can be read as a borderland of Europe, a place mapped by the historical interpenetration of Africa and Europe. *O Cidadán* foregrounds the power relations that structure social and political relations in Galicia and in Quebec. It also signals the limits of the mobility and connectedness that are the promise of both cosmopolitanism and worldliness. In dedications, footnotes, and other paraliterary gestures, the text makes legible the effects in lives and bodies of various acts of resistance.

The limits of worldliness are brought sharply into focus by a dedication in the opening pages of Mouré's text: "to two young Africans who tried to call out to Europe, with the body (mortos) of writing (escritas nos seus petos): Yaguine Koita and Fodé Tounkara" (1).[19] Simon Gikandi, in his discussion of the boys, cites a letter "left behind by two Guinean boys whose dead bodies were found in the cargo hold of a plane in Brussels in August 1998" (630).[20] If we read the parts of Mouré's dedication written in English, the boys call out "with the body of writing"; if we add the parentheses written in Galego, we understand that the "body" is dead and that there is writing in the boys' pockets. In the place of money, the boys have writing, writing that has currency, is read and published, only after they are dead. The words in Galego, then, expose what it means to "call out to Europe" for those who are outside its flows of capital and its circuits of political representation. They underscore the fact that very few are likely to understand what this writing really says; yet the dedication does not construct the boys as victims. It focusses not on their attempt to *get to* Europe but on their attempt to *call out to* Europe. The boys' agency is not unlike that of the young woman, Bhubaneswari Bhaduri, whose interventionist suicide Spivak reads in "Can the Subaltern Speak?" In both cases, subjects attempt "to 'speak' by turning [their] bod[ies] into [texts]" (Spivak, *Critique* 308). In the case of Koita and Tounkara, their bodies and their letter, which ask to be read together, inscribe the (im)possibility of subaltern speech and the boys' contestation of this position.

If, as *O Cidadán* suggests, citizenship is an act of resistance, an act of border-crossing, what does it mean that an act of resistance, of crossing borders, requires the citizens' deaths in order to be recognized? In one poem, the writing subject asks, "Is the citizen a being who risks harm?" (34). In fact, the word "harms"—both harms risked and harms inflicted—is one of the most frequent words in the titles of Mouré's poems. The two boys would seem to be a limit case of harms. Another case, and a helpful point of comparison, is Portuguese consul-general De Sousa Mendes who admitted refugees to Portugal in 1940, and who, we read in a footnote, was "forcibly retired, denied full pension, and died in 1954, destitute" (98). In both cases, citizens place themselves in harm's way; yet the terms are radically different. De Sousa Mendes did not need to die in order for his signature to be recognized or to be effective in allowing refugees across the border. Being punished for civil disobedience is not the same as being read and recognized because one dies. What is more, even after their deaths, the boys' act is not certain to be read as one of resistance; it would be relatively easy to explain it away as suicide or to attribute it to difficulties in Guinea.

One of the limits of a worldliness (or a cosmopolitanism) based on acts of inclusion, based upon the "in-/-corporation of the stranger, l'autrui" (*O Cidadán* 87), is that some subjects defy "inclusion"—or are simply not looking for inclusion. Mouré's text uses dedications and footnotes to signal this limit and, in effect, to diagram its own exclusions. There is no act of civilian love and no subversive resignification of a border that can make dead boys part of Europe. The boys' writing is only read, the text suggests, because they die on the way. Had they lived, they would have become illegal immigrants, a category that is thrown radically into question by *O Cidadán*'s work with intelligibility. What Mouré's text is less able to do, however, is to write the act of resistance by which an illegal immigrant might *claim* citizenship. *O Cidadán* does not highlight such acts of resistance; it is far more likely to highlight the act of the official that lets the illegal immigrant in. The potential in Mouré's text for the kind of border thinking

Mignolo proposes—a conversation initiated from the perspective of those who have lived with colonialism, imperialism, underdevelopment, racism, war, enslavement, exploitative monetary arrangements, and exclusionary immigration practices—is limited. The dedication to Koita and Tounkara gestures in the direction of such a conversation insofar as it recognizes the boys' agency and uses words in Galego to specify the terms in which they died. The neo-colonial relations that underwrite movement between Africa and Europe are not an explicit preoccupation of the text, however; and the problematic of subaltern speech is not the same as the censorship of Galego. In other words, there are limits to the transnational links that can be made when the histories are not adequately delineated from the perspectives of those who live them.

"How humanity is attributed to beings"

The discourses and practices of citizenship are in some ways so overdetermined that it is difficult to break their hold on the political imaginary. Mouré's text, by refusing the prevailing codes of intelligibility that legitimize and regulate those discourses and practices, allows them to materialize differently. O Cidadán raises the question of citizenship in conjunction with that of "how humanity is attributed to beings" (106). Locating the affect of citizenship in the relations *between citizens* rather than in the relations between citizen and state, the text also maps a relation of care among bodies, even among bodies that will never know one another. O Cidadán's practice of "civilian love" recognizes as legitimate those who are without papers, who are stateless. It also resists models of citizenship based on exclusion, that is, models in which some bodies belong and therefore "matter," and other bodies do not. All bodies, the text suggests, matter. The bodies in the dedications and the footnotes—whose humanity has been, in various ways, denied—are in this sense part of the question of citizenship and must be part of Mouré's text. They are a reminder of the contradictions of cosmopolitanism and the limits of worldliness. They are also, to use the text's own terms, the text's "constitutive outside" (133); but here the deconstructionist mode of analysis, with its economy of inside/outside, needs to be interrupted, to give way to modes of analysis and intervention that would allow the bodies along the edges of Mouré's text to speak. O Cidadán is a lyric, a song to the citizen, yet a song that arguably is looking for such interruptions in the interests of fostering the unruly public relation that is citizenship.

TRANS-SCAN
GLOBALIZATION, LITERARY
HEMISPHERIC STUDIES,
CITIZENSHIP AS PROJECT

The Ends of CanLit: Scanning the Trans

// "TransCanada" and "The Ends of CanLit," the polysemic titles of the conference and the session for which this paper was originally written, invoke the multiple, often contradictory, enabling, and problematic dimensions of the category of nation. Among the sites of previous debate about that category is a discipline that both presupposed national literature and constituted its negation: comparative literature. In the discipline's representative text of the postwar period, René Wellek and Austin Warren remarked that the "great argument for 'comparative' or 'general' literature or just 'literature' is the obvious falsity of the ideal of a self-enclosed national literature" (49). Many varieties of comparative literary studies themselves, however, also "tended to reinforce an identification of nation-states as imagined communities with national languages as their natural bases," as the scholars observed who signed the 1993 Bernheimer Report of the American Comparative Literature Association (Bernheimer 40). The essentializing strictures of national pedagogies and critical perspectives, the nexus that shortly before the Bernheimer Report Homi Bhabha titled *Nation and Narration*, have also been critiqued by scholars from within national North American literatures, in fields that had fought hard for recognition as national literatures in their emergence against English and French literature. In a 1991 article entitled "The End of American Literature," Gregory Jay thus suggested that it "is time to stop teaching 'American' literature" (264). In a field whose recognition had come much later, looking back at the reading practices that had helped institute the project of "littérature québécoise," Pierre Nepveu similarly asked in 1988 whether, from a position of consolidated strength, it was not time to think about "la *fin* de la littérature québécoise" and to explore a "littérature *post*-québécoise" (*L'Ecologie* 14).

The discussion of the literatures of Canada, of course, has probed conjunctions of literature and "nation" relentlessly from its beginnings (Siemerling, "Rereading"). Among the many examples, think of Edwart Hartley Dewart's 1864 belief in the existence of a Canadian literature or Archibald Lampman's 1891 doubts; Octave Crémazie's 1867 lament for having to share the language of Bossuet and Racine or Camille Roy's 1904 considerations of "La nationalisation de la littérature canadienne" (Gauvin; Siemerling, "Rereading"); the cosmopolitan/native disagreements between Smith and Sutherland (Kokotailo; Sugars, "Can the Canadian") or the reception of Nelligan and the exotiques/régionalistes controversies (Garand); the concerns of Frye, Atwood, and the other thematic critics, or more recent studies like Frank Davey's 1993 *Post-National Arguments*, with its scrutiny of transnationality in Canadian novels since 1967. Most recent positions recognize the social constructedness of nation and calculate carefully the risks of essence; yet often they continue to insist on nation, in the face of many perhaps premature dismissals, as an important category of literary and cultural studies. This pertains equally to other fields that are often conceived transnationally, such as Black studies or postcolonial studies. André Alexis, George Elliott Clarke ("Contesting"), Lawrence Hill, and others thus insist on national specificity against a one-size-fits-all "model blackness" (see Siemerling, "May I"). Cynthia Sugars, who rightly argues that postcolonial registers are pervasive in CanLit from its beginnings, acknowledges postcolonialism's interest in deconstructing nation yet also notes that the "vector of the nation continues to have profound psychic resonance for Canadians" and that "to discard the concept of national identity as an oppressive construct seems counter-productive, as is true of notions of the 'subject' generally" ("Can the Canadian" 117).

What are we to make, then, of the invitation to think about the ends of CanLit and consider TransCanada? Let me preface this position paper and its navigations of possible TransCanadas with a preliminary trans-scan. Given the prodigious signifying power of the prefix "trans," and the ease with which it is sometimes fashionably employed, some warnings may be in order. The *Oxford English Dictionary* reveals "trans" also to be an older form of "trance," suggesting possibly "a swoon, a faint" or "a more or less prolonged suspension of consciousness and inertness to stimulus; a cataleptic or hypnotic condition." From there it is not far to related meanings such as "great apprehension or dread of coming evil" and "to pass, depart (esp. from life)"; or perhaps, closer to home, "to benumb or be numbed by fear of cold." Does the conference invite us to consider the case of Canada in "A state of extreme apprehension or dread; a state of doubt or suspense"? Doubt and suspense persist when we consult (our very own) *Canadian Oxford Dictionary*. The glosses of the prefix "trans-" include here "across, beyond," "on or to the other side of," "through," "into another state or place," and "surpassing, transcending."

These are double-edged directions. Such doubleness and doubt, however, speak to my sense of what is possible and potentially valuable in "Trans-Canadian" perspectives. These perspectives combine well with the idea that local positionality by definition is relational, and thus requires mediation, difference, and multi-perspectival recognitions; and that desires and projects of self-certainty need relativizing thresholds to limit the projections of transcendence. To anticipate: I think it is important to go "through" Canada in the double sense of both across and beyond, while avoiding any "trans" that suspends consciousness of, "passes over" (one meaning of trans-scendere), or "departs from" its situated problematics. For my trans-scan, I have selected five stops, with windows opening on hemispheric studies and globalization, the results of the first Social Sciences and Humanities Research Council (SSHRC) Strategic Research Cluster competition in 2004, linguistic difference, nineteenth-century Black writing, and then again hemispheric studies.

TransCanada?

If to go "trans"-Canada is also to go "beyond" Canada, what's on the other side? In a perspective that sees national borders as phenomena to be studied rather than a priori delimiters of a field of study, one possible answer is "America" or the "New World." As I will argue in the last section of this paper, I think such a perspective is indeed helpful, and often even necessary. Intertextualities and shared cultural contexts suggest mutual relevance here that points also in the direction of what Gayatri Chakravorty Spivak envisions as a mutual renewal of comparative literature and revised forms of area studies (*Death* 1–23). Such interdisciplinary cross-examinations—Bernheimer cited both area and period studies as productive possibilities in this respect (14–15)—can preserve attention to the specificity and materiality of language(s) while reasserting literary and other artistic practices as socially, historically, and internationally implicated processes of signification, and make space for cultural studies while preventing it from floundering in thematicism. However, while in such perspectives new Americas remain to be discovered and "The Moment of the Discovery of America Continues" (Kroetsch 1), we have also to remain aware of economico-cultural imbalances and neo-colonial potentials suggested, for instance, by Carolyn Porter's 1994 critique of "the synecdoche of a US read as 'America'" (468), or by Janice Radway's related question in an article based on her 1998 Presidential Address to the American Studies Association, "What's in a Name."

In these "trans-Canadian" discussions "on … the other side of" the border, many critics in the United States have problematized national paradigms in the teaching of "American" literature. Gregory Jay also mentions Canada in this respect. In response to Carolyn Porter's justified remark that his project of teaching "Writing in the United States" reasserts nationalist boundaries just when critiques of essentialism challenge "American Literature" (Porter 499–502), he offers the following caveat:

> we should recognize that calling for an end to the study of a national American literature means calling for an end to the study of a national Mexican or Canadian or Colombian literature as well. Do "we" in the United States want to prescribe such an abandonment of local and regional cultural traditions? Do we have the right? Would this call for postnationalism return us to the widely discussed observation that the criticisms of identity politics arise just at the moment when those whose identitities have been marginalized demand recognition? (*American Literature* 182)

Jay's questions seem well worth pondering in the context of the end(s) of CanLit. Consider the 1991 *Columbia History of the American Novel*, which contained Arnold Davidson's chapter "Canada in Fiction." Canadian fiction was getting exposure south of the border; yet while the United States academic institution took note of Canadian literature and other "American" literatures, this inclusion was conducted under the slippery signifier of the "American novel." The double-edged semiotics of this process seem to cut both ways: the demarginalization of Canadian and other literatures potentially strengthens the non-hegemonic connotations of the word "America" here, while at the same time risking assimilation and homogenization in a battle with a habitualized synecdoche that reflects neo-colonial power and privileges the United States. These are figurative negotiations that continue to be problematic. José Martí in 1891 expressed his views of hemispheric possibilities under the Spanish title "Nuestra América," with a strong emphasis on the pronoun. In translation—for instance in the *Heath Anthology* (Martí, "Our America")—the expressive geopolitical and cultural anchoring of the possessive pronoun and the (literally and in a Bakhtinian sense) accented noun is transmuted or lost. While I am interested in TransCanadian perspectives that are also transnational, I think that for now, at least in English, phrases like "Studies of the Americas" or "North American Studies" seem preferable to designate transnational fields that clearly avoid the problematic force of an unqualified "America." Those wider projects, however, are best undertaken as part of, or contrapuntally together with, more local Trans-Canadian explorations across Canada.

From a Canadian perspective, for all the critical sense that we should be "through" with essentializing narratives of nation and "go beyond" or "transcend" them, I think the only way to do so is by also going further through and across Canada. This is relevant, first of all, for the continued critique of essentialism itself, since the effects of the signifier do not simply disappear with the critique; on the contrary, they are displaced and differently delimited but remain an important field of cultural and literary inquiry. Furthermore, compared with research in other national literatures, there remains so much to go through here, areas and questions and texts for which the category of nation represents a constitutive mediation. Finally, our ability to pursue this still-necessary project is intimately linked to the impact of our globalized condition on the public sphere; the effects of that impact, I will argue, require a renewed reflection on the role of literary scholarship in the project of democratic citizenship and its national dimension.

Globalization has been understood as an accelerated movement of people, goods, and information, which Mary Louise Pratt in her response to the Bernheimer Report saw linked to democratization in higher education and to processes of decolonization ("Comparative" 59). For Anthony Appiah, it is associated with the increasing presence of strangers within heretofore presumably unstrange communities (*Ethics* 216). Yet globalization can also be scanned as "the imposition of the same system of exchange everywhere" (Spivak, *Death* 72), in ways that more specifically produce what Jürgen Habermas, in his 2001 essay "The Postnational Constellation and the Future of Democracy," named "democratic deficits" (*Postnational* 71). Such "democratic deficits" can hijack accountability to democratically elected constituencies, and spirit this principle away like the *desaparecidos* subjected to extraordinary rendition in the aftermath of what is metonymically called 9/11 (Derrida, qtd. in Borradori 86).

While there are more dramatic recent examples, even the older North American Free Trade Agreement Chapter 11 clause, under which investors can sue governments over the outcomes of democratically implemented legislation, is enough to argue that economic changes linked to globalization cause scenarios in which "governments are losing their ability to be responsive to constituents" (Klein, *Fences and Windows* 57–58). More generally, Habermas highlights "democratic deficits" in the wake of transnational movements of capital, employment, and investments that erode the tax base of the state and thus increasingly reduce the scope of democratically controlled choices in the shaping of society: "There is a crippling sense that national politics have dwindled to more or less intelligent management of a process of forced adaptation to the pressure to shore up purely local positional advantages" ("Postnational" 61).

Globalization and postnational constellations not only force individual disciplines to reposition themselves (Saussy 2006); they also alter the general conditions of the production of knowledge and directly influence the working parameters of universities. Research and teaching are pressured by state priorities that seek quantifiable results to enter into equations of national competitiveness under global circumstances. The consequences can be positive, as the concept of Canada Research Chairs demonstrates: yet one of the problems linked to these transformations of the national public sphere under increasingly trans- or postnational pressures is that many state decision-makers see global competitiveness more easily linked to the sciences than the humanities. Such constellations call for renewed attention to the end(s) of Canadian literature in the projects of the Canadian state.

Research in the Time of Globalization

This problem has been vividly demonstrated by the results of the initial, 2004 SSHRC competition for Strategic Research Clusters Design Grants. Literary studies were massively sidelined both in the competition outcome and at the subsequent Knowledge Project event in Ottawa. In a letter to ACCUTE president Keith Wilson on February 7, 2005, former president Marjorie Stone pointed to a "pattern of marginalization" affecting humanities projects and, in particular, literary studies in this competition, with "*no* project out of the 33 successful ones [focussing] on literary or textual studies or the arts, judging by their titles." This result is all the more alarming since the SSHRC website announced the program as "the first concrete step in the plan to transform SSHRC from a granting council to a much more comprehensive knowledge council," and thus presented it as being indicative of future orientations of state-funded academic research in Canada.

Occasionally, questions have been raised about the value of funded research for literary scholarship: does it unduly promote science models, quantitative approaches, or policy-oriented questions in a discipline that has produced some of its most celebrated results in quite different ways and areas? Northrop Frye labouring over a standard research grant application is not what comes to mind when we think of the *Anatomy*; yet, while such concerns deserve attention, it is important to remember that research funding has not only enabled most of the important large collaborative projects in the field, but also facilitated many of the smaller initiatives and individual monographs that relay research to peers, educators, and a wider public here and abroad. It is certainly vital for a project of democratic citizenship that the case for the study of literary and cultural production is clearly heard in debates over Canada's research resources, that its importance for the nation's democratic and multicultural fabric is understood, and that its role for Canada's successful participation in a globalized state of affairs is emphasized. In this context, national research networking is certainly one of the most effective options in the "TransCanadian" business of going "through" and "across" Canada and its literatures and cultures, of which there remains much to be carried out. In addition, such networking is equally effective in cases where "TransCanadian" research is carried out best by also going "beyond" Canada. Let me cite two of many examples, selected from problematics of language and race.

TransCanada? Oui!

Associations evoked by the conference lead to a title by Roy Kiyooka that begins its Transcanadian journey in Montreal, Quebec (*Transcanada* 5–24), and announces, "i am moved by the fervor with whc Montreal painters / poets / sculptors / & Others confront public apathy" (5); and to a poem by F. R. Scott, the poet, political activist, and public intellectual who was also a translator of Hector de Saint-Denys Garneau and Anne Hébert, and one of the most important mediators between francophone and anglophone writers of his time (F. R. Scott; Godbout 67–120). Another association, reinforced by the conference website's imagery, is the Trans-Canada Highway, which crosses not only different regions but also different languages. TransCanadian citizenship inclusive of more than one language, however, remains in many contexts a project yet to be carried out. Research in the languages and

cultures of Canada would seem essential to that project. To my mind, opportunities in our field lie in the fact that current research in postcolonial studies or diasporic studies, for instance, has so much to gain from multilingual
TransCanadian perspectives. One example is the reception of discourses of
decolonization in the early 1960s in Quebec, where Fanon was avidly read
long before his texts appeared on anglophone radar screens (Siemerling
New, 120–29). This reception was instrumental in the emergence of the project of a "littérature québécoise," yet has been rarely studied or used in the English Canadian postcolonialism debate. This problematic would have
complicated some early "investments" in Canadian postcolonial issues beyond
the triangulations effected by inclusions of First Nations issues, and it is certainly relevant for a complex debate about TransCanada.

One frequent argument against such TransCanadian purviews is that
the limits of individual linguistic ability are the limits of our scholarship.
Precisely such predicaments and unrealized potentials, however, should
help us argue for the importance of multilingual or interdisciplinary national
research networks that can overcome these isolations, and for the inclusion of literary scholars in the planning of national research agendas. The
strength of arguments based on the necessities of linguistic collaboration
increases even further if one moves beyond the French–English divide. The
inauguration of graduate studies in comparative Canadian literature at the
Université de Sherbrooke in 1963, for instance, was based mainly on the
desire to study literature and criticism in English and French; the current
edition of those graduate programs, however, hosts the SSHRC-funded *Bibliography of Comparative Studies in Canadian, Québec, and Foreign Literatures / Bibliographie d'études comparées des littératures canadienne, québécoise,
et étrangères* (Sirois et al.). This project has recently affiliated a specialist in
Hispanic Canadian and Québécois writing; it seeks to enlarge its linguistic
capabilities beyond its current collective access to texts in approximately
ten languages.

The example of linguistic difference certainly points to TransCanada as
a move both across and beyond Canada. The study of many diasporas in
Canada is undoubtedly enriched by the inclusion of literary production in
TransCanadian languages beyond English and French. Italian diasporic writing in Montreal, for instance, is a trilingual phenomenon, and its study benefits from knowledge about Italy. A class discussion of texts by Wayson Choy
or Ying Chen, likewise, can prosper significantly if a Chinese-speaking student is present with advanced knowledge of a diasporic culture that functions both across and beyond Canada and Quebec.

Around 1852

Let me select another TransCanadian example that illustrates the need to go further through but also beyond Canada, this time regarding the broad issue of race. I want to evoke briefly the question of the role of Black writing in "foundational" narratives of Canadian literature.

Take, for example, the year 1852, a somewhat canonical date in most narratives of Canadian literature, evoking Susanna Moodie's *Roughing It in the Bush*, and sometimes her sister Catharine Parr Traill's *Canadian Crusoes*. For scholars of United States literature, the date likely summons (at least since Jane Tompkins's *Sensational Designs*) Harriet Beecher Stowe's 1852 *Uncle Tom's Cabin*, written in response to the 1850 Fugitive Slave Law. This law made it legally binding for authorities in the non-slavery northern states to enforce southern slave ownership and assist slave catchers, the reason behind most Black emigration to Canada West at the time. In connection with this development, 1852 also saw the *First Report of the Anti-Slavery Society of Canada*, Mary Ann Shadd's *A Plea for Emigration, or, Notes of Canada West* (1852), and her planning, as the first Black female editor in Canada, of the *Provincial Freeman* (1853–60), which published its first issue in the following year and entered into competition with Henry Bibb's *Voice of the Fugitive* (founded in 1851). These texts are part of the production of Black writing in Canada that included a substantial number of types of texts, before and after this date, including numerous slave narratives.

While these authors and publications are not unknown to historians and have in the last few years begun to be cited or discussed by specialists in African Canadian literature (e.g., Almonte 25–33; Walcott 27–49; Clarke, *Odysseys* 329; A. Stone), they are not scanned by our standard literary histories and anthologies, and were not included in the important pilot bibliography by Lorris Elliott.

Consider the merits of possible arguments against the inclusion of these texts into narratives of CanLit. The argument that some of these texts should not be considered because they were printed or published outside of Canada West evokes the textual and publication history of Moodie's *Roughing It* (originally published in London; first Canadian edition in 1871), and thus leads to the counter-argument that publication outside Canada does not normally apply as a criterion for exclusion. Being foreign-born is also rarely cited as an exclusionary criterion when it comes to Canadian authorship. Perhaps the fact that many of these authors returned to the United States during or after the Civil War might be adduced; but such reservations seem questionable in a country that embraces Mavis Gallant and Dany Laferrière as Canadian authors. Finally, there are arguments about "literary quality." These might lead us back to the debates caused by the opening of Northrop Frye's first "Conclusion" to the *Literary History of Canada* in 1965, and such debates would not sit well with current interest in settler narratives, autobiography, postcolonial and diasporic writing, and literature as an institution.

In addition, there is the case of the Black emigrationist Martin Robert Delany, one of the first Black medical students admitted to Harvard (though he was not allowed to complete his degree), who was also a co-editor, with Frederick Douglass, of the *North Star* between 1846 and 1848. In 1854 he moved to Canada, where he collaborated with Mary Ann Shadd and the *Provincial Freeman*. Here he also wrote most of what could lay claim to being the first Black novel in Canada, *Blake, or the Huts of America* (Ullman 193; Clarke, *Odysseys* 329, 338n6). The beginning of the novel was first serialized in the *Anglo-African Magazine*. Of the proposed 80 chapters, 74 were published in the *Weekly Anglo-African* from November 1861 to May 1862 (Sundquist 184), breaking off, for unknown reasons, just as the hero is implicated in an armed revolt in Cuba.

The text is interesting not only because it would be difficult to exclude it on the grounds of literary quality, but also because it illustrates the need for TransCanadian perspectives to go further through and beyond Canada at the same time. Delany's novel itself was produced in a Canada–US crossborder context, but includes Cuba in its consideration of the implications and reaches of slavery. Questions about what role nineteenth-century Black writing might play in our narratives of Canadian literature thus strongly reinforce arguments—which can be drawn from many other areas—that transborder and comparative contexts will assist us in going through the issues relevant for Canadian literature.

TransCanada? Sí!

My last TransCanada stop on this trans-scan takes me beyond United States–Canada transborder questions again to contexts of wider North American and hemispheric studies. In addition to the obvious and steadily increasing relevance of Caribbean and other Latin American diasporas in Canada, the "Cuban connection" in Delany's text is but one further example of the importance of these areas in truly TransCanadian studies. Another example of that particular connection is evident in current research on transculturation, a term that may also have inspired the title of this conference. It was introduced in Spanish by the Cuban scholar Fernando Ortiz in his work *Contrapunteo cubano del tabaco y el azúcar*. He employed it to critique previous models of deculturation and acculturation, and in an effort to account for processes of selection and invention. The term transculturation was popularized in anglophone literary studies by Mary Louise Pratt in her influential study *Imperial Eyes: Travel Writing and Transculturation*. In francophone usage, however, *transculture* had already been established as an imported, important, and contested term in Quebec. It was disseminated in particular from 1983 on via a trilingual journal rooted in the Montreal Italian diaspora, *Vice Versa: Magazine Transculturel, Transcultural Magazine, Rivista Transculturale* (see Siemerling, *New* 130–33). The term was subsequently used and much debated in the work of influential critics and intellectuals such as Lise Bissonnette, Jean Lamore, Lucie Lequin, Pierre Nepveu, and Sherry Simon. In Quebec contexts, the implications of *transculture* are very different from those surrounding the inception and Cuban reception of Ortiz's work, and the uses in anglophone contexts and discourses vary again widely. Since the multilayered dimensions of such conceptual transfers emerge in the contrasts and parallels of comparative analysis, a TransCanadian approach to transculture in Canada arguably works best both across and beyond its internal and external boundaries.

The advantages of such wider comparative perspectives support the practice of North American and hemispheric studies together with, or as part of, the study of Canadian literature and culture. The problems I began with, however, certainly continue to require our engagement. One such occasion—and my last example—was the Second World Congress of the International Association of American Studies in August 2005 in Ottawa. The congress was part of ongoing attempts at internationalizing "American" studies. The issues evoked by Martí and the problem of the signifier were as present as ever, but there was also a question here again as to whose "America" was being invoked or what it might become. The congress was held in four languages; some papers fell in the more traditional, anglophone understanding of American Studies as US studies, but many spoke to the much wider field of Studies of the Americas. In response to the title of the congress, *America's Worlds and the World's Americas*, I organized two sessions entitled Canada and Its Americas, to debate further the pitfalls and possibilities of (TransCanadian) hemispheric studies.

The papers and debates in these sessions demonstrated that there is both a strong concern about protecting Canadian culture and literary scholarship in a North American, US-dominated context and a strong interest in discussing Canadian culture and literature in the wider context of the Americas. In other sessions, it became obvious that specialists in US literature who were theoretically interested in internationalizing their field did not necessarily seek to take advantage of the Canadian conference setting to inquire actively into transnational issues that would include Canadian topics. Little is gained by splendid isolation, however; articulations of Canadian vantage points in literary and cultural discussions of the Americas offer important opportunities to counteract the continued invisibility of Canada in these debates. The very fact of the routine marginalization of Canadian culture in hemispheric scholarship requires active intervention.

I think it has become clear throughout my discussion that, for me, Trans-Canada and the ends of Canadian literature suggest *neither* remaining within the boundaries of Canada *nor* departing into postnational approaches that disregard attention to national borders and formations as quaint reminders and remainders of twentieth-century scholarship. In the interests of democratic citizenship that actively participates in global contexts, it seems crucial to both maintain and reinforce nationally designated fields of cultural and literary inquiry in Canada *and* to engage in relational and comparative perspectives that also highlight local specificity.

ASHOK MATHUR

TRANSUBRACINATION
HOW WRITERS OF COLOUR BECAME CANLIT

I n this position paper for TransCanada, my initial thoughts were to focus on literary practices, most particularly the shifting position held by, and perceptions held of, writers of colour in the putative canon of CanLit over the past two decades. Hence the title's play on deracination and transubstantiation: what processes are at work such that a particular subject position enters into the maw of consumer culture and transmogrifies into something entirely different? That is, if as literary and cultural critics we can agree that the notion of "writers of colour" came into a national literary consciousness as a marginal notation in the 1980s, then it is with considerable alarm that we should note the mainstreaming of many of these writers in that they have begun to *represent* CanLit in many quarters. What began as a brown wafer begging to be tasted has become the body it once opposed. I do not want to suggest that developing a wider appeal or marketability is a necessarily bad thing, though I am loathe to suggest that because writers of colour and progressive communities of readers and critics demanded a visible presence of racialized writers the current milieu is therefore a good thing. In the context of cultural production by racialized artists, Richard Fung and Monika Kin Gagnon write that "if no one writes about your work it's hard to gain the legitimacy to get the resources to produce the work" (23); but the flip side, when that work *is* being written about, read, and sought, is that such consumption is driven by a market desire for a particular direction or focus. Fung and Gagnon refer to this as one of the paradoxes created by demands for inclusionary practice: "that slippery ground that artists of colour walk between commodification and cultural pertinence" (76).

As I considered the implications of various literatures, constructed by notions of nation and race, I found myself compelled to seek direction from outside the normative bounds of not just the literary canon, but literary practice. Reflecting on the movements of the eighties and nineties, I recall that there was a swelling of political agency through numerous forms of artistic expression, all interconnected and dependent on a domino-type of history-making. "Writing thru Race," a gathering of some 200 racialized writers in Vancouver in 1994, did not come out of an overtly literary concern or politic, but from an overarching movement of arts and cultural production. Movements around the visual and media arts, such as interventions by the Minquon Panchayat within the Association of National Non-Profit Artist Run Centres, were similarly informed by and through literary actions. Through all this was the practice and pedagogy of identity politics, at once liberating and constraining, full of potential and contradiction, presenting to us opportunities (at times somewhat mercurial ones) to disturb a social fabric that had become complacent in its homogeneity and lack of attention to power relationships.

With this in mind, I wanted to fashion this position paper around a general sense of movement outside of literature and, rather than present definitive conclusions about how (or if) writers of colour have, indeed, become CanLit, land instead on a series of talking points. Such points might help us investigate not just past political shifts but also potential futures for those who want to engage in what Monika Kin Gagnon refers to as "cultural race politics" (*Other Conundrums* 21) within a contemporary framework. To that end, I am presenting here a version of a piece commissioned by the Canada Council as part of its Off the Radar program, piloted through Inter-Arts. As rapporteur for a panel put on by the Powell Street Festival organizers in Vancouver, my role was to produce a critical commentary on the subject at hand, explained in greater detail below. This narrative, versions of which were subsequently published on the council's website and more recently in *FUSE* magazine, is an attempt to come to terms with shifting political frames and how to negotiate effective futures within this context. Notable in this narrative is the focus on visual and media arts rather than writing and publishing; at the conclusion of this narrative, however, I want to return to a number of points that, I hope, will allow us to lift off in particular directions and discussions during TransCanada and beyond.

Leaving It Be: The Invitation

It is late morning on a warm September day in 2004, and I'm occupying myself with that twenty-first-century part-procrastinative, part-requisite habit of checking my day's email. I'm sitting in my office on Granville Island, taking periodic breaks from the onslaught of messages by looking out at the cement plant across the road, reflecting on the academic term to come and the past two-and-a-half years I have spent at my job teaching and developing arts-based courses at the Emily Carr Institute. On this particular day, I'm remembering the phone call from the then-dean who offered me my current position, and how I tried to negotiate time so that I could coordinate, with other faculty of colour, the diverse needs of a campus like Emily Carr. My request was met with resignation; faculty of colour, she told me, was me. That was 2001. Today, checking my email, there is a note from a former Emily Carr student, Vanessa Kwan, wondering if I would be available to act as respondent for a Powell Street festival panel entitled "Leaving It Be: Apathy, Activism, and Ethnicity in Contemporary Practice." Its intent would be to investigate how the identity politics of the nineties have become passé in a contemporary art world, giving way to related expressions of diversity articulated through interdisciplinary models—and, if this is the case, how we might track the relationship between the interest in race and identity activism in the nineties and the contemporary interest in new media and cross-disciplinarity. I respond almost immediately. While it is some thirty months since I was hired at Emily Carr, and in that time I have been joined by three more permanent faculty of colour, I want to make and hear noise about where we think we've come to in terms of equity. There have been seismic shifts in the last decade, more pronounced in some areas than others, but significant and troublesome to various degrees. So, yes, I write to Vanessa, I will respond to this panel. Lights up, let's talk.

The Panel

It turns out that several of the panelists participated in the IntraNation residency that I directed at the Banff Centre in the summer of 2004, an event that focussed on artistic production in contexts framed by national and other forms of identity. That residency makes for an easy transition to this panel, plus there is an overarching familiarity amongst the panelists as their work and ideas have travelled within similar circles. As moderator, Ken Lum, nationally and internationally known for his large-scale photo installations, sets the tone by posing the question of the meaning of the nation-state in the context of diasporic populations. He bends this back to the local, suggesting that the Vancouver conceptual arts scene made attempts to peer outside its borders and incorporate internationalist concerns, but that this ultimately failed. Lum's introductory notes, delivered to an attentive and engaged audience of about a hundred, allow the panelists that follow—Cindy Mochizuki, Linda Sormin, Henry Tsang, and Jin-Me Yoon—to explore more fully, through their own practices and historical specificities, the intersections of identity, cultural activism, and art.

This is a well-orchestrated and polite panel, with participants showing their work, raising pertinent points, and staying on time. Upon closing of the formal presentations, questions from the floor are equally polite and searching, and, when the day is done, participants from the panel and the audience retreat to a nearby watering hole to continue the conversation. It is, as they say in organizing circles, a success; but, perhaps swayed by nostalgia and yearning, I leave the event with a sense of ennui. Where was the passion, the anger, the deliberate provocations that spilled the debates of the early nineties out of artist-run centres and gathering halls onto the culture-war pullout sections of the *Post* and the *Globe*? Where was the delight, the laughter, and excitement as new cultural arenas were broached, old systems were obliterated and rejuvenated? Given that none of this was present, only slightly ironic in that apathy was the first-named subject of the subtitle, where are we, as an intellectual, activist, artistic community? Where are we going, on which trajectory, triggered by which history? Far from being overcome by nostalgic longing, I find myself investigating the tactics of the panel and panelists further because these artists are most certainly responding to the climate we now endure, and while the immediacy of change-by-protest that delineated the nineties may now be, well, a thing of the past, there is still an urgency at work, albeit one marked by uncertainty.

Identity Reformation

If the mythic nineties were marked by an insistence of presence—disenfranchised groups and individuals demanding to be seen, heard, and included—the current decade, awash with the re-emergence of unapologetic militarism and fresh new enemies in the mist of a globalization that means everything and nothing, is typified by a desire to keep up. That keeping up often amounts to a type of shape-shifting, or, more accurately, the grand extension of postmodernity's desire to slip freely between identities—

not just an ability to rustle off one's skin in serpentine manner, but a type of reverse-ecdysis, a shuffling *into* another's shedded outer layers, embracing a type of passing through borrowed appearance.

In such a space, a voicing of identity-location is lost in an echoey chamber where claims bounce off metaphoric walls, amplifying themselves in creative and grotesque manners. One case in point is Tsang's *Orange County*, a video-installation that takes viewers to a very different Orange County (yet frighteningly similar in a way that would do Baudrillard proud) than the one they may see on television. Tsang documents a body, his body, a body-read-as-Asian, walking through the streets of Orange County, California, and Ju Jun, the replica of Orange County built by a wealthy Beijing development company for China's elite, who want to live the American Dream but still be able to commute to work.

Henry Tsang, *Orange County*: Video File in QuickTime (.mov) format

Tsang's installation shows him walking through these two same/different neighbourhoods whereby the figure moves from one space to the next almost seamlessly. There is a lag time in between; is it the time zone difference, the jet lag? Where does he go? When he reappears, nothing has changed: the clothing is the same, the knee-length black jacket, the slightly scruffy black jeans that don't quite match but don't quite position him as a target for police questioning. He is Chinese, so he flows from America to China and back without restriction, without question. Twenty years ago, he would not have been able to pass; he would have been too western in one, too Asian in the other; but now, the worlds have collided, we are the world, and there will be a Starbucks nearby soon. Tsang goes on to question how the very nature of "normal" is shifting radically, dependent on information, perception, and power relationships. We may revisit the theoretical notion of the mimic men, whom Homi Bhabha once cast as "white, but not quite" ("The Location of Culture" 86), although today's mimic men, at least in certain circles of profit and wealth, might be read as attaining a quality of Whiteness without leaving the comforts of wherever home may be. Identity is reformed and resituated.

For her part, Mochizuki frames the notion of interdisciplinarity and ethnicity in contemporary arts as a place of struggle with positive implications. She looks back to the legacy of artists such as Roy Kiyooka, whose model of interdisciplinarity, Mochizuki suggests, informs a much larger practice, acts as a bridge between work as a cultural activist and visual artist. She proposes a revisitation of identity politics that pays attention to the theoretical construct of Mary Louise Pratt's "contact zone." In other words, as an artist whose practice emerged as public interest in identity politics were waning, Mochizuki sees the continuing contact zone between various cultural groups as a critical entry point to this discussion. By example, she refers to her co-performance with Rita Wong during the IntraNation residency: the duo, calling itself FeastFamine, performed a perambulatory piece in downtown Banff. Strolling up and down the main drag pushing a dim sum cart filled with "decolonization wishboxes," the duo gave these away along with information sheets detailing First Nations histories in the geographic area of the park. Mochizuki and Wong have talked about how this performance was variously read as an act of intervention into the social fabric, a commodifying act (as in, what are you selling?), and a performance that placed their gendered, raced bodies into a place of contention. To have bodies that are read as young, female, and Asian addressing directly issues of colonized land and responsibility to First Peoples marks a categorical shift from the identity politics of old. Here we have not a representation of the self but, like Tsang's reconsideration of how his body is read in different geographic and political climates, a representation that foregrounds neither its own particularities nor its specific histories, but a relational and ethical position.

The work of Mochizuki and Wong clearly indicates a shift from what Yoon calls the "stakes around identity" (Powell Street Festival) that prevailed when she was entering the field of artmaking. Yoon calls attention to the former valorization of marginalization and emphasizes that contemporary times call for new forms, among them a continued contextualization of the nature of identity. She expresses an interest in the "hauntings," the spectres—that is, the notion of the body as cipher—particularly as the racialized body is constituted. Following the gestures made by Mochizuki, Yoon notes that we need not shift away from taking positions, but that to be most effective we need to structure these positions within the material aspects of our work. She exemplifies this in projects like her *Unbidden* installation at the Kamloops Art Gallery, in which the artist refuses to present literal representations of place or action but allows viewers to situate themselves in a space of their own memory and contemporary reality. The body is troubled, disturbed, but very much present in such a space.

Courting Risk

How does it look, then, to inhabit a racialized body in a racialized world that is largely informed by events that affect us locally and globally? If Yoon, Mochizuki, and Tsang are correct in pursuing a critical analysis that, on one hand, embraces a continued awareness of subject positioning but, on the other, wants to engage with political and artistic concerns beyond the frailties of the skin, the question of strategy comes into play. Of course, employing multiple strategies in the pursuit of theorizing a minoritized discourse is hardly new, but the urgent question is how to work so that such strategies have a progressive, political effect. Linda Sormin talks about moving to an abstract narrative, seeking out ways of embodying a physicality that becomes a metaphor for living in a particular body. Her ceramic sculptures epitomize this movement.

Linda Sormin, *Sculptures*: Video File in QuickTime (.mov) format

"At once aggressive and vulnerable, the massive, precarious forms have the capacity to injure me, and I to destroy them," Sormin writes:

> My practice is an attempt to persuade the clay to behave (and misbehave) in ways that are new to me. The possibility of ceramic material moving, distorting or "failing" in the firing is something that excites me. This speculative approach offers a high level of drama and delight for me as a maker. The bravado involved with my working large scale, and the macho—and oxymoronic—activity of "orchestrating risk" is at odds with the compulsive, fussy, dolling up of my pieces with gold, copper and silver leaf, ribbons and flowerets. (n.p.)

Sormin's work and critical approach may not represent the body in any literal way, but like the projects of her contemporaries—Tsang's *Orange County*, Mochizuki's *FeastFamine*, and Yoon's *Unbidden*, where the body clearly matters in a visually represented way—Sormin situates the body in relationship to her precarious sculptures. It is impossible to stand beside her labyrinthine sculptures without being enticed to slip a finger, a hand, into the foreboding lattices and thereby inhabit the physicality of the work itself, and, in so doing, read one's own body into the art.

Palimpsestry and Overwritten Narratives

Some months after the panel, I am poring over notes I jotted down during the event and received from panelists in response to my desperate plea for language that will help me address the critical topics of the panel that, at once, excite and confuse me. No, not the panel itself, which was clear, cohesive, and, as I suggest in the opening of these maunderings, quite polite—but the ideas that brought the panel into being at once excite and confuse me. This is what the Powell Street organizers were intent on investigating:

> In the contemporary art world, identity politics are said to be passé, a theoretical and practical model associated with work that had currency through the 1990s. Contemporary art institutions, funding bodies and critics now emphasize work that is "interdisciplinary," work that embraces "new forms," work that, having sufficiently dealt with the inequalities of the past, looks firmly to the future. This panel is concerned with the point at which identity politics and its embedded struggle for new modes of expression intersects with the emergence of interdisciplinary practice as an increasingly legitimate (and appropriate) approach to art-making. In a context where many young artists seem reluctant to tackle "cultural issues," but embrace cross-disciplinary practice and new media freely, it seems an appropriate time to address the place of ethnicity and activism in contemporary art practice. (Powell Street Festival)

During the question period of the panel, there was considerable focus on seeking out the narratives that describe where we are, who we are, in a contemporary reality. Yoon summed this up succinctly when she noted that such a desire for meaning could only be satisfied by looking at what lies underneath our constructed realities. This palimpsestic process is not as evident as it might first seem, for Yoon's comments suggest not an existential search for meaning in the depths, but a peering through and at the layers of history and practice. We might readily acknowledge that we construct ourselves through various histories, written or unwritten, well-known or rumoured, authentic or questionable; but how do we learn (and what remembrances do we bring forward) from our evolving past, a past that is constantly rewritten as we reflect upon its value and substance? Such a palimpsestic reading, a squinting, peering, microscopically intense gaze, allows us to pick out fragments of what once was, not to reconstruct them wholly, but to take them in proprioceptively, pull them into our bodies directly, let those fragments inhabit us as much as we might inhabit a Sormin sculpture.

If the recent past is a palimpsest, partially erased but readable in its remnants, then we cannot help but view the identity movements of the nineties—full of bombast and righteousness as well as acute criticality and political awareness—as historically significant and omnipresent. We have not left the politics of identity behind us, nor constructed an elaborate camouflage to continue working in the same old ways. What we have done is build upon the tremulous ground beneath our feet. Certainly, there has been some loss of political will and compromises have been made in the name of leaving it be and getting on with our collective lives. The narrative I want to suggest, however, is one where we have not turned our back on our past but have scrutinized it, sorted carefully through the bits and pieces, and cobbled together a comprehensive response. Whether we call it new forms that owe their existence to previous ones, or interdisciplinary practices that developed out of oppositional politics, this is still an artmaking that comes from urgency, from political need. Our strategies might shift, our causes might mutate, but we will continue to read our pasts into our contemporary lives, and, in doing so, we will write out our potential futures.

Back to the Future: Transubracination and Some Talking Points

There are a number of key elements that I hope to translate or transliterate from the visual/media arts context to that of literature. I don't mean to suggest there exists a rupture in the various discourses, nor that the LitCrit and CanLit industries are themselves without a trajectory in the realm of cultural race politics; but I think that by borrowing from fields that are much more interdisciplinary and, by extension, more fluid in addressing material concerns around the body, we might be more aware both of the gates installed by market forces and how to negotiate our way past these barriers as writers of colour and critics of a supposedly national literature.

Talking Point #1

The literary publishing industry, inflected by the associated industries of big-box bookstores and nationalized and globalized literary legitimizers such as the star-system of book prizes and media awards, is most interested in creating a reading public that will bring it maximum revenue. To do this, the industry must manufacture not just a particular kind of taste, but a great equalizing taste. That is, the big titles it puts out have to be successful in the big-box stores, the academy, and the media in order to move the number of units required to create maximum profits with minimum costs. Writers of colour, many of whom cut their eyeteeth in the small and niche press scene, are affected in various ways. Certain writers must be pushed to the top, become household names. In order to do so, they have to provide a particular sensibility to the reading public. Consider the place of Asian Canadian literature within the larger frame of CanLit, exemplified by the import and media presence of Asian Heritage Month. Contrast the relatively mild political focus of Asian Heritage Month with its predecessors, such as Desh Pardesh. The difference is in the ability (or desire) for Asian Heritage Month to be all things to all people (read: consumers). Where Desh, a localized festival in a specific tight four-day frame, focussed on progressive, queer, South Asian, innovative practices, AHM is pan-Asian and industry-sponsored. Its program headliners are relatively conservative writers, filmmakers, and content-providers, its outreach to wide communities in urban centres nationwide. The bottom line is to make "Asian" cultural work turn a profit. What is to be done to develop strong creative and critical practices from a plethora of literary communities without taking our lead from market forces?

Talking Point #2

In the summer of 2004, more than sixty creative arts practitioners met at the Banff Centre for a residency to work on, through, and against questions of the nation. More specifically, the artists at IntraNation were concerned with how various nation-like structures were rising from within and across pre-existing nation-states. What kinds of connections are possible when writers, artists, curators, and their various audiences are at once focussing their means of production from within particularized nation-states while simultaneously resisting that form of nationhood? I resist calling this an international gathering of artists since the very question of national belonging was subject to such question; nor would I characterize this as a group of cultural producers prioritizing borders or border crossings since, while this was inevitable, it was often incidental to the reinvestigation of the various critiques of the state occurring from inside and outside its putative borders. How might we upset the logic we keep returning to, the sometimes protectionist, often relativist, focus on Canada as a site for cultural production?

Talking Point #3

In *The Souls of Cyberfolk: Posthumanism as Vernacular Theory,* Thomas Foster draws the lead portion of his title from a 1990 comic book that depicts an African American scientist who has been transformed into a cyborg to do the bidding of his right-wing controllers. The character sees his physicality as monstrous and notes, "I am worse than a monster. I'm a weapon. I've become the walking embodiment of all I despise" (144). To return to the role of the writer of colour (if, indeed, that very term is still useful or productive) working within a nationalist literary context, how do we function in an environment that is so able to co-opt, rebrand, and market? In effect, for writers of colour concerned with performing a progressive politic through creative production, how do we not become such despicable embodiments, and to what purpose might alliances and coalitions aid us in this desire?

Talking Point #4

In May and June 2005, installation artist Aiko Suzuki showed her *Bombard/Invade/Radiate: Witness* show at A Space in Toronto. Ostensibly, her work addresses public and private responses to cancer, but it also reconfigures traditional ways of seeing. Inside what looks to be a large rain barrel, the artist has placed a video monitor that loops World War II footage of American fighter planes dropping bombs while the word "witness" appears periodically across the screen. The footage is without sound but "droplets of water fall onto the monitor's surface in a slow rhythm that overrides the soundless dropping of bombs. We wait for some final moment, some end, but it never arrives. The images play ominously to the slow drip of time. Only then do we notice that the monitor is enclosed in a rusted bomb casing, a relic of war that is antiquated but not obsolete" (Sakamoto n.p.). Through this interdisciplinary practice, the artist relocates a sense of perception and agency in ways that may be difficult to accomplish within disciplinary-bound models such as mainstream literary production. How might we breach disciplinary boundaries? How might we broach interdisciplinary discourses such that we can address critically our collective concerns around constructions of race, nation, literature, and related questions that have brought us together here at TransCanada?

JULIA EMBERLEY

INSTITUTIONAL GENEALOGIES IN THE GLOBAL NET OF FUNDAMENTALISMS, FAMILIES, AND FANTASIES

> ... the world of speech and desires has known invasions, struggles, plundering, disguises, ploys.
> — Michel Foucault, "Nietzsche, Genealogy, History"

In "Nietzsche, Genealogy, History," Michel Foucault characterizes the importance of the genealogical method in terms of its capacity to "[oppose] itself to the search for 'origins'" (140). Naming this oppositional strategy a genealogy is, of course, somewhat ironic, especially when considered in relation to the filiative legacies drawn up in such religious histories of "mankind" as those which appear in the Judeo-Christian Bible. The patrilineal accounts of father/son inheritances are seemingly endless, and in the exclusion of mothers, daughters, and sisters, function as a standard-bearer of the archetypal and autocthonous "search for origins" beyond the female reproductive body. Thus, to overturn the search for origins is to insist upon its sites of construction and, in so doing, denaturalize whatever dominant (i.e., racist and patriarchal) origin stories currently exist, be they religious or secular (e.g., oedipal). It is also to put into question the reduction of the female body to a reproductive categorical imperative; for to erect a patrilineal genealogy of pure descent is to assume that what has been excluded—the female reproductive body—is its natural (taken for granted) correlative, and is therefore excluded a priori from the domains of culture and society. Although the implications I am drawing out of Foucault's understanding of a genealogical method may not have been included in his original vision of it—and, yet, in keeping with its opposition to the search for origins—I would like to suggest mobilizing institutional genealogies that are responsive to the formation of sexual and racial differences in nineteenth- and twentieth-century discourses and representational technologies. By tracing such institutional and institutionalized genealogies, it becomes possible to write a different sort of history; one, for example, that can take into account the institutional linkages that maintain origin stories and their filiative bonds of inheritance at work in the formation of colonial and decolonial nationalisms. This different genealogy, this genealogy with a difference, lies perhaps somewhere in the future, somewhere in the journals, diaries, poems, and notebooks of anti-racist feminists who already know how history has failed to tell the "other stories" at stake in colonial modernity. Nevertheless, I would like to imagine mobilizing genealogies of difference here—in the academic institution—for the particular purpose of discussing how religious fundamentalisms have relied upon familial relations to perpetuate an ideological web of fantasies about power, sexuality, and domination.

The institutional limits of "the family" are currently being negotiated by discourses of religious fundamentalism, on the one hand, and gay and lesbian marriage, on the other, especially in the domain of public media.[1] The larger question to which these concerns are directed in this essay is how this global competitive discourse on the family impacts on the significance of cultural practices, such as literature and film, and their role in the academy (i.e., the classroom) and in contemporary society. Thus it is my intention to address, in the context of Canadian educational and media institutions, the ethical and political responsibilities that shape our intellectual sites of research, writing, and teaching by way of attending to these pressing global developments. While the research for this essay builds upon my studies of Aboriginality in the representational technologies and techniques of colonial power used to reproduce "the family," my focus here will be on how global religious fundamentalist movements are currently using the heteronormative domain of "the family" to establish their hegemony in everyday life.[2] Furthermore, I am interested in how this so-called "religious revolution" is impacting on and being challenged by multiple institutions of public learning, including not only educational institutions but also less obvious sites of knowledge acquisition and transmission, such as television programming, the Internet, and other aspects of public media.

Religious fundamentalism, at least as it appears in Canadian media over the last decade or so, is largely represented as a phenomenon that happens "elsewhere," either in the US and the broader Middle East, or in Canadian immigrant communities, where it is circumscribed by notions of cultural difference that function as racist codes for otherness and exclusion. Debate about religious difference in the public arena is directed toward questions of religious rights, freedoms, and equalities, and not those of power and religious oppression. The latter is often subsumed, for example, under the rhetoric of "religious tolerance" (or intolerance) toward the existence, teachings, and practices of multiple and, in many cases, monotheistic religions, and somewhat ironically, of course, since these particular religious practices are opposed to the very idea of plural godheads. In his critique of the cultural dimensions of religious fundamentalisms, Tariq Ali argues that the problem of religion and society today is that they are dominated by "religious nationalism or its postmodern avatar, religious multiculturalism" (6). One of the more problematic aspects of the multicultural alibi is how it silences and censors critical opposition to religious oppression. An additional problem emerges, however, when the ideology of nationalism dominates the discussion of religion because of the tendency to ignore everyday life and thus to misrecognize the mediatory role played by religious fundamentalisms in creating as well as maintaining separate realms of private and public governance.

Although feminist critical debates of globalization have taken into account questions of identity formation and the impact of global political and economic forces in shaping the interrelated categories and experiences of gender, race, and sexuality, along with those of class and imperialism,[3] the separation of public and private spheres has not been sufficiently recognized as an important site for interrogating how transnational hegemonies create and maintain themselves. As a result, critical globalization studies are reproducing at the level of epistemology the separation of political powers within nation-states, thus continuing to render micro-political or domestic political governance either supplemental to, secondary (as in "ideological"), or entirely distinct from the macro-political and economic interests of transnational capitalism. At the level of the global political economy and knowledge production, the actual mechanisms that make the process of establishing global hegemonies possible remain hidden, thereby reinscribing the devaluation not only of particular arenas of study but also of the subjects whose lives are directly affected by the domestic politics of everyday life, including the poor, who are also predominantly women and children.

Questions of "difference" have preoccupied intellectual and institutional horizons of academia for some time now. If a post–World War II socialist consciousness challenged the elitism and ideological class biases of literary study, the 1980s and 1990s were dominated by feminist, lesbian and gay, and anti-racist critiques of the "canon" and its humanist and not-so-humanist exclusions. Literary critics have learned and unlearned how different histories, bodies, and experiences constitute the writing, reception, and critical response to literature and the academic production of literary knowledge. While this history of difference(s) challenged colonial and neo-colonial narratives of the nation and beyond, the emergence of new contradictions and conflicts among various social movements (e.g., sexuality and decolonization) suggest that a genealogical approach to how such differences are imbricated in each other's political formations must be sought if the emerging tensions between domestic and public domains of power and governance currently being mediated by religious nationalisms are to be addressed and transformed. Of particular importance here is why a cultural semiotics of "the family" has become the most intense site of violent contestation for furthering the oppressive aims of religious nationalisms and familialisms. Moreover, we might consider how heteronormativity is implicated in the histories of imperialism and colonization, as well as the connection between heteronormativity and recent neo-liberal and neo-conservative global practices. To address these questions means going beyond the rhetoric of religious and cultural diversity and towards destabilizing the very notion of "religious fundamentalism"—and examining how religion is a site of both imaginary re-signification and political power. This cultural politics approach to the intersection of religion and literary studies is designed to focus on religious fundamentalists' own investments in cultural signification; this approach makes it possible to comprehend and transform the violent opposition mounted by religious fundamentalist movements toward literary and cultural works, such as Deepa Mehta's film *Fire* (1996), which was attacked in India in 1998 by Hindu fundamentalists for its depiction of a lesbian relationship in a Hindu family.[4] Cultural practices have become significant targets for religious fundamentalist violence precisely because, in many cases, they constitute an effective means for the dissemination of a critical resistance to and disclosure of the limits of democracy. Thus, I would argue, it is important to open up the discussion of "religious fundamentalisms" to their imaginary as well as their social and political interests. By doing so, Canadian literary scholars can participate meaningfully in important debates in educational institutions and elsewhere about the formation of the real and imagined communities of religious fundamentalisms as global and "domestic" forces of power.

In pursuing these and other questions, I aim to move beyond the postmodern dilemma—what Jean-François Lyotard termed a postmodern incredulity toward metanarratives or, in Habermasian terms, the state of "enlightened bewilderment" (qtd. in Torpey 1) that currently exists toward grand projects of social change—by offering a different way of thinking about political affinities across the division between public and domestic or private spheres, especially as the latter are circumscribed by current notions of the "familial." While the critical attention currently directed toward public institutions is obviously important, the failure to understand how oppressive regimes of power operate through familial relations, parental and patriarchal authority, and heteronormative and racialized structures of knowing and being means that the analysis of the public domain is complicit in perpetuating key mechanisms of power, such as sexual and domestic violence and the control and regulation of human reproduction and sexuality. These mechanisms of corporeal power provide the public domain with its authority and governance over everyday life and human subjectivity. To ignore these avenues of corporeal power will ensure that democracy will never reach women and the poor.[5]

To shift critical perspectives away from a grand enlightenment project of social change that privileges Europe at the expense of its many global others and towards building political affinities and kinships across the boundaries of the international division of labours and the differential articulations across the fields of gender, sexuality, race, class, and colonization would involve

i. Transforming the meaning of the "public intellectual" by attending to various spatial regimes of knowing and knowledge production that exist today, especially those that fall outside the all-too-familiar and sanctioned institutions of learning that "we," university academics, inhabit. Different spaces of knowing might include media, television, popular print culture, and the Internet, along with institutions such as the family.
ii. Moving beyond incredulity and bewilderment in the struggle for social change by refusing to locate ourselves in fixed binary oppositions, and, instead, working toward establishing strategically mobile social positions across particular geopolitical and economic contexts.
iii. Making connections globally, across similar political and cultural movements, by building networks of political affinity through the Internet,

email, museums, art exhibits, conference travel, and other connecting systems of communication and knowledge production. As academically inclined cultural workers, university teachers and researchers might use our access to such forms of material wealth to learn and educate for the purposes of disrupting hegemonic forces of religious fundamentalist, nationalist, and familial violence.

iv. Reading transactionally[6] cultural practices, such as literature, film, popular culture texts of various kinds, and performance art, in order to disclose how we negotiate meaning and signification with and in everyday life, thereby contributing to de-authorizing and disrupting neo-liberal and neo-conservative powers of exclusion and dispossession.

∾

In his discussion of the geneaology of the Muslim Brotherhood, a notable right-wing Islamic religious and political organization that was founded in Egypt in 1928, Tariq Ali observes that its agenda was to revitalize the politics of the seventh century, to the extent that, like the prophet Mohammed, the Brotherhood must defeat rival orthodoxies by putting into place a new socioeconomic and political system, and create "new laws that could serve as a complete code for everyday life" (97). Ali goes on to note that a primary motive for the Islamist jihad against secular nationalists and Marxists in Muslim countries, such as that of the Muslim Brotherhood throughout the twentieth century, was its opposition to "materialism" in all is varieties:

> What Hasan al-Banna, the Brothers and their numerous successors today can never accept is materialism: not as a school of thought or a doctrine in the narrow sense of the word, nor even as a chance occurrence, but as an undeniable reality. Something that cannot be altered regardless of who rules the state. The materialism of all living creatures—animals, Wall Street Bankers, politicians, priests, nuns, mullahs, and rabbis—is fueled by the same subconscious instincts. Thinking people search for truth in matter because they are aware that there is nowhere else for them to search. (99)

I cite this passage from Ali's *The Clash of Fundamentalisms* because it provides an important trajectory for this discussion of the materiality of religious fundamentalist practices in everyday life, including commodity practices, as well as the new contradictions that are currently emerging between religious fundamentalisms, racism, neo-colonialism, and the struggle for lesbian and gay marriages. Specifically, I am interested in asking to what extent relations between the personal and political and between the private and public are being mediated by religious fundamentalisms, and what new forms of mystification are being created to render invisible and unseen new global economies of labour and desire. It is easy to think of an object as something material, composed of concrete matter, but what of human relations? What is material, for example, about the family, familial relations, and familiarity? In the 1980s, socialist-feminist critics such as Christine Delphy, Michèle Barrett, Mary McIntosh, and others took up Louis Althusser's notion of ideology to examine the family as a site of woman's oppression. While their studies served to demonstrate the intellectual value of ideological critique, they never quite achieved an analysis of the materiality of human relations produced in and by the so-called family. While the family became another sort of repository for the containment of critical thought, its production of corporeal powers through the body remained a mere fantasy of conflict resolution, rather than a key object and subject of a sustained analysis into the material production of life, power, violence, and affectivity. Such an analysis demands a materialist approach to corporeality and biopowers in which both are examined as sites of materiality rather than supplemental or semi-autonomous spheres of the political-economic base.

~

In January 2005, an advertising flyer from Bell Canada found its way into my home through the mailbox. Bell Canada declined to allow the image to be reproduced here. The flyer contains a photograph of a textbook open to a page with the heading "The Female Body." Below the heading is an illustration of a young, naked, and white femaled body with the breasts and genital areas cut out from the page. A couple of smaller anatomical illustrations to the right and left of the main illustration are also cut out. To the left of the photograph is a text box containing the words

> You'll do anything to
> protect your kids from
> inappropriate content.
> So will we.

Below this text and photograph is another text box with the words in large print "Protect your family with B— S— Basic service!" Parental Controls is one of the key features advertised.

The Lewinsky–Clinton affair in the US in the late 1990s made it clear that no amount of media manipulation could save the US nor its neighbouring nation from the "inappropriate content" of the Oval Office; today in post–9/11 Canada, however, corporate communications monopolies claim to be able to "do anything to protect your kids from inappropriate content," principally by cutting out those parts of the female anatomy that threaten to confuse or destabilize the boundaries of what counts as desire in the internal spaces of home, homeland, and household. The political economy of communication networks is represented in the semiotic anatomy of this advertisement as a highly libidinalized circulation of partial bodies and body parts, thus underscoring, for the purposes of my analysis here, a corporeal materiality. Nothing is more indicative of the success of capitalism than its control, regulation, and exploitation of the reproductivity of the female body, the greatest "natural resource" of generative power, even before oil, water, trees, and fur-bearing animals. Industrial capitalism, at least since the late eighteenth century, has been policing this body for the purposes of managing its labouring and desiring forces. I am going to engage in a sort of corporeal reassemblage here by putting the femaled body back into the economic picture, not as a supplementary ideological blip on the supposedly larger economic radar, but as the central biopolitical object of imperial and global economic practices and representations.

If we contemplate further this body that has been cut into, this anatomically correct body taken from a science textbook, signified by the notepad and pencil beside it in the Bell advertisement, that has had its parts subjected to extermination, we might wonder what the ad is attempting to accomplish. Of course, the ultimate goal is to coerce the viewer into purchasing Bell's basic service plan, which includes the security feature "Parental Controls." In order to do that, the advertisement must communicate with the parents, those with the money. Thinking back to the early 1990s and the Benetton ads that contained media images of current political significance dealing with social issues such as racism, ethnic cleansing, and AIDs, reframed to provoke controversy and thus gain the attention of a youthful viewer who, at that time, could still be considered to be invested in such social causes, perhaps the Bell ad is also seeking to draw in its viewers through the dissemination of a controversial ad. The increasing commodification and simulation of political movements for social change that occurred throughout the 1980s and 1990s left the individual with the purchasing power to buy into whatever political movement struck his or her fancy and to feel morally absolved of any actual engagement with political activism that might not involve shopping. Things have changed since then and not necessarily for the better. The family, rather than the individual, has become the dominant locus of a naturalized affectivity (i.e., purchasing power) and right-wing fundamentalist agendas for familial control and regulation have become the new controversial signifier in this Bell advertisement. In other words, the ad signifies religious fundamentalism, creationist origin stories over scientific truths, and the violence of the curtained femaled body that results, as the site of communicative interest today. After all, one of the justifications used on the part of the US to invade Afghanistan in order to advance the security of the nation was to "save" Afghani women and protect them from the fundamentalist abuses of the Taliban. To protect "our" kids is to protect "our" women, is to infantilize children, women, and Third World subjects, all of whom allegedly need the protection and security features of the global military *and communication networks* of North America. Bell's objectives are, perhaps, much larger than we suspect, but I would venture to guess that a primary objective is to further their global economic agenda by becoming another link between everyday life and the "security" of the family and the nation.

The materialities of communication and communication networks exist in various forms of transmission and reception. Print culture is of course a primary source, as are television and movies, and the image/text compositions of printed advertisements, billboard signs, and Internet screens:

> Bell Globemedia is a dynamic multi-media company, comprised of Canada's premier media groups: CTV Inc., Canada's number-one private broadcaster and The Globe and Mail, the leading daily national newspaper.
>
> Bell Globemedia's diverse collection of media brands creates an environment where different Canadian voices support each other, without compromising each other's strength. For example, TSN and Report on Business Television leverage their authoritative and expert content to CTV for its local newscasts, to The Globe and Mail for enhanced perspective, and on to companion Web sites TSN.ca and robtv.com. Bell Globemedia also owns RDS, the world's first French-language sports channel, which complements TSN and CTV's sports-related properties.
>
> With stations, news bureaus and offices in all of Canada's major cities, Bell Globemedia employees are connected to local communities, ensuring that what interests Canadians—locally, nationally and internationally—makes it to the screen, into print and onto the Internet. More than $285-million over seven years has been allocated for the creation of new programming and support for organizations, educational institutions and associations in our industry. (*Bell Globemedia*)

In addition to print culture, the body is also a site of communication and communicative strategies. Perhaps this is nowhere more obvious today than in the regulated politics of female reproductivity, either through genomic technological production of what we euphemistically call test-tube babies or through a highly effective religious fundamentalist politics and its cultural hegemony in the media. Either you labour to produce babies for the labour market, or you are liberated from the curse of your reproductive potential and you can proceed to simulate the baby of your dreams online. The disappearing femaled body today stands at the centre of capitalist and religious fundamentalist interests and objectives: the disappearance of the reproductive body through technology and the spectacle powers of mechanical, technological, and digital representational reproduction.

∽

Religious nationalisms and domestications claim to mediate between matter and spirit. Their mediations are, rather, ideological. I understand ideology, and especially its emergence since the nineteenth century, not as a representation of or reaction to economic or political realities, nor as something semi-autonomous from, yet supplemental to, the economic and political spheres, but as the force of mediation, if not mystification, between domestic and national, personal and public, formations of power.

Advanced capitalism demands that we have relationships with things, with commodities, and not with people. The intensification of this commodity materialism is such that it easily flips into its opposite "spiritualism" or religiosity. Shop at Walmart on Saturday; Sunday go to church. No doubt this captures something of the spirit, if not the letter, of Marx's notion of commodity fetishism. Not surprisingly, then, the best thing that could happen to Christian religious fundamentalisms in the US is when they can convert spiritual rhetoric back into the commodity form.

Marianne Williamson, televangelist "hottie," dons a brown leather jacket buttoned up tightly, the fabric stretching almost to bursting across her breast, a little lacy chemise peeping over her cleavage like some sort of token of modesty. She appears Sunday evenings on her television show *Everyday Grace*, where she struts across the stage, rubbing her nose once too self-consciously. She talks non-stop about "the unforgiven": "Who did you judge today?" she asks, continuing, "And I prayed to God to stop me from judging that woman too hard." Williamson is speaking to a live audience and her evocative manner of speech and dress has the uncanny effect of turning her question upon herself. It is as if she is challenging the audience to judge her for commoditizing her body as an object of desire. Televangelist programming manufactures a world of desire through the phantasmatic reproduction of an age-old trope—the fallen woman.

A Screen Allegory of the Disappearing Citizen

Iraqi woman votes in Basra, 30 January 2005. Photograph by Atef Hassan. Image reproduced by permission of Reuters.

Women are also disappearing into the folds of Islamic fundamentalism. From the spectacle of the veiled woman in Algerian postcards at the turn of the century to the spectacle of the veiled woman as a sign of Islamic power in Iran or Afghanistan, the veiled Muslim female body has become a mere phantasm of existence (see Alloula). Western metropolitan sexual politics in the 1980s saw the emergence of prostitute political organizations struggling against police brutality and agitating for safe-sex practices. In addition to these political practices, the performance art of Annie Sprinkle, Valie Export, Linda Montano, and others in the US and Canada revolutionized the rhetoric of pornography (Juro and Vale), transforming it from its signification of female domination (qua Monique Wittig[7]), to a symbol not simply about sexual domination but about labouring and sexual practices in a time of AIDS. What international studies feminist scholar Cynthia Enloe calls "the Western media's seeming addiction to the visual image of the veiled Muslim woman" is emerging to supplant the pornographic female body as the dominant sign of female subjugation (271). This figure is positioned in opposition to the liberated Western metropolitan woman and is racistly othered as the product of ignorance and poverty elsewhere and in immigrant enclaves scattered throughout urban centres and small towns; she is meant to signify a primitive past and a handmaid's future for what we might call, post-Foucault, "the species woman."

One important challenge to the spectacle violence of this disappearing woman/citizen has been the counter-emergence of the figure of the cross-dresser, or transgendered representations in films such as Mohsen Makhmalbaf's *Kandahar: Journey into the Heart of Afghanistan*. *Kandahar* is the fictional docudrama based on the story of Nelofer Pazira, who immigrated to Canada in 1989 to seek refuge from the tyranny of the Taliban in Afghanistan. One day, as Makhmalbaf's tells it, "a young Afghan woman, who had taken refuge in Canada, came to see me. She had just received a desperate letter from her friend who wanted to commit suicide because of the harsh conditions in Kandahar. She wanted to go back and help her friend at all cost. She asked me to go with her and film her journey." The story is based on Pazira's experience. In the film, Makhmalbaf created a central character named Nafas; her name means respiration: "it's an Afghan name. The *burka* (a gown worn by Afghan women which covers the entire body) prevents women from breathing and from being free." The narrative of the film is a travelogue that documents Nafas's journey into Afghanistan. In one story on this journey, a group of women covered in their flowing and colourful *burkas* are walking across the Iranian desert to attend a wedding. At one point, the group splits, half going to the wedding and the other half going in the direction of the Afghanistan border. At the border, the women must lift their *burkas*, only to reveal, in many cases, that the majority are men and not women. In *Kandahar,* transgendering allegorizes the disappearing democratic citizen and how its disappearance is being furthered on the basis of familial corporeal power mediated by religious nationalisms.

Shelley Niro's film *Honey Moccasin* is another take on desire and the palimpsest of colonial power in everyday life. The film begins with a newscast on a slew of recent thefts in the reserve community. Someone is stealing pow-wow dress materials. Zachary John, the owner of the Inukshuk Café, is clearly the culprit. Honey Moccasin, owner of The Smokin Moccasin (MOCK-A-SIN as it appears on a stage backdrop in the bar), a bar once owned by Zack's father, Johnny John, discovers not only that Zack is the perpetrator of the crimes but that he is using his stolen goods to cross-dress as a jingle dancer in his basement. Zack is gay, in love with Bow, Honey's bouncer at the bar, and a cross-dresser. In addition to an avant-garde fashion show of pow-wow regalia, the film contains two pieces of "metropolitan" cultural representation, one a performance piece based on Peggy Lee's song "Fever" and the other a film, based on "Inukshuk," a poem by Daniel David Moses; both are performed and filmed by Honey's talented daughter, Mabel, an art student. These brilliant artistic interventions in the film challenge the romantic myths of Aboriginality, especially I would suggest, in the current critical context in which the figure of the berdache (Indigenous male homosexual) is being deployed as a site of distinction between modernity and "savagery" or traditionalism. Niro's film critically engages with a prevalent social problem, homophobia, but its social critique is launched not in order to insist upon the denial of continuing ways of life in favour of their so-called modernization, but as a strategy of decolonizing the multiple and complex forms of colonial violence and brutality.

Creating strong and healthy individuals within communities means embracing their sexuality and gender, as in Witi Ihimeara's novel, *The Whale Rider*, and its filmic version, directed by Niki Caro, *Whale Rider*, in which a traditional Maori elder in New Zealand fails to see the leadership qualities in his grandchild simply because she is a girl and not a boy. Within such works, the question of desire pulls in multiple directions and the desire to be "human" supersedes the sexualization of such desires. In the performance piece based on the Peggy Lee song, the lyrics are reclaimed and parodied, and the song's sexual connotations dissolve away as the trope of fever recalls the smallpox epidemic that wiped out a large proportion of the Indigenous peoples in the seventeenth century:

> Captain Smith and Pocahontas
> Had a very mad affair
> When her daddy tried to kill him
> She said daddy oh don't you dare. (*Honey Moccasin*)

The correlation of sexual desire and disease, of course, also casts its ugly shadow over the meaning of homosexuality; and yet in the face of these horrific historical and material modes of violence, Zack emerges as a strong and healthy, gay, cross-dressing man. Having paid his debt to society by suffering the humiliation of going on television and giving back all of the stolen goods, Zack is revealed in the final scene in red lipstick, being embraced by and embracing his father. The question of colonial and homophobic violence is intimately woven into this scene and recalls the words in Moses's poem, "Inukshuk," where he writes of "hunters, who only hunt their brothers." These hunters are discredited in the face of fathers who love their sons—and grandfathers who love their daughters—regardless of their gender.

Of course transgendering is about gender and sexual identity, but it is also about crossing multiple zones of desirability and commodification: crossing borders between the spectacle and the commodity, between the technologically produced image and the materialities of economic and political power, and between the public and private negotiations of identity, sexuality, love, and labour. In *Vested Interests: Cross-dressing and Cultural Anxiety*, Marjorie Garber traces the way the transvestite figure in a text "that does not seem, thematically, to be primarily concerned with gender difference or blurred gender indicates a *category crisis elsewhere*, an irresolvable conflict or epistemological crux that destabilizes comfortable binarity, and displaces the resulting discomfort onto a figure that already inhabits, indeed incarnates, the margin" (17; emphasis in original). Garber's post-Foucauldian emphasis on the epistemic effects of transvestism tends, however, to relocate the power of social and political forces elsewhere, not acknowledging the active dimension of such figures of transformation as deeply political engagements with changing political events of violence and oppression. In other words, such figures in the context of globalization and Third Worldism are not simply a response to binary difference or a way of trying to achieve an ideological resolution to a binary conflict. They not only constitute a response to ideological forces containment, but also actively go beyond such forces by signalling the necessity for transformation and change. Contrary to Marjorie

Garber's theory of transgendering as a symptom of cultural anxiety, a "categorical crisis," films such as *Kandahar* and *Honey Moccasin* make use of the transformative codes of transgendering, with its emphasis on masquerade and binary crossovers, to allegorize the transcultural powers of oppression that exist in today's neo-colonial globalization by signifying a semiotic rupture with "the Real" as a necessary critical response to the ideological mediations of religious nationalisms, familialisms, and other imperial fundamentalisms. Such necessary ruptures self-consciously mimic and overturn the weapons of mass deception delivered up by the likes of Ann Coulter and others in the US religious fundamentalist mainstream.

The cultural work of Niro and Makhmalbaf engages in various strategies of de-authorization that persistently critique as well as destabilize the making and remaking of religious fundamentalisms, familialisms and nationalisms. In his *Genealogies of Religion*, Talal Asad examines the debates over history and authorship in the discourse of anthropology. He argues that when the anthropologist Marshall Sahlins protested that "local peoples are not 'passive objects of their own history,' it should be evident that this is not equivalent to claiming that they are its 'authors.'" Asad goes on to say that

> The sense of author is ambiguous as between the person who produces a narrative and the person who authorizes particular powers, including the right to produce certain kinds of narrative. The two are clearly connected, but there is an obvious sense in which the author of a biography is different from the author of the life that is its object—even if it is true that as an individual (as an "active subject") that person is not entirely the author of his own life. Indeed, since everyone is in some degree or other an object for other people, as well as an object of others' narratives, no one is ever entirely the author of her life. People are never only active agents and subjects in their own history. The interesting question in each case is: In what degree, and in what way, are they agents or patients? (4)

The European imperial bourgeois class defined itself and its authority in determining the meaning of civilization through cultural practices such as literature in the late nineteenth century. In other words, authority is not only about who had access to the printing press and who was included, but also about the use of literary authority as a discursive and material site of power and domination. Equally important, then, is the history of resistance to that authority; but why does Asad offer, in his post-Foucauldian set of choices, a choice between agent or patient? Is it really a question of the degree to which one is agential or pathologized, or is it a question of the degree of violence to which one has been subjected, economically, culturally, politically, and socially?

Postscript

One of the consequences of the use of the family and, more generally, personal, private, and intimate relationships by religious fundamentalists to achieve political power is that those critical of its homophobic, misogynist, and violent agenda have in response attempted to transform this domain of intersubjectivity and affectivity into a counter-political force for social change through notions of "compassion" and "love." A key problematic emerges from this conjunction of political and social change and the semiotics of subject-affectivity. As theistic values, notions of love and forgiveness have always been part of neo-colonial discourses of repatriation and forgiveness, as witnessed by such made-for-television movies as *Where the Spirit Lives*. Tropes of compassion and empathy are becoming affective signs of a human dimension rooted in religious notions of belief: Joy Kogawa's book *The Rain Ascends* is another case in point. Blurring the lines between religion and Buddhism, the theme of compassion emerges as the anecdote to the historical violence of colonialism and especially sexual abuse in residential schooling. The novel is written in a didactic style, using different characters to articulate multiple points of view on sexual violence and familial relations of power and forgiveness. However, the history of sexual violence in the Christian residential schools calls for a new critical investment in political kinships across the multicultural/neo-colonial divide, so that the problem is not imagined as one of a lack of compassion or the comprehension of a human dilemma but as a political problem with social consequences that can be understood from the perspective of state oppression and, in particular, the family as both a new and false site of resolution. It is no longer the "individual" who must solve today's problems but "the family."

Some readers will recognize in this problematic a somewhat familiar, if only partially articulated, reference to "the personal is political." During the late 1960s and 1970s, the political efficacy of this phrase drew attention to the social and political construction of heterosexuality as a compulsory, if not compulsive, method of social and human reproduction. If the redistribution of wealth was not the only answer to the impoverishment of social life and the cure to social injustice, the redistribution of the zones of pleasure would provide another sort of antidote. Thus, the figure of "desire" and the social control and regulation of sexual pleasure and longing were put on the agenda, and, while we knew that not all vaginas spoke equally, Luce Iri-garay's "When Our Two Lips Speak" happily expanded the "talking cure" and many embraced the new dia-lick-tic (*This Sex*).

Something changed between then and now. The invention of so-called "family values" during the Reagan/Thatcher regime turned "desire" back into a dirty fold that supposedly threatened the stability of the workplace, schooling, and racialized, gendered, and classed boundaries. Hanif Kureishi's script for the film *Sammy and Rosie Get Laid*[8] is one of the most powerful representations of the conflict of "family values" in a late-capitalist Thatch-erite new imperialism. The film narrates a series of tangled relationships during the infamous Brixton riots in London, England, during the 1980s: the imperial spectator was given a jolt of Brechtean distantiation as fundamen-talist discourse went postnational and the intertwined histories of British imperialism and the struggle for Indian independence came together on the streets of Brixton to rehearse the hypocrisy of the nationalization of decolonization and shore up the limits of First Worldist desire in the face of racial and cultural Third World–ed otherness. The personal is political, yes, and its counter-politics resist not only heterosexism and patriarchy but also imperialism; yet only in a partial and provisional way can these embodied resistances inhabit each other's terrain in order to bring about an enlight-ened and alternative sketch of an anti-imperialist, anti-homophobic, anti-racist representation of social life—and never all at once because the contradictions are unevenly distributed even across the most intense sites of oppression and exploitation, materially, sexually, and affectively. They are not uniform, they cannot be resisted uniformly, and they cannot remain unopposed.

Thus, it was with some surprise that I read Aniz Nafisi's strong challenge to the politics of the personal in *Reading Lolita in Tehran*:

> It is said that the personal is political. That is not true, of course. At the core of the fight for political rights is the desire to protect ourselves, to prevent the polit-ical from intruding on our individual lives. Personal and political are interde-pendent but not one and the same thing. The realm of imagination is a bridge between them, constantly refashioning one in terms of the other. Plato's philoso-pher-king knew this and so did the blind censor, so it was perhaps not surpris-ing that the Islamic Republic's first task had been to blur the lines and boundaries between the personal and the political, thereby destroying both. (273)

The public domains of culture are being destroyed by the "blind censors" of religious fundamentalism, and the somewhat idealized private domains of sexualities and intimacies become (as if they were not already for many) zones of sexual and emotional coercions; but where do the complicities and interdependencies lie between the public and the private, between public cultures and personal ones? If the imagination has created a bridge between them is it not through the synecdochic mechanism or a supplementation in which "the silent gift of the subaltern and the thunderous imperative of the Enlightenment to 'the public use of Reason'" emerge, "one filling the other's gap?" (Spivak, "Afterword" 201). How can we formulate an "ethics of love" that does not play on the synecdochic machine of political hopelessness by evoking affectivity as the domain of a transgressive Indigenous politics? Is it because Indigenous societies are so relentlessly oppressed today under the new regime of biopolitical subjugation and commercial exploitation that non-Indigenous, Western, industrial, capitalist intellectuals assume they are more emotional (i.e., "weaker," "effeminate")? Because to love is not to kill? Anyone familiar with domestic violence will be at odds with such a "post-colonial ethics of love," let alone those weary of other intellectual romanticisms, noble, personal, colonial, patriarchal, familial, and otherwise. If the interdependencies between "the family" and the "postnation" are to be realized, a closer reading of the domestic, private, intimate, and personal spheres, as well as what counts as the imagination (and to whom and at what cost) must be examined. The lesbian/Indigenous woman is now the site of the production of the distinction between tradition (i.e., savagery) and late capitalist imperial modernity. Deepa Mehta's film *Fire* and the response to it by Hindu fundamentalists attests to this moment of "postcolonial" contestation played out over whose bodies will occupy the territory of desire and whose bodies will be territorialized for the purposes of regulating desire.

While public institutions of knowledge seem to be the most invested sites of critical engagement among leftist intellectuals today, I suggest that the more accessible and commodified sites of cultural practices, including television, films, newspapers, and magazines, are actually having the greatest impact and must, therefore, be important areas of critical engagement. In addition, perhaps the most interesting sites of resistance are found in alternative cultural practices that resist such commodification. The domain of public culture is today probably the most important site of contestation. To state that cultural practices are important sites of resistance to national and religious fundamentalisms is not new—the number of writers, artists, and filmmakers being put on trial increases daily. Considering the areas in which religious fundamentalisms operate to gain social and political power—the family, the constitution of marriages, public protests against films ranging from Scorcese's *The Last Temptations of Christ* to Mehta's *Fire*—should tell us where the battles are really being fought. Talking about his film *Kandahar*, director Mohsen Makhmalbaf notes that

> At the beginning of the XXI century, the Talibans have a problem with images! There is no cinema, they have even taken away television. Their newspapers do not print pictures. Taking photographs or painting is considered "impure." Music is forbidden. Girls' schools have been closed down. Girls do not have a right to anything, not even public baths! In 1996 the Talibans ordered a big library in Katoul, containing 55,000 books, to be burnt to the ground. According to a report by the United Nations, one million Afghans are today in danger of being killed, without mentioning the millions of people who have lost their legs due to the mines. The world is more distressed at the destruction of stone Buddhas than at the fate of human beings. (Makhmalbaf)

The critique of late-capitalist imperialism is well articulated among those most affected by it. That "articulation," however, may not come in the forms acknowledged and recognized by academic discourses and practices. To exclude the voices of those people in a critique of colonialism, neo-colonization, and globalization is to perpetuate a certain kind of institutional violence. In the clash of sign systems that occurred in the period of contact, for example, the colonial project instituted various forms of knowledges, disciplines, and representations to silence and even deny the existence of other ways of writing, communicating, teaching, learning, seeing, representing, and producing knowledge. Has any "progress" been made if the perspectives of Indigenous transglobal subjects are not part of the critical debates on imperialism, colonization, and globalization? I seriously doubt it. Social movements in the so-called developed nations have created themselves on the basis of their material wealth and prosperity, access to education, systems of communication, and other technologies of power, such as the nuclear family; however, poverty among women, children, and immigrants abounds and under globalization is steadily increasing. Thus, political kinships and networks of critical engagement and practices cannot be limited to the educational institution, nor the institutional practices of the family.

Cultural practices and the study of them are a meaningful alternative to many discursive regimes, including the discourses of the social sciences and their neo-Foucauldian fascinations with the ubiquity of power in juridical and medical discourses of the body, to the exclusion of labouring and predominantly Third World, female, Indigenous bodies. We may be tempted to turn away from the study of culture to these other empirical and discursive sites of power, but the global cultural practices of decolonizing transglobalizing subjects will and do provide another way of critically engaging with the tensions and daily negotiations over what constitutes "reality." Although we delight in the study of how the Reality Principle Has Been Sold (i.e., reality TV), critical perspectives on the effects of such events come from a variety of sources and practices, collaborative networks and communities. Those of us within the academic institutions must work hard at building connections with and providing support to those most egregiously subjected to the semiotic violence of everyday life. Moreover, we need to work collaboratively on how to transform our teaching and research practices to include other ways of knowing, and varied and different cultural practices, such as the performative pedagogical techniques of Augusto Boal, who started the Theatre of the Oppressed movement in Brazil, or the making of testimonial writings and videos that expose the history of colonization and its sexual violence against women and children. We must make use of visual as well as textual materials and everyday media objects such as music, film, television, the Internet, websites, magazines, and newspapers, and read and study them alongside poetry, drama, novels, and essays. We need to continue to de-authorize "literature" and use multiple cultural practices, knowledges, and representations to disrupt the claims to authority or the re-authorizing of knowledge in the hands of a "few" to the exclusion of the "many."

LEN FINDLAY

TRANSCANADA COLLECTIVES
SOCIAL IMAGINATION,
THE CUNNING OF PRODUCTION,
AND THE MULTILATERAL SUBLIME

> The village idiot takes the throne
> — Bruce Cockburn, "All Our Dark Tomorrows"

In the current conjuncture, weapons of mass sedation have been joined by weapons of mass devotion in the furtherance of reactionary political and social agendas. Vatican imperialism, for example, has aligned with American imperialism and its academic advocates in the reduction of moral authority to the marketing of Cold War versions of freedom and faith from prosperous metropoles to vulnerable peripheries. Resistance to this neo-diffusionism has been much in evidence too: in many registers, many locations, and various media, with scholars singing the song of embeddedness but also the songs of dissent. Meanwhile, Canada is seen as stranded far from the tables where the "real" players gather, but also as aligned with the allegedly lesser forces who want to change the nature of the game being played.[1] The Martin government acted expediently on immigration laws while belatedly publishing its take on foreign policy as a "statement" rather than the full review that was promised. Happily, the thoughts, imaginings, and actions of citizens (and *citoyens et citoyennes*) remain unruly, as do those of students as "unruly subjects" (Boren) and, in the case of First Nations, even *sui generis* (Henderson, "*Sui Generis*"). Where are the spaces and structures for the nurturing of unruly communities and collectivities—political, creative coalitions that are Canadian only in the spectral sense—whereby figurations of the nation haunt the pretensions and practices of the state (Cheah, *Spectral*), employing cunning against the current circuitry and surveillance of power-knowledge economies? Where, indeed, is the "cybertariat" (Huws)? Where is the "cognitariat" (Berardi)?[2] Where is the *kallocracy* governed by the beauties of the sustainable-yet-incommensurable? How can we push transgressive practices to the fore in the name of TransCanada? Finally, where and who are "we" in such instances? To help begin to answer these and related questions, this position paper[3] offers first some critical culturalism, then three versions of citizenship—bourgeois, artisanal, and Aboriginal—and finally a TransCanadian collectivist imaginary that I am trying to develop under the aegis of the multilateral sublime (Findlay, "When I hear" 21).

Social Imagination

One of the major sites of contradiction in Canada today is cultural policy. Social cohesion is an ongoing concern of governments, and, more often out of desperation than conviction, they look to culture as a form of nation-building that will produce political stability and hence support economic growth. But the cultural cohering of the nation cannot mediate between stability and growth, the one stubbornly national and the other incurably transnational; at least it cannot do so without requiring substantial adjustments to the cultural nation's own singularity. Ergo, official bilingualism and multiculturalism function as balm for the wounds that the nation as sovereign singularity incurs from the postnational and anti-national agencies of capital. Canada in the singular needs Canadas in the plural (supplemented by immigrant capital and skills, and by seasonal foreign labour) to contain and conceal the damage done to (and by) Canada as convenient logo and nominal home for investment capital whose expectations of profit and spheres of action are unbounded.[4] As a trading nation apparently dependent on its exports for improving its standard of living, Canada is a concept at once coherent and dispersed, but neither that coherence nor that dispersal can be easily enlisted from below or from a periphery so as to change Canada's paradoxical status as a First World / Third World client state, especially when culture as a favoured locus of individual freedom and collective identity is claimed for venting and obedience-training so as to swell the ranks without unduly altering either the politics or the pigmentation of "canonical Canadians" (Day 166).

The creative imagination is, then, construed from above as profoundly but sedatively social, in the sense of harmoniously socializing citizens, activating commonalities, and "permitting" or "respecting" differences, in what is not so much John Porter's vertical mosaic as the violable mosaic. In contrast, creative imagination, produced from below and from the "regions," can be a powerful instrument of resistance and change, precisely in its refusal of dominant forms of instrumentality, if not of instrumentality *tout court*. What warrant is there for imaginative production from below or from the boonies? Historians like Jacques Rancière, Jonathan Rose, Dipesh Chakrabarty, and Bryan Palmer demonstrate compellingly the imaginative capacities and accomplishments of the world's underclasses. Here I want to feature an important theoretical analogue to their work in the notion of the cunning of production and the forms of citizenship resisted or nourished by that cunning.

The Cunning of Production: Track One

In referring to "the cunning of production," I am following in part the example of Greek political scientist Alexander Chryssis and Hungarian émigré Istvan Meszáros (cited by Chryssis from Meszáros's *Beyond Capital*). Chryssis points to the paraphrase of the cunning of nature in Kant and the actual coinage, "the cunning of reason," in Hegel (*die List der Vernunft*). He does so in order to argue that "the concept of *cunning* ... was the cornerstone upon which the most eminent representatives of the classical German philosophy grounded their own philosophical interpretations of history" (97).

A bourgeois liberal cosmopolitan like Michael Ignatieff, always on the lookout for threats to "Western intellectual hegemony" (*Human Rights* 61), attempts in the 1999–2000 Tanner Lectures at Princeton to forestall one such internal threat by travestying critics' arguments thus:

> Human rights is seen as an exercise in *the cunning of Western reason*: no longer able to dominate the world through direct imperial rule, western reason masks its own will to power in the impartial, universalizing language of human rights and seeks to impose its own narrow agenda on a plethora of world cultures that do not actually share the West's conception of individuality, selfhood, agency, or freedom. This postmodernist relativism began as an intellectual fashion on Western campuses, but it has seeped slowly into Western human rights practice, causing all activists to pause and consider the intellectual warrant for the universality they once took for granted. (*Human Rights* 61–62; emphasis added).

Ignatieff is right to see the cunning of reason as a point of vulnerability in the philosophical derivation of modern statehood and citizenship, but he

cannot see much beyond that defensive sense of the Euro-American investment in exportable, transcendent selfhood. Instead, he casts opposition to
imperialist absolutism in the patronizing terms of fashion and slow seepage,
while locating that opposition—and the apparent problem of "paus[ing]"
to reflect rather than acting on assumption—entirely within the intellectual superstructure of "the West." Ignatieff then defends his position even
more dogmatically: "Rights language cannot be parsed or translated into a
non-individualistic, communitarian framework. It presumes moral individualism and is nonsensical outside that assumption.… it is precisely this
individualism that renders it attractive to non-Western peoples and explains
why human rights has become a global movement" (*Human Rights* 67–68).
Note how effectively this passage anticipates the doctrines of military humanism, military humanitarianism, and pre-emptive war, and also the apologia
that is *Empire Lite* and the intensifying commodification of democracy and
citizenship it demands and selectively rewards. More importantly, I wish to
identify here a source of increasing danger for Canada's understanding and
recognition of collective rights and Canadian understanding of multilateralism as something very different from Ignatieff's reclamation of "global
movements" in the name of an ultra-diffusionist civilizing mission. In some
ways, Ignatieff is not worth my time or yours. However, his palpable influence on emergent Canadian foreign policy, and his prominence among the
federal Liberals, persuades me that his thinking represents a major threat to
TransCanadian collectivities, especially when they are artisanal or Aboriginal.[5] The acquisitive/compassionate individualism he continues to advo-
cate ignores cunning as a means of collective resistance rather than a
hegemonic alibi. Ignatieff's moralizing citizen of the world implicitly discour-
ages and discredits the artisanal and Aboriginal citizenship I wish to argue
for and the multilateralism I wish to oppose to the resurgent unilateralism
and exceptionalism of the Bush administration and its Sharonian epigone
(see Agamben, *State*).

The Cunning of Production: Track Two

I return, then, to a leftist rather than a liberal engagement with the cunning
of reason, and to the discernment in a famous Hegelian formulation of a crisis that can be claimed for underclass hope rather than bourgeois faith.
Chryssis claims that Engels and Marx feel obliged to make a move similar
to Hegel's but involving history rather than reason. They do so in the *Manifesto* because of the complications of realizing a proletarian revolution *in*

history. This move Chryssis calls an appeal to the notion of the cunning of production. In his paraphrase of Hegel's argument, agents in history pursuing their own interests are also at the same time (in Hegel's words) "the *means and instruments of a higher power* and wider enterprise, of which they themselves are ignorant and which they nevertheless unconsciously carry out" (97; emphasis in the original). Note that Hegel's articulation sounds like the mysterious dichotomy in Mandeville between private vices and public virtues, and even more like Adam Smith's "invisible hand" attributed to the "free market." Such mystery is directly related to psychoanalysis by Gilles Deleuze and Felix Guattari, in their attempt to assert the primacy of production, and "the production of productions" (4), through reconceptualization of the machine and of Marxian nature as the body without organs in furtherance of the miraculation of production and its delirium (9–15). The recording of alienated production under capital is the representational contradiction and stress of concealment that can be read in the double move of deterritorializing and reterritorializing.

Chryssis identifies Engels's engagement with Hegel's argument in *Ludwig Feuerbach and the End of Classical German Philosophy*, where Engels appeals to surface "chance" and "inner hidden laws" that "only have to be discovered" (387). For Chryssis, this is evidence that Engels "does not try to negate but to substantiate the function of cunning within the theoretical context of historical materialism" (98). In Meszáros, Chryssis met with revisionary wordplay, mostly as *mere* wordplay, as in Meszáros's comment on Engels: "the fundamental difference between a speculative and a materialist conception of history is not established by renaming the 'cunning of reason' the 'cunning of history'" (*Beyond Capital* 446). Chryssis wonders whether Meszáros is right in distinguishing between Marx and Engels on this question. Chryssis then adjusts the argument he wishes to make very pointedly:

> Marx and Engels' theory of revolution, as included and expounded in the *Manifesto*, presupposes a certain "cunning of production" in the sense of a socioeconomic process, within which the bourgeoisie, while promoting its particular interests, prepares almost unconsciously and unwittingly the final overthrow of capitalism and the transition to communism. Furthermore, as we are going to argue in this article, this "cunning of production" plays a determinant role in the Marxian theory of revolution and critically affects the subject/object dialectic of the revolutionary process itself. (90)

The capitalist bourgeoisie is wed to increased efficiency in existing modes of production and the assimilation of pre- or non-capitalist modes

of production to this model of commodified labour and restricted ownership of productive means, in an apparently never-ending narrative of growth
and progress. It is a commitment to interim advantage deriving from surplus value but also a recipe for ultimate decline and displacement as capitalism accomplishes its own demise. Domination of the market in its fullest
domestic and international articulations creates conditions of enhanced
dependency that even a transnational global bourgeoisie will eventually be
unable to confine and manage. Engels and Marx offer an analogy or allegory
of frantic activity and ultimate loss of control in the figure of the "sorcerer"
(67) who seems to function somewhere between sorcerer's apprentice and
Faustian compact. The emphasis in this passage is on the amazing spectacle of transformation going on before the very eyes of people around the
world. The sense of magic intensifies with *hervorzaubern* (as the term for conjuring) and the explicit introduction of the figure of the *Hexenmeister*. The
powers summoned only to escape his control are literally subterranenean (*die
unterirdischen Gewalten*). Chryssis takes from this the inference that Engels
and Marx are compelled to admit that the "cunning of production, as
described above, affects the formation of the proletariat not only as a class
in itself, but also as a class for itself" (99). Here is why they go so far as to
conclude that the "bourgeoisie not only produces its gravediggers (the pro-
letarians), but also furnishes them with all the necessary theoretical and
practical weapons for fighting capitalism" (Chryssis 99).

Chryssis then feels entitled to see the cunning of production as the
implicit but necessary mechanism of transformation from slavery to revolutionary class-consciousness, from exploitation to emancipation. Chryssis
recognizes here the force of Meszáros's contention that the answer is to be
found in alienation understood as an "inherently *dynamic* concept: a concept that necessarily implies change" (100); but how exactly in given historical conditions does this inherent dynamism differ from the Hegelian
movement of the concept or idea? Historical materialism would seem to
shift from the realm of necessity to the realm of possibility.

What does this move then do to the cunning located hitherto in necessity? Now there is a Hegelian escape possible in the linking of necessity to
freedom, but Chryssis at this point goes to Hegel's *Logic* in order to redefine
possibility as "the *maturation* of the conditions for the transition of the Idea
to the next stage of its necessary development" (102). (He cites G.H.R. Parkin-
son in support of the importation or convergence whereby possibility is not
the opposite of necessity but its precursor.) This he goes on to see as "the
materialist transfiguration of the Hegelian freedom/necessity dialectic" (103).

This transfiguration, I would argue, should be seen as refiguring aesthetic freedom and proletarianizing the arch-bourgeois concept of *Bildung*. On this basis can be developed a radically productionist version of intellectual and imaginative work that can facilitate convergence with other kinds of labour in the resignification and empowerment of artisanal citizenship in the post-bourgeois state.[6]

What, then, can producers of TransCanada learn from this? First, there is the general strategy of revisionary citation, so that, for example, the Last Spike's racist photographic and cultural framing of the unified nation in images constantly reproduced (as in Gillmor, Michaud, and Turgeon 22) might now become the Latest Spanner in the works of ideological railroading as nation-building. In the federal budget speech of March 23, 2004, Finance Minister Ralph Goodale observed,

> Initiatives such as the Canada Foundation for Innovation, Genome Canada, the Canadian Institutes of Health Research, Millennium Scholarships, the Canada Research Chairs, and others have helped position Canada at the forefront of a knowledge-based world. Dr. Peter MacKinnon, the Chair of the Association of Universities and Colleges of Canada [AUCC], has said that this federal focus on knowledge and innovation can "be in the 21st Century what the construction of the transcontinental railway was in the 19th Century. It can be a new National Dream." (8)

When powerful politicians cite academic leaders approvingly, one needs to attend carefully to what is being legitimated, and why. MacKinnon is president of the University of Saskatchewan, home of the Canadian Light Source, Canada's most expensive research installation; and Goodale at the time was the province's sole Liberal Member of Parliament, a connection apparently too parochial to be mentioned in a federal budget speech. One of the nation's most influential ministers quotes the chair of a national organization in order to recoup nation-formation in a new register with a Liberal brand rather than the Tory stamp of *the* father of Confederation, Sir John A. Macdonald. The University of Saskatchewan's current mantra of "Renewing the Dream" is replayed in a TransCanadian way that shows AUCC explicitly on side with federal policy, and lending that highly targeted and directive policy legitimacy, lustre, and the convenient amnesia that attends the uncritical redeployment of a problematic icon. An appeal to part of the history of the railroad's construction provides oneiric satisfactions, past and present, but only by ignoring the political scandals, the racial division of labour, and the ruthless appropriation of First Nations' lands (Creighton 353–99), while recentring the White male entrepreneurs who dominate the photos and prose accounts of the driving of the last spike in (revealingly renamed) Craigellachie in November 1886. Canadian capital still wields the hammer only on ceremonial or recreational occasions. Canadian labour and Canada's Indigenes must look to their own considerable cunning, and to the knowledge and courage of unembedded academics and artists, to counter the exclusions and distortions that attend the triumphalist ceremonies and recyclings of market rationality.

In addition to revisionary citation, we can learn from the specifically Marxian capacity to rework Hegel, not only by turning him on his head, but also by substituting one term for another—in this instance production for reason—as a necessary but insufficient condition for the demystification and ultimate displacement of bourgeois-capitalist social and economic relations that host rather than haunt the modern state. This particular procedure, like taking on Ignatieff, can have a very direct Canadian impact, given the prominence of Hegelian idealism in the formation of Canadian intellectual life (as Alan McKillop and others have shown).

Information technology and the knowledge economy, insofar as they urge the primacy of mental power as computing power more or less divorced from mental and manual labour, require and produce the cunning of production, in part as cyber-solidarity and withholding of labour. This latter moment of refusal, like the unmoved–mover model behind Marx's discussion of the value form and Hegel's cunning reason, is the foundational difference that makes versions of the system of differences *work*. But how does this consort with the "self-forgetfulness of production" (Adorno 28) or with Negri's claim that "we have all the tools we need to work in our heads" (qtd. in Stein 59) and that "This is the end of the distinction between production and life … work has identified itself with life.… Our challenge is to invent new forms for organizing liberty in life and production" (59)? Warnings such as these about romanticizing labour are very important, but the notion of cunning remains especially apt for moderating or overturning the post-labour claims of the knowledge economy, because cunning is a kind of capacity and a kind of knowing that refuses to be confined within the (commodifying) grids, standards, and regulation of information, its effective transfer, and what is built on this transfer: in the name of knowledge and modernity and growth, but in conditions as brutally enforced as they are zealously concealed.

Producing a Cunning Canada: A Lesson from Treaty Federalism

So what sort of cunning Canada should we seek to produce? How can a robustly inclusive artisanal citizenship that refuses hierarchies based on mental versus manual labour challenge the aspirations and actualities of the bourgeois state? Treaty federalism holds some clues to the cunning in question, and a promise of much needed collaboration of artisans and Aboriginals.

On August 15, 1876, two thousand Native people camped on the plains outside Fort Carlton on the North Saskatchewan River, waiting to meet with Treaty Commissioner Alexander Morris and sign the largest land treaty in the history of the continent. The transfer of more than 350,000 square kilometres was being negotiated. Morris opened the ceremony with a vision of the Natives' future, and he did so with what on the page appears to be considerable fluency, this being his fourth such performance: "I see the Queen's Councillors taking the Indian by the hand saying we are brothers, we will lift you up, we will teach you, if you will learn, *the cunning of the white man*" (231; emphasis added). The impression of delivering a well-rehearsed, discreetly sexist script is reinforced in part by the use of the phrase "the cunning of the white man," which had first appeared in negotiations of Treaty Four in September 1874 (92, 96). On that occasion, this cunning was recommended as only a part or smattering ("something") of White knowledge, to be used when natural scarcity was inevitably aggravated by colonization of the great plains. The following day in 1874 Morris had resorted to the phrase again: "The Queen wishes her red children to learn the cunning of the white man and when they are ready for it she will send schoolmasters on every Reserve and pay them" (96). Consistent with the policy and practices of infantilizing the Indigene, the expression seems designed to reduce knowledge to the kind of unlettered lore on which Indigenous survival practices are based. Cunning will allow the Indigene to supplement tradition when times are hard, but readiness for receiving a fuller education from professionals will come only once the First Nations are on reservations, having signed the treaties and apparently ceded much of their land for White settlement. White cunning functions on these occasions as a commodity with multiple strings attached, and cunning will become formal, systematic education not to empower Aboriginal people but only to make more efficient their dispossession and betrayal.

There is, however, another cunning at work in the production of the treaty, a cunning of the other, a cunning that resists in its own way the cunning of bourgeois capitalist reason and the Government of Canada's ongoing role as "cunning intermediary" (Indian Claims Commission, qtd. in "Sask. Natives" A1). Indigenous cunning evinces a mysteriousness far different from the encrypted greed of the Crown's representatives. However, it was and remains mysterious to many because it is protected by protocols within the inalienable, residually inappropriable treasury of Indigenous knowledge. This cunning of Indigenous production remains today a powerful instrument of restorative and distributive justice and *collective* rights increasingly recognized by Canada's courts and increasingly resisted by federal and provincial governments as they choose to contest, case by case, the colonial damage done in the name of the nation and in violation of the Honour of the Crown. Morris's offer to dole out White cunning while grabbing the land was reiterated on a number of different occasions but not well received by everyone. For example, Poundmaker (Pitikwahanapawiyin), a Plains Cree critic of the provisions of Treaty Six (1876), responded to Morris in terms that were omitted from the Lieutenant Governor's published account of proceedings: "This is our land! It isn't a piece of pemmican to be cut off and given back to us. It is our land and we will take what we want" (Peter Erasmus, qtd. in Christensen 246). This affirmation is rich in implications for the role of commodification and education in colonization. The Indigene's options are cunningly constrained by Morris: either accept the tutelage in cunning, or (by implication) die (out). In refusing such infantilization, Poundmaker uses the apt image of pemmican—an example of Indigenous knowledge eagerly appropriated by the first waves of White intrusion—to stress that the land is not reducible to any particular product, even one as key to survival as this compact and highly nutritious mix of meat, fat, and berries, and that the current lack of food in no way undermines Aboriginal title to the land. Poundmaker refuses the White version of a gift economy and the paternalistic fiction of giving back that which was freely given but never given up. Pemmican represents Indigenous knowledge and prudence regarding the natural scarcity brought by Canadian winters and natural fluctuations in populations of game. It is the product of the land and Indigenous knowledge. The claim to ownership of that land is a claim to hold it in collective trust; it is a claim of stewardship to be taken on trust rather than seen as a weakening of individual legal entitlement and tenure. Pemmican is not whiskey, and should not be used to anti-Aboriginal ends that would immobilize and disempower just as alcohol was designed to do.

The Multilateral Sublime: Track One

One of the most ominous convergences of the moment, one most evident in the United States, is the convergence of the military and the market sublime. It is my contention that the military sublime works in tandem with the market sublime in an often-obscene symbiosis to direct the fortunes of war and war profiteers, especially within the ominous singularity of the world's only remaining superpower. In other words, they collude in order to entrench and defend capitalist values, including that pre-eminent First World freedom, the freedom of capital to move unencumbered across the world. The idea of investors' rights trumping citizens' rights became especially clear on July 29, 2003, when the Pentagon sent some of its finest to Capitol Hill to unveil (coloured flow charts and all) its Policy Analysis Market, which would allow investors to predict and profit from new hotspots and forms of conflict around the world. Pre-emptive destruction paves the way for lucrative reconstruction of "rogue" or "failing" states in what Naomi Klein has recently termed "disaster capitalism." The current "sophistication" of the capital market drives not only the military-industrial complex but also American foreign policy and international relations more generally. The Policy Analysis Market website was rapidly pulled and the media coverage was minimal, though my local paper did have an editorial after the long weekend, a piece entitled "Terror trading terrible tactic." Apparently, the goal remains to tap into predictive successes of the economic marketplace on everything from interest rates to orange juice prices to terrorist futures, building on the University of Iowa's political futures market that has outperformed the polls and experts in calling the outcome of presidential elections. This enhanced and literalized version of making a killing allows security analysts and other speculators to clean up in the name of democratization. Complementary forms of the sublime entrench the categories and consequences of force and finance, army surplus and surplus value, which equally require a reserve army of the underemployed and unemployed. Immanuel Kant's opposition between a properly conducted war with "something of the sublime about it" (*Critique* 112; *Kritik* 263) and a "mere commercial spirit ... that tends to degrade the character of the nation" (*Critique* 113) is itself understandably naïve about the capacity of economic modernity to colonize and commodify every aspect of human endeavour and to wage war by other means than main force. That opposition is still around today in the American maxim that security trumps trade. This is not realpolitik at its best but rather a serious patriotic error focussed on the episode of insurgency rather than the master narrative of transnational economic hegemony, an error that ignores or elides the convergence pursued under cover of the fog of war and the political lies and obfuscations that attend it. Security *is* trade (Singer).

I choose the sublime as my key concept or cultural category because of its apparent *un*Canadianness outside the realm of nature or wilderness. The sublime, after all, has strong associations with such apparently unCanadian matters as terror and obscurity, shock and awe, invasiveness and excessiveness, as well as an ability to intimidate and subordinate beauty to power, representation to conquest. For Edmund Burke, in the section on power added to the 1759 edition of his *Philosophical Enquiry into the Origin of Our Ideas of the Sublime and Beautiful*, there is "nothing sublime which is not some modification of power" (64–65). I allude to Burke in part to remind us of the special prominence of the sublime in the later eighteenth and early nineteenth centuries, a period that marked the rise of the modern nation-state, the "discovery" of nature by the engines and self-absorbed apologists of acquisitive culture, and the rise of economic modernity and what Germaine de Stael, in a telling fusion of market intimidation and market rationality, called "the calculating sublime" (10). Burke witnessed the proliferation of nations and a singular, endlessly expanding market, a place where national culture was invented and enlisted in the service of oppression at home and possession overseas, a place where the possessive individualism of national entities was moderated and periodically intensified by the ideas of Europe: progress, virtue and the commonalities and differences at work within a civilizing mission deriving from the White enlightenment. For those working in the Burkean tradition, and hence against the "swinish multitude" and "geographical morality," multilateralism must be subverted, discredited, and prohibited because it intimates an alternative sublime that diffuses and hence diminishes overwhelming presence and imperial control. It represents a loss of power by the dominant as well as the redefinition of power itself by the dominated.

The Multilateral Sublime: Track Two

Not surprisingly, the TransCanadian multilateral sublime defines itself in part by difference—difference from the British and American empires and the awe and acquisitiveness at the heart of both operations and their ideas of plenary/exclusionary citizenship. In this defining by difference, there is a constant temptation to recentre sanctimonious nordicities at the expense of Canada's hurtful history, as Sherene Razack has recently shown in the canonical Canadian domain of peacekeeping. This reminder argues against the uncritical embrace of multilateralism as unproblematic multiculturalism at home and honest brokerism internationally; but that does not mean the abandonment of the multilateral as imposture or covert imposition. American unilateralism is a strong source of multilateralist Canadian identities. Such identities are not only reactive formations originating with an anxious yet well-meaning middle power; they are also produced by seeds and afffiliations of multilateralism integral to and immanent within Canada. Aboriginal collectivism has produced an impressive resurgence of the Assembly of First Nations (AFN) after the attempt to fragment this collective by Minister Nault in the last Chrétien administration. The Background Papers produced by the AFN on a "Framework for Advancing the Recognition and Implementation of First Nations Governments" (*Our Nations*) and for the Negotiations Sectoral Roundtable in Calgary in January of 2005 (*Renewal*) offered a compelling version of collective rights and the kinds of reconciliation and renewal only they can bring. These un-Ignatieffian papers, when read in tandem with the federal government's neo-Ignatieffian *International Policy Statement: A Role of Pride and Influence in the World* (Foreign Affairs Canada), suggest that political vision and citizenship for a TransCanada future and for what Prime Minister Martin called "The New Multilateralism" is more convincingly and inspiringly articulated in the AFN documents where orality and insurgent textuality work together rather than offering more opportunities for White cunning to flourish. This carries through into the more recent *First Nations–Federal Crown Political Accord*, derided by the mainstream media as the last of a doomed and desperate administration's irresponsible giveaways but in fact the next phase in the education of the dominant by Indigenous knowledge and thinking. The Government of Canada disappointingly links the US version of the terrorist threat to the more efficiently targeted projection of Canadian power internationally, because we Canadians "will have to be smart, focused, agile, creative and dogged in the pursuit of our interests" (Foreign Affairs Canada 2). The AFN drafters have clearly benefitted from their involvement in Indigenous multilateralism at the United Nations, while Foreign Affairs Canada, because of a desire to reassure the US and economic elites at home, has couched its vision in language such as this:

> Today, companies increasingly operate across national boundaries, not only to improve access to markets, but more significantly, to allocate elements of the value chain to their most economically efficient location.... The drivers of international

and domestic competitiveness are one and same: our economy, and every player in it, must be supported by an open, secure and competitive business climate in Canada.... By benchmarking our policies with those of major markets, we will facilitate new investment flows. (7–8)

This may sound like a university integrated plan, but it is certainly not what Antonio Gramsci meant by an "illustrious vernacular" operating as the sociolinguistic guarantor of justice across the nation (see Findlay "When I hear" 13–18). There is no sublimity in Canadian bureaucratese, except the sullied sublime of the military and the market as solutions to each other's problems.

Aboriginal and artisanal citizens employ vernaculars where people are pre-eminent and economic processes subordinate to collective interests. This is language where power can be more readily uncoupled from terror, collectivities displace mono-immensities and the overshadowed individual, and the sublime can be claimed for the collectivizing cunning of multilateralism from below. Political leaders and elite institutions of our capitalist state-nation need to shut their mouths and listen to what these vernaculars are expressing, so that they can move from the single to the triple bottom line: economic, yes, but always also social and environmental. This needs to be a big production, but not in the deeply complicit Hollywood sense. It is an agenda that will not put an end to difference but rather put differences to work in serial declarations of interdependency (Borrows)—an intimidating task, no doubt, but not beyond the cunning of production as undertaken by Aboriginal and artisanal hands and minds. New forms of solidarity combined with the necessary indeterminacy of an otherwise too readily hijackable agenda—imagine that!

NOTES

Preface / Smaro Kamboureli

1 See http://www.sshrc.ca/web/whatsnew/initiatives/transformation.
2 All quotations are from http://www.transcanadas.ca/transcanada1. The conference's website, called "TransCanada: Literature, Institutions, Citizenship," also includes the full program of the event, as well as the original versions of some of the essays in this volume and audio recordings of the plenary sessions.

Metamorphoses of a Discipline: Rethinking Canadian Literature within Institutional Contexts / Diana Brydon

1 For an exemplary investigation of this problematic, see Jonathan Kertzer's *Worrying the Nation*, which "studies the convergence of three formative terms: national, literary, and history" to ask "What happens to a national literature when the very idea of the nation has been set in doubt?" (5). As I read them, Imre Szeman and Adam Carter seek to reframe this question by indicating the ways in which Canadian literary criticism (most notably in the work of Northrop Frye) was "underwritten by a literary nationalism" and expressed "the view that it is no longer sensible to speak of a specifically Canadian sensibility or culture" (Szeman, *Zones* 183). In this chapter, I choose to follow Szeman's suggestion that it might be helpful to "think of the nation as a potential space for political activity, while at the same time unthinking the unitary vision of the *polis* that it has often implied" (196). Kertzer comes to a similar conclusion: "It is precisely because Canada has so many conflicting constituencies that we need a national space in which to meet, dispute, and negotiate" (188). To construct such a space, as the TransCanada project attempts to do, one must divert attention from the nation to the nation-state and the ways in which it mediates how, as Kertzer puts it, "the nation as social imaginary always relies on both a narrative of justice and the justice of narrative" (12). In Kertzer's view, "Nation

and literature thus regulate each other insistently but inconsistently" (13). How they do so is complex and requires further examination.

2 This is how I understood the task that I was assigned when asked to deliver the opening address at a conference called "TransCanada: Literature, Institutions, Citizenship," in Vancouver in June 2005. The conference was based on an open call designed to be the first stage in thinking through a collaborative research project. I am grateful to the conference organizers for the opportunity to test these ideas with such a dynamic group and to the Social Sciences and Humanities Research Council of Canada for a standard research grant that enabled me to research and write this. I have also benefitted from discussions with audiences in the Department of English at the University of Auckland and at the Stout Research Centre for New Zealand Studies at the University of Wellington, who further helped me to refine my understanding of these questions. My thanks to the Association for Canadian Studies in Australia and New Zealand for funding this trip and to Mark Williams for organizing it.

3 George Bowering makes this clear when he states, "I don't particularly want to live in a country that considers itself the best in the world. I want us to look around and see what needs fixing" (14). See also Adam Carter, quoting Northrop Frye to the effect that the "Canada to which we really do owe loyalty is the Canada that we have failed to create" (96).

4 Canadian history has been going through a similar debate, highlighted by J. L. Granatstein's polemical *Who Killed Canadian History?* but taking much more interesting shape in studies that resituate the nation from a variety of perspectives. For an interesting examination of the history of Canadian governance through perspectives generated by discourses of law, rhetoric and irony, for example, see Michael Dorland and Maurice Charland, *Law, Rhetoric, and Irony in the Formation of Canadian Civil Culture.*

5 For analysis of these challenges in the Canadian context, see texts edited by William Bruneau and Donald C. Savage, William Bruneau and James L. Turk, and James L. Turk in the Canadian Association of University Teachers (CAUT) series of studies.

6 While I recognize that discourses of crisis and turning points are tropes of literary criticism in the modern era, I am also convinced by the arguments of world systems theorists in books such as *The World We Are Entering: 2000–2050*, edited by Immanuel Wallerstein and Armand Clesse, that the current period provides an exceptional challenge and opportunity for shifts in culture, economics, and society.

7 Stephen Slemon elaborates a similar argument elsewhere in this volume.

8 My thanks to David Chariandy for raising this question.

9 Winfried Siemerling provides a fuller argument for understanding Quebec within TransCanadian and transcontinental traditions elsewhere in this volume and in *The New North American Studies.* My interest here is in simply noting the ways that these particular institutional structures create a division of responsibilities that produces blockages for thinking TransCanadianly outside comparative literature, which has far less of an institutional presence than English, for example, and which has its own protocols for studying national literatures. To focus on "literature, institutions and citizenship" may afford fresh ways of conceiving the Quebec/Canada relation beyond those currently institutionalized through forms of naming that depend on notions of reified nation-states and their nationalisms, such as the Association for Canadian and Quebec Literatures.

10 While I tried to address some aspects of this challenge in my chapter in Laura Moss's *Is Canada Postcolonial?* and there exist a number of books and essays tackling dimensions of this topic, there is much more work to be done in this area. For essays working through some dimensions of these questions see *Reclaiming Indigenous Voice and Vision*, edited by Marie Battiste, and "Readers' Forum, Part II: Always Indigenize!", the special issue of *ESC: English Studies in Canada* 30.3 (September 2004). For an overview of some of these challenges, see also J. Edward Chamberlin, *If This Is Your Land, Where Are Your Stories?*

11 For extensive analysis of how these structures operated, see the three volumes of *The History of the Book in Canada*, edited by Fleming et al. (vol. 1, 2004), Lamonde et al. (vol. 2, 2005), and Gerson and Michon (vol. 3, 2007). For a personalized account of how they operated within daily life in the latter half of the twentieth century, see George Bowering, *Left Hook*. Canadian literary studies also exists internationally, often within individual disciplinary departmental structures and occasionally within North American studies, but also through the support of Canadian studies associations.

12 A related shift happens when attention turns from theorizing the nation to seeking to understand the nation-state.

13 For one such study, see Sherene H. Razack, *Dark Threats and White Knights: The Somalia Affair, Peacekeeping, and the New Imperialism*. Razack writes, "A Canadian today knows herself or himself as someone who comes from the nicest place on earth, as someone from a peacekeeping nation, and as a modest, self-deprecating individual who is able to gently teach Third World Others about civility" (9). For unquestioning acceptance of this myth, see Jennifer Welsh, *At Home in the World*.

14 Complicating this assessment are the ways in which the 2003 invasion of Iraq has alerted us to the dangers of embedded viewpoints of an issue. As Razack's study makes clear, we need the viewpoints of those who are excluded or marginalized by hegemonic myths if we are to learn to read their power effectively. See also *Situating "Race" and Racisms in Space, Time and Theory*, edited by Jo-Anne Lee and John Lutz.

15 As an act of patriotism, I think. I remember reading Leacock, Callaghan, and MacLennan but nothing else at that time. See Robert Lecker, *Making It Real*, for an analysis of this series.

16 In noting the importance of rhetoric in the formation of citizens and the creation of a public sphere, Michael Dorland and Maurice Charland note, for example, that "rhetorical training was widely offered in eighteenth- and nineteenth-century Canada, although that instruction in a *culture oratoire* was often reserved for elites who already shared social, and hence pre-political commonalities and by the late nineteenth century, had been collapsed into the teaching of literature on the one hand and on the other had been reified in the formulaic prose of mass newspapers" (277). In recognition of such a history, Robert Scholes, in his 2004 Presidential Address to the Modern Language Association of America, counsels a return to pre-Renaissance studies in "grammar, rhetoric, and dialectic" as the route to the renewal of English studies today (733). The implications of a renewed engagement with citizen formation, he suggests, will involve broadening the range of study rather than "allowing that range to shrink to a specialization" (732). Part of the TransCanada project will involve thinking through the implications of such a proposal for teaching Canadian

literature in Canada, where the framing institutions are quite different and where citizenship is differently conceived and practised.

17 For complementary analyses of these processes, see Dorland and Charland, and Anthony J. Hall. For Hall, working within the Canadian tradition of critiquing what C. B. Macpherson termed "possessive individualism," the indigenous image of the bowl with one spoon "is consistent with the creative and humane use of the state to achieve a variety of shared purposes" (*American* 422). This is a vision of the role of the state very much at odds with current trends toward dismantling the social welfare state, but attuned to certain Canadian traditions that these books trace back to the eighteenth century. How such attempts at partial retrieval of a residual ideology may interact with critiques such as Razack's of the racism and sexism embedded in imperialism is the major task facing the TransCanada project as I see it.

18 For a wide-ranging engagement with these questions, see *Is Canada Postcolonial?* edited by Laura Moss, and *Unhomely States*, edited by Cynthia Sugars.

19 See the review article by Jacinta O'Hagan for an analysis of this phenomenon.

20 I elaborate my views in the chapter "Situating Multiculturalism: Contemporary Canadian Citizenship Debates," forthcoming in a volume titled *Culturalisms*, which is co-edited by Diana Brydon, James Meffan, and Mark Williams.

21 The forthcoming special issues of *Essays on Canadian Writing* on *Poetics and Public Culture in Canada: Essays in Honour of Frank Davey*, edited by Diana Brydon, Manina Jones, Jessica Schagerl, and Kristen Warder, of *Open Letter* on *The Poetry Reading Is a Public Tuning*, edited by Melina Baum-Singer and Lily Cho, and of *Rampike*, co-edited by Susan Holbrook, Richard Douglas Chin, Louis Cabri, Nicole Markotic, and Christian Bök, will address this problematic more fully. They follow from the earlier conference and published proceedings, *The Recovery of the Public World*, edited by Charles Watts and Edward Byrne.

22 See Michael Hardt and Antonio Negri, *Multitude*, and Ian Angus, *Emergent Publics*, for examples of two texts that pin their faith for progressive change on emergent social movements rather than established institutions.

23 For theses on how these operate, see Engin F. Isin, "The Neurotic Citizen," and William Walters, "Secure Borders, Safe Haven, Domopolitics."

24 Pico Iyer's *The Global Soul* was published at the height of euphoria celebrating the porous borders and global flows promised by globalization only months before the darker side of such a world was revealed by the attacks on New York's World Trade Center on September 11, 2001. Iyer celebrates Toronto as an ideal global city and Michael Ondaatje's *The English Patient* as providing a vision of what Iyer terms "this new order" (146). He writes of Ondaatje's novel: "Sitting above all provincialisms—and privatizing even the most famous conflict among empires—it dares to suggest a 'New Age' in which people can live with a nomad's (or a monk's) freedom from attachments" (146).

25 For Rosaldo, a "classic act of cultural citizenship" entails "using cultural expression to claim public rights and recognition" (36).

26 In this respect, I disagree with Imre Szeman, if I understand his argument in *Zones of Instability* correctly, on the relation of literature to the nation although I find him interesting on Canadian criticism nonetheless.

27 It strikes me as an interesting coincidence that I wrote this before Margaret Atwood released her *Penelopiad*. Although the explicit account of the weaving and unweav-

ing of the shroud called "Penelope's web" occupies only a small part of her text, it clearly evokes the unfinished and ongoing task of storytelling, brilliantly exemplified in the very existence of this text itself, which revises the Homeric story to expose its violently sexist underpinnings. Atwood's insistence on interrupting the standard account of the Homeric myth with a dissident chorus performed by the twelve hanged maids provides a creative counterpart to Razack's analysis in *Dark Threats and White Knights*, critiquing the values embedded in imperialist ideologies from Homer to George W. Bush and thereby undermining myths that claim civilization and civility as the legacy of the West.

28 The Metropolis Project is an international forum for research and policy on migration, diversity, and changing cities. See http://canada.metropolis.net for details.

29 In her contribution to the "Roundtable on the Future of the Humanities in a Fragmented World," Gayatri Spivak laments that "The humanities, with their slow learning model and their lack of policy orientation, do not make the grade" (718). In this respect, valuing literature increasingly appears to be a residual ideology in Raymond Williams's terms; yet it is not one that I am willing to surrender.

30 The state has suspended citizenship rights in the past, but it is also the state that holds the power to grant redress.

31 The role of *Obasan* in the Japanese Canadian Redress movement is the best known example.

32 For a fuller analysis of her argument, see Stephen Slemon, "Lament for a Notion." I have also discussed this at more length in a forthcoming essay, "Earth, World, Planet: Where Does the Postcolonial Critic Stand?" For less sympathetic accounts of Spivak's project, see Didier Coste, "Votum mortis," and Alfred Lopez, "The Repeating Apocalypse."

33 See Macpherson and also Joseph Carens, "Democracy and Possessive Individualism," for further analysis and development of Macpherson's critique of democracy and possessive individualism. I remain attracted to autonomy as the signifier of "the unlimited self-questioning about the law and its foundation as well as the capacity, in light of this interrogation, to *make*, to *do*, and to *institute*" (Gezerlis 471). These are Castoriadis's claims for autonomy as explained by Gezerlis. Without this kind of questioning, we seem unlikely to ensure justice and equity for all, remote as that goal may seem. At the same time, we need to remember Gilroy's point, that discourses of autonomy have been employed—and continue to be employed—to disqualify various groups from citizenship, including women, slaves, Natives, Blacks, children, animals, and the disabled.

34 See Rauno Kuokkanen, "The Responsibility of the Academy," for an elaboration of this argument.

Against Institution: Established Law, Custom or Purpose / Rinaldo Walcott

1 In 1992, young Black people and others rioted on Yonge Street in Toronto. The riots grew out of a protest march to denounce the acquittal of a Toronto police officer in the shooting death of a Black man. The protest march was also in solidarity with African Americans who were protesting the acquittal of police officers in the Rodney King affair by rioting in LA. The Canadian media reports that followed the riot in Toronto demonstrated in no uncertain terms that Black people were not seen as

constitutive of the Canadian polity. The Stephen Lewis Report (1992) published soon after confirmed the previous assertion by specifically pointing to anti-Black racism as a cause of the youth riots.

From Canadian Trance to TransCanada: White Civility to Wry Civility in the CanLit Project / Daniel Coleman

1 I would like to thank Donald Goellnicht and Lorraine York, my colleagues at McMaster, for their comments and suggestions on earlier drafts of this paper.

2 For the purposes of consistency, this volume uses the upper case for racializing words that refer to people whether as nouns or adjectives—thus, "Blacks," "White settler," "Aboriginal knowledge," and so on—because they parallel the national and ethnic uses of similar terms such as "Canadian," "Chinese," or "Mohawk." Some consideration was given at the copy editing stage to using the lower case when referring to the conceptualization of these categories—thus, "whiteness," "blackness," "indigeneity," etc. This distinction was, however, extremely difficult to maintain consistently because the conceptualization cannot be separated completely from the capacity of these terms to refer to people, and so the volume uses the upper case throughout. I have come to the conclusion that there is no adequate system for referring to these racialized terms, and that their typographical awkwardness and inconsistency are signs of their constant capacity for mutation and reinvention.

3 Bill C-38, known as the Same-Sex Marriage Law, was passed in Parliament a few days after the conference on June 28, 2005.

4 I would like to thank Peter Dickinson, who drew the connection between Walcott's use of "rudeness" and my discussion of White civility in the response he read to the conference version of this paper at the TransCanada Conference in Vancouver on June 25, 2005.

5 For an overview of these ongoing projects, see Daniel Coleman and Donald Goellnicht, "'Race' ... Into the Twenty-First Century."

6 See "The Broken Word" in my *The Scent of Eucalyptus* for an account of Negussie Kumbi's imprisonment.

7 As my characterization of the various approaches to Canadian literary studies shows, I do not see literary studies as separable from cultural studies. I agree with Germaine Warkentin and Heather Murray, who argued, in their introduction to their special issue of *Canadian Literature* on *Reading the Discourse of Early Canada*, that Canadian literary culture can only be read intelligently in a wide discursive realm of "stories and sense-making, power and persuasion" (7).

8 I share Étienne Balibar's conception of civility as that form of politics that does not suppress all violence but creates a civil public sphere by removing violence to that space's borders ("Three Concepts" 29–30), but I do not share his desire to unlink "civility" from "civilization" and the latter's association with the colonialist- Enlightenment idea of history as progress from barbarism to civilization (39 n. 6). The continuity between this evolutionary concept of history and civility is fundamental to my analysis. See also Anindyo Roy for a study of British civility in the context of Indian colonial history.

9 See Michel Foucault's "Governmentality" essay on the linkage of self-government to state government, and Jennifer Henderson's *Settler Feminism and Race Making in*

Canada for the development of this theory in relation to Canadian settler feminism (19ff).

10 R. B. Bennett, the Conservative MP for Calgary East, gave a speech at an Empire Day banquet sponsored by the Empire Club of Toronto in 1914 that expresses this civilizing mission in its triumphalistic mode: "We are [in India and Egypt] because under the Providence of God we are a Christian people that have given to the subject races of the world the only kind of decent government they have ever known. (Applause.) We are the only colonizing race that has been able to colonize the great outlying portions of the world and give the people that priceless boon of self-government, and we have educated men year after year until at last those who were once subjects became free, and those who were free became freer, and you and I must carry our portion of that responsibility if we are to be the true Imperialists we should be.... An Imperialist, to me, means a man who accepts gladly and bears proudly the responsibilities of his race and breed. (Applause.)" (qtd. in Berger 230–31).

11 See Eva Mackey, *The House of Difference* (2–3), and Richard Day, *Multiculturalism and the History of Canadian Diversity* (5, 42), for discussion of this process in a Canadian context.

12 In "Country, Cadence, Silence: Writing in Colonial Space," Dennis Lee describes how he experienced four years of writer's block during the years of the Vietnam War when he could not put his finger on the cadence or pulse of Canadian culture. This block ended, he writes, when he read George Grant's *Lament for a Nation*, which mapped for him the failures of Canada to withstand the pressures to become a branch plant of the American economic empire. This book, he says, gave him a new understanding of Canada's colonial condition in relation to the United States, which in turn broke his writer's block. The revised version of *Civil Elegies* that resulted went on to win the Governor General's Award for poetry in 1973.

13 I take the term "*Canadian*-Canadianness" from Eva Mackey's *The House of Difference*, where she derives it from one of the people she interviewed in a small Ontario town during a festival celebrating Canada's 125th anniversary. The interviewee used this term to distinguish hyphenated or "multicultural" Canadians from *Canadian*-Canadians, who have no need to hyphenate their identities with ethnic or national markers (104).

14 In an interview with Patricia Saunders in the *Journal of West Indian Literature*, M. NourbeSe Philip comments on the racialized effects of this Canadian anxiety of belateness: "Canada is a very insecure place culturally speaking. It doesn't have the same long history in the arts compared to the United States or Britain, both of which are far more culturally confident societies, different societies, and for very different reasons. So whereas, for instance, in the late 1980s the *Times Literary Supplement* would run an article on Linton Kwesi Johnson; here, the dub poets could not get even into the League of Canadian Poets because the latter organization didn't consider their work as poetry. Because of the cultural uncertainty that exists here that in turn is wedded to issues of white supremacy, there is this sense of not quite knowing what to accept, or not knowing whether it's 'art' or not. This makes for an, at times, stinking brew of ethnocentricism, racism, and cultural superiority. The flip side of this is the blanket acceptance of anything ethnic with very little critique" ("Trying" 213).

15 See also Razack's chapter on the Somalia mission in *Dark Threats and White Knights: The Somalia Affair, Peacekeeping, and the New Imperialism*.

16 See Kamboureli's second chapter in *Scandalous Bodies*, "Sedative Politics: Media, Law, Philosophy" (81–130).

17 "There is no 'human individual,'" Castoriadis writes. "There is a psyche that is socialized, and in this socialization, in the final result, there is almost nothing individual in the true sense of the term" (190).

18 See Cornell West's "A Genealogy of Modern Racism" for a discussion of the classical revival in European Enlightenment thinking that "Whitened" Greek aesthetic and philosophical principles to establish a genealogy for European civilization.

19 In a conversation reproduced in Taiaiake Alfred's *Peace, Power, and Righteousness*, Atsenhaienton, a Kanien'kehaka diplomat and leader from Kahnawake, Ontario, says a more accurate translation would call the Iroquoian law "the big warmth" or "the big harmony" (102). See Alfred for alternative spellings for the Rotinohshonni (Haudenosaunee) and *Kaienerekowa* (*Kayánerénhkowa*).

20 For a discussion of the dating of Deganawidah's establishment of the Law of Peace, see Paul A. Wallace, "The White Roots of Peace" (32–33).

21 The Tuscaroras joined later (Wallace 46).

22 See Wallace for a historical and Alfred for a recent discussion of the Six Nations' system of governance.

23 In her influential *Epistemology of the Closet*, Eve Sedgwick writes, "Insofar as ignorance is ignorance *of* a knowledge—a knowledge that may itself, it goes without saying, be seen as either true or false under some other regime of truth—these ignorances, far from being pieces of the originary dark, are produced by and correspond to particular knowledges and circulate as part of particular regimes of truth" (8).

24 See Len Findlay's "Always Indigenize!" for an exhortation to refuse the reproduction of sanctioned ignorance about First Nations' histories in the settler colonies.

TransCanada, Literature: No Direction Home / Stephen Slemon

1 The Centre for Cultural Renewal's home page reads, "The United States is, by far, Canada's largest trading partner.... We require a better understanding of the US economy and politics if we are to have enlightened US policy development in Canada."

Diasporic Citizenship: Contradictions and Possibilities for Canadian Literature / Lily Cho

1 Sassen distinguishes de-nationalized from postnational citizenship and suggests that "The understanding in the scholarship is that postnational citizenship is located partly outside the confines of the national. In considering denationalization, the focus moves on to the transformation of the national, including the national in its condition as foundation for citizenship. Thus it could be argued that postnationalism and denationalization represent two different trajectories. Both are viable, and they do not exclude each other" (56).

2 See Michel Laguerre, *Diasporic Citizenship: Haitian Americans in Transnational America.*

3 In *Flexible Citizenship*, Ong focusses "on the agency of displaced subjects and attempts by the state to regulate their activities and identities as a way to explore new cul-

tural logics of transnationality" (23). The subjects of Ong's study are thus mainly multiple-passport-carrying entrepreneurs and other transnational elites.

4 I take the phrase from the title of the final chapter of *Going Native*, "Rituals of Citizenship: Going Native and Contemporary American Identity" (199–202). Huhndorf argues specifically that the occupation of Native identities by White America is part of a process "of constructing white identities, naturalizing conquest, and inscribing various power relations within American culture" (6). Thus, the rituals of citizenship involve a continual process of "going Native," of taking the place of Native identities in mainstream culture and, in the case of a film such as *Dances with Wolves*, evoking "the conquest of Native America ... only to assuage the guilt stemming from that painful history" (4). As I have argued throughout this paper, Native Canadian identities are not minoritized in the same ways as other racially minoritized identities are, but we can productively think through the relationship of these minority positions within the rubric of diaspora.

Acts of Citizenship: Erin Mouré's *O Cidadán* and the Limits of Worldliness / Lianne Moyes

1 I would like to thank Rachid Belghiti, Pauline Butling, Richard Cassidy, David Chariandy, Barbara Godard, Heike Härting, Smaro Kamboureli, Catherine Leclerc, Nicole Markotic, Robert Majzels, Roy Miki, Erin Mouré, Tunji Osinubi, and Robert Schwartzwald for their dialogue during the writing of this paper. I am especially grateful to Heike Härting for her intellectual generosity and critical acuity in our conversations about citizenship. Her own work on citizenship, to which this essay is indebted, is forthcoming in *Essays on Canadian Writing*. Research for this essay was supported by a small-projects grant from SSHRC. Some of the ideas I develop here were published in fledgling form in an essay on representations of Montreal in the poetry of Robyn Sarah, Mary di Michele, and Erin Mouré, an essay translated by Catherine Leclerc for *Voix et images*. The English-language version of that essay appears in *Language Acts: Anglo-Quebec Poetry, 1976 to the 21st Century*.

2 The text's preamble has no page number.

3 A language with Celtic and Latin roots as well as Germanic and Arabic influences.

4 The word means "urban dweller." Unless otherwise indicated, all translations are mine.

5 "To where can you deport a citizen?" asks Mouré's writing subject, remembering the "75,721 citizens of France deported during WWII" (*O Cidadán* 108). In Canada, the attempt on the part of the Mackenzie King government to "repatriate" Japanese Canadians to Japan after the Second World War is another example of a government deporting its own citizens.

6 During the Middle Ages, Galicia had the same status as Mecca as a religious centre, and its language was the principal language of lyrical poetry in the Iberian peninsula. In the early nineteenth century, confronted with the economic and cultural privilege of those who spoke Castilian, over a quarter of Galicians emigrated, many to the Americas. Claims for political and cultural autonomy initiated during the first half of the nineteenth century intensified in the early twentieth century. However, Galego was suppressed during Franco's regime and had to wait until 1980, following the 1978 democratization of Spain, to be recognized as an official language

of Galicia. In order to extend the use of Galego beyond the colloquial (to which it had been reduced during the mid-twentieth century), language laws have been in place since 1983 to promote Galego in the spheres of public life, education, culture, business, and the media.

7   English is, she reminds us, a "hegemonic" language.

8   Mouré's work on citizenship can be traced to the essays "Poetry, Memory and the Polis" and "The Anti-Anaesthetic," published in the late 1980s, as well as to *Sheepish Beauty, Civilian Love.*

9   In her work on affect, Clare Hemmings notes that in matters of sexuality it is the woman who carries the shame of gendered impropriety and marks its limits. In the words of Jennifer Biddle, "It is, after all, the prostitute who is shameless, but the gentleman ... who is discreet" (qtd. in Hemmings 561).

10 Scholars antagonistic to poststructuralism, Hemmings explains, frequently invoke affect as a way of freeing themselves from the "yoke" of language and of power relations. Hemmings points to the work of feminist and postcolonial thinkers for analyses of signification and power that do not overlook "emotional investments, political connectivity and the possibility of change" (557).

11 Scott Malcomson exposes the "cosmopolitan" as little more than "someone empowered to decide who is provincial" (238).

12 Edward Said's "Reflections on Exile" are helpful here in understanding the lived reality of dislocation and dispossession that subtends the modernist myths of cosmopolitanism, homelessness, and exile (364).

13 See Pheng Cheah's "Introduction Part II" (30–38) and "Given Culture" (310–24) for further discussion.

14 Among theorists of cosmopolitanism, there are also those who insist upon the need for citizens to intervene in the politics of nation-states. Pheng Cheah, for example, makes the argument that "to be effective at the level of political institutions or the popular masses, transnational networks have to work with and through the nation-state in order to transform it. They have to negotiate directly with the state in the hope of influencing its political morality and/or mobilize local support into popular *national* movements that press against the state" ("Given Culture" 312).

15 See Audré Lorde on "sisterhood"; see Gayatri Chakravorty Spivak ("French Feminism in an International Frame") and Inderpal Grewal and Caren Kaplan on "global feminism"; see also Susan Stanford Friedman.

16 See also "The citizens herselves broke down the coasts" (*O Cidadán* 130).

17 Note Kristeva's use of "brotherhood"—"fraternité" in the original—instead of "sororal."

18 In English: "to be a stranger here is to be a part of everything understood by citizenship."

19 In English: "who tried to call out to Europe, with the body (dead) of writing (writing in their pockets)."

20 Gikandi cites the English translation of the letter found with the boys, a translation published in the November 1999 issue of *Harper's Magazine* (299.1794: 22). The original letter was written in French. Guinea gained independence from France in 1958.

Institutional Genealogies in the Global Net of Fundamentalisms, Families, and Fantasies / Julia Emberley

1 Further to the rhetoric of globalization and its intersection with lesbian and gay bodies see Mary K. Bloodsworth-Lugo and Carmen R. Lugo-Lugo, "'The War on Terror' and Same-sex Marriage: Narratives of Containment and the Shaping of U.S. Public Opinion." In this article, the authors state their intent to "explore the connections between U.S. presidential rhetoric regarding 'The War on Terror' and that involving lesbians and gay men. Specifically, we argue that official post–September 11 discourse has delineated the contours of the category 'American' in juxtaposition to the category 'un-American.' Due to worries about terrorist 'uncontainability,' the year 2003 witnessed a concerted effort to protect 'America' by containing the 'un-American' body. In this movement, lesbian/gay bodies are easily conflated with terrorist bodies. The same-sex marriage debate, and the increase of HIV/AIDS cases in gay and bisexual men, presented sites of requisite 'terrorist containment.' The rhetoric of military fundamentalism also positions itself against lesbians and gay men."

2 See, for example, *Defamiliarizing the Aboriginal: Cultural Practices and Decolonization in Canada* and articles "The 'Bourgeois Family,' Aboriginal Women, and Colonial Governance in Canada: A Study in Feminist Historical and Cultural Materialisms"; "The Power in Written Bodies: Gender, Decolonization and the Archive"; "Colonial Phantasms: Aboriginality in the Photographic Archive"; and "Colonial Governance and the Making and Unmaking of the Bourgeois Eskimo Family in Robert Flaherty's *Nanook of the North.*"

3 See, for example, Seyla Benhabib, *The Claims of Culture: Equality and Diversity in the Global Era* and Iris Young, *Inclusion and Democracy.*

4 Movie theatres showing *Fire* in New Delhi, Bombay, and other cities were attacked for showing the film in December 1998. For a useful list of newspaper articles reporting the controversy during 1998–99, see "Deepa Mehta's *Fire* Creates Controversy and Protests in India" at the website of the South Asian Women's NETwork (SAWNET).

5 John Torpey astutely observes both "the declining trust in alternative visions of society" and "the simultaneous upsurge of concern with memory, history and 'coming to terms with the past.'" He also notes that "the lessons of twentieth-century history have facilitated a shift from the labor movement's traditional rallying cry of 'don't mourn, organize' to a sensibility that insists we must 'organize to mourn'" (1). As the public meaning of mourning is defined through acts and practices of reconciliation, reparation, and repatriation, the question remains, however, as to who or what is being "mourned"—the loss of bourgeois imperial and patriarchal power and its separation of private and public domains of power and governance that made that governance possible?

6 In *The Cultural Politics of Fur*, I developed this process as follows: "A transactional reading not only maps the commerce of textual exchange; it also participates in the negotiations and has the potential to mobilize antagonistic oppositions such as woman/man and human/animal out of their fetishistic regimes of truth" (5–6). Here it is the spirit/matter opposition that is being mobilized out of its fetishistic status in the discourses of religious fundamentalisms.

7 See Monique Wittig's essay "The Straight Mind" (1980) in which she writes that "Pornographic images, films, magazine photos, publicity posters on the walls of the

cities, constitute a discourse, and this discourse covers our world with its signs, and this discourse has a meaning: it signifies that women are dominated" (Wittig 25).

8 For a discussion of the film, see my "Fantasies of Contact in a Transnational Frame: A Transactional Reading."

TransCanada Collectives: Social Imagination, the Cunning of Production, and the Multilateral Sublime / Len Findlay

1 Those who lament Canada's diminished presence in international affairs include Andrew Cohen, Michael Ignatieff, and Margaret MacMillan. For a contestation of their views, see my "Intent for a Nation."

2 Ursula Huws is most concerned with the gendered division of cyber-labour, while Franco Berardi is more broadly intent on forming of a new class of revolutionary "cognitarians" to resocialize information capitalism.

3 My notion of a position paper is indebted to Antonio Gramsci's version of a "war of position" preceding a "war of movement" (324, 350). An anti-capitalist intervention like mine from within the academic trench seeks to facilitate a shift of location from professional/civil society to political society, and to TransCanada interventions that not only unsettle but change the liberal state's allegiance to the insanities of market rationalty. It is a war of ideas and imaginings, and a developing praxis undertaken from within academic and literary institutions against the most tenacious features of Canada's hurtful history and the neo-liberalism that currently profits from and promotes those very features.

4 For unboundedness (*Unbegränztheit*) as a property of the sublime in general rather than of the market that so gleefully reduces nature to an infinity of resource development opportunities, see Immanuel Kant's treatment of *das Erhabene* in the second book of his *Critique of Judgement*.

5 Ignatieff's attempts to deny his role as inadvertent apologist for American violations of the human rights of so-called enemy combatants have simply added an imperious element to the impression of embeddedness conveyed by his defence of Operation Iraqi Freedom (Taylor).

6 Jacques Rancière provides an excellent precedent for this in his fusion of the technical and the banausic in ancient Greece, while John Guillory reveals the deep integration of aesthetic and economic modernity in Adam Smith, but Rancière's and Guillory's arguments have not had the impact on literary studies that they ought to have had.

WORKS CITED

"Aboriginal Children in Poverty in Urban Communities: Social Exclusion and the Growing Racialization of Poverty in Canada." *Canadian Council on Social Development.* 10 June 2003. Canadian Council on Social Development. 14 June 2005 <http://www.ccsd.ca/pr/2003/aboriginal.htm>.

Adorno, Theodor. *Hegel: Three Studies.* Trans. Shierry Weber Nicholson. Cambridge, MA: MIT P, 1994.

Agamben, Giorgio. *Means without End: Notes on Politics.* Trans. Vincenzo Binetti and Cesare Casarino. Minneapolis: U of Minnesota P, 2000.

———. *State of Exception.* Trans. Kevin Attell. Chicago: U of Chicago P, 2005.

Akenson, Donald Harman. "The Historiography of English-Speaking Canada and the Concept of Diaspora: A Sceptical Appreciation." *Canadian Historical Review* 76.3 (1995): 375–409.

Alexis, André. "Borrowed Blackness." *This Magazine* May 1995: 14–20.

Alfred, Taiaiake. *Peace, Power, Righteousness: An Indigenous Manifesto.* Toronto: Oxford UP, 1999.

Ali, Tariq. *The Clash of Fundamentalisms: Crusades, Jihads, and Modernity.* London: Verso, 2002.

Alloula, Malek. *The Colonial Harem.* Trans. Myrna Godzich and Wlad Godzich. Minneapolis: U of Minnesota P, 1986.

Almonte, Richard. Introduction. *A Plea for Emigration; Or, Notes of Canada West.* 1852. By Mary A. Shadd. Ed. and introd. Richard Almonte. Toronto: Mercury, 1998. 9–41.

Altamirano-Jimenez, Isabel. "North American First Peoples: Slipping into Market Citizenship." *Citizenship Studies* 8.4 (2004): 349–65.

Anderson, Amanda. "Cosmopolitanism, Universalism, and the Divided Legacies of Modernity." *Cosmopolitics: Thinking and Feeling beyond the Nation.* Ed. Bruce Robbins and Pheng Cheah. Minneapolis: U of Minnesota P, 1998. 265–89.

Anderson, Benedict. *Imagined Communities: Reflections on the Origins and Spread of Nationalism*. 2nd ed. London: Verso, 1991.

Andrew, Caroline. "Multiculturalism, Gender, and Social Cohesion: Reflections on Intersectionality and Urban Citizenship in Canada." *Insiders and Outsiders: Alan Cairns and the Reshaping of Canadian Citizenship*. Ed. Gerald Kernerman and Philip Resnick. Vancouver: U of British Columbia P, 2005. 316–28.

Angus, Ian. *Emergent Publics: An Essay on Social Movements and Democracy*. Winnipeg: Arbeiter Ring, 2001.

Anti-Slavery Society of Canada. *First Annual Report Presented to the Anti-Slavery Society of Canada, by Its Executive Committee*. Toronto: Brown's, 1852.

Appadurai, Arjun. "Grassroots Globalization and the Research Imagination." *Public Culture* 12.1 (2000): 1–19.

———. *Modernity at Large: Cultural Dimensions of Globalization*. Minneapolis: U of Minnesota P, 1996.

Appiah, Kwame Anthony. *The Ethics of Identity*. Princeton: Princeton UP, 2005.

Aquin, Hubert. *Trou de mémoire*. Ottawa: Cercle du livre de France, 1968.

Asad, Talal. *Genealogies of Religion: Discipline and Reasons of Power in Christianity and Islam*. Baltimore: Johns Hopkins UP, 1993.

Assembly of First Nations. *Our Nations, Our Governments: Choosing Our Own Paths. Report of the Joint Committee of Chiefs and Advisors on the Recognition and Implementation of First Nations Government*. Ottawa: Assembly of First Nations, 2005.

———. *Renewal Commission Annual Report 2004-2005*. Pp. 85–92. <http://www.afn.ca/article.asp?id=120>.

Attridge, Derek. *The Singularity of Literature*. London: Routledge, 2004.

Atwood, Margaret. *The Penelopiad*. Toronto: Knopf, 2005.

———. *Survival: A Thematic Guide to Canadian Literature*. Toronto: Anansi, 1972.

Baldwin, J. *Go Tell It on the Mountain*. New York: Dial, 1970.

Balibar, Étienne. "The Borders of Europe." Trans. J. Swenson. *Cosmopolitics: Thinking and Feeling beyond the Nation*. Ed. Bruce Robbins and Pheng Cheah. Minneapolis: U of Minnesota P, 1998. 216–29.

———. "Three Concepts of Politics: Emancipation, Transformation, Civility." Trans. Chris Turner. *Politics and the Other Scene*. Trans. Christine Jones, James Swenson, and Chris Turner. New York: Verso, 2002. 1–39.

Bannerji, Himani. *The Dark Side of the Nation: Essays on Multiculturalism, Nationalism, and Gender*. Toronto: Canadian Scholars' Press, 2000.

Barrett, Michèle. *Women's Oppression Today*. 2nd ed. London: Verso, 1989.

———, and Mary McIntosh. *The Anti-Social Family*. London: Verso, 1982.

Battiste, Marie, ed. *Reclaiming Indigenous Voice and Vision*. Vancouver: U of British Columbia P, 2000.

Baum-Singer, Melina, and Lily Cho, eds. "Poetics and Public Culture." *Open Letter*. Twelfth Series, No. 8 (Spring 2006).

Bauman, Zygmunt. "Soil, Blood and Identity." *Sociological Review* 40.4 (1992): 675–701.

Bell Globemedia. 12 June 2006. Bell Canada Enterprises. 4 Apr. 2005 <http://www.bellglobemedia.ca>.

Benhabib, Seyla. *The Claims of Culture: Equality and Diversity in the Global Era.* Princeton: Princeton UP, 2002.

———. "Models of Public Space: Hannah Arendt, the Liberal Tradition, and Jürgen Habermas." *Habermas and the Public Sphere.* Ed. Craig Calhoun. Cambridge: MIT P, 1992. 73–98.

Berardi, Franco [Bifo]. "The Factory of Unhappiness." Interview. *Makeworlds.* 4 Aug. 2004. NEURO. 30 Sept. 2005 <http://www.makeworlds.org/node/142>.

Berger, Carl. *The Sense of Power: Studies in the Ideas of Canadian Imperialism, 1867–1914.* Toronto: U of Toronto P, 1970.

Berlant, Lauren. *The Queen of America Goes to Washington City: Essays on Sex and Citizenship.* Durham: Duke UP, 1997.

Bernheimer, Charles, et al. "The Bernheimer Report, 1993: Comparative Literature at the Turn of the Century." *Comparative Literature in the Age of Multiculturalism.* Ed. Bernheimer. Baltimore: Johns Hopkins UP, 1995. 39–48.

Berton, Pierre. *The National Dream: The Great Railway, 1871–1881.* Toronto: McClelland and Stewart, 1970.

Bhabha, Homi K. *The Location of Culture.* New York: Routledge, 1994.

———, ed. *Nation and Narration.* London and New York: Routledge, 1990.

———. "Of Mimicry and Man: The Ambivalence of Colonial Discourse." *October* 28 (Spring 1984): 125–33.

Birney, Earl. *Down the Long Table.* Toronto: McClelland and Stewart, 1955.

Bissonnette, Lise. "La transculture, entre l'art et la politique." *Métamorphoses d'une utopie.* Ed. Jean-Michel Lacroix and Fulvio Caccia. Paris: Presses de la Sorbonne Nouvelle / Triptyque, 1992. 311–20.

Bloodsworth-Lugo, Mary K., and Carmen R. Lugo-Lugo. "'The War on Terror' and Same-Sex Marriage: Narratives of Containment and the Shaping of U.S. Public Opinion." *Peace and Change* 30.4 (2005): 469–88.

Boren, Mark Edelman. *Student Resistance: A History of the Unruly Subject.* New York: Routledge, 2001.

Borradori, Giovanna. *Philosophy in a Time of Terror: Dialogues with Jürgen Habermas and Jacques Derrida.* Chicago: U of Chicago P, 2003.

Borrows, John. *Recovering Canada: The Resurgence of Aboriginal Law.* Toronto: U of Toronto P, 2002.

Bourdieu, Pierre. *Firing Back: Against the Tyranny of the Market 2.* Trans. Loïc Wacquant. New York: New Press, 2001.

———. "Structure, *Habitus*, Practices." *The Logic of Practice.* Trans. Richard Nice. Stanford: Stanford UP, 1990. 52–65.

Bowering, George. *Left Hook: A Sideways Look at Canadian Writing.* Vancouver: Raincoast, 2005.

Boyarin, Jonathan, and Daniel Boyarin. "Diaspora: Generation and the Ground of Jewish Diaspora." *Theorizing Diaspora.* Ed. Jana Evans Braziel and Anita Mannur. Oxford: Blackwell, 2003. 85–118.

———. *Powers of Diaspora: Two Essays on the Relevance of Jewish Culture.* Minneapolis: U of Minnesota P, 2002.

Brah, Avtar. *Cartographies of Diaspora: Contesting Identities.* London: Routledge, 1996.

Brand, Dionne. *What We All Long For.* Toronto: Knopf, 2005.

Brennan, Teresa. *The Transmission of Affect.* Ithaca: Cornell UP, 2004.

Brennan, Timothy. *At Home in the World: Cosmopolitanism Now.* Cambridge: Harvard UP, 1997.

———. "Cosmo-Theory." *South Atlantic Quarterly* 100.3 (2001): 659–91.

Brodie, Janine. "Introduction: Globalization and Citizenship beyond the National State." *Citizenship Studies* 8.4 (2004): 323–32.

Brown, Nicholas, and Imre Szeman. "What Is the Multitude? Questions for Michael Hardt and Antonio Negri." *Cultural Studies* 19.3 (2005): 372–87.

Bruneau, William, and Donald C. Savage, eds. *Counting Out the Scholars: The Case against Performance Indicators in Higher Education.* CAUT Series. Toronto: James Lorimer, 2002.

Bruneau, William, and James L. Turk, eds. *Disciplining Dissent.* CAUT Series. Toronto: James Lorimer, 2004.

Brydon, Diana. "Metamorphosis of a Discipline: Rethinking the Canadian Literacy Institution." TransCanada: Literature Institutions, Citizenship Conference. Vancouver 2005.

Brydon, Diana. "Cross-Talk, Postcolonial Pedagogy, and Transnational Literacy." *Home-Work: Postcolonialism, Pedagogy, and Canadian Literature.* Ed. Cynthia Sugars. Ottawa: U of Ottawa P, 2004. 57–74.

———. "Earth, World, Planet: Where Does the Postcolonial Critic Stand?" *Cultural Transformations: Perspectives on Translocation in a Global Age,* ed. Chris Prentice, Henry Johnson, and Vijay Devadas. Forthcoming.

———. "Introduction: Reading Postcolonialty, Reading Canada." *Testing the Limits: Postcolonial Theories and Canadian Literatures.* Ed. Diana Brydon. Spec. issue of *Essays on Canadian Writing* 56 (Fall 1995): 1–19.

———, Manina Jones, Jessica Schagerl, and Kristen Warder, eds. *Poetics and Public Culture in Canada: Essays in Honour of Frank Davey.* Spec. issue. Forthcoming.

Buell, Lawrence. *The Future of Environmental Criticism: Environmental Crisis and the Literary Imagination.* Malden, MA: Blackwell, 2005.

Burke, Edmund. *A Philosophical Enquiry into the Origins of Our Ideas of the Sublime and Beautiful.* Ed. James T. Boulton. Notre Dame: Notre Dame UP, 1968.

Butler, Judith. *Bodies That Matter: On the Discursive Limits of Sex.* New York: Routledge, 1993.

———. *Gender Trouble: Feminism and the Subversion of Identity.* New York: Routledge, 1990.

———. "Performative Acts and Gender Constitution: An Essay in Phenomenology and Feminist Theory." *Theatre Journal* 49.1 (1988): 519–31.

"Campaign to Stop Secret Trials in Canada." 2004. Homesnotbombs. 8 Nov. 2005 <http://www.homesnotbombs.ca/secrettrials.htm>.

Campbell, Maria. *Stories of the Road Allowance People*. Penticton, BC: Theytus, 1995.

Canada. "Detention." ENF 20. *Citizenship and Immigration Canada*. <http://www.cic .gc.ca/manuals-guides/english/enf/enf20e.pdf>.

Canada. Royal Commission on National Development in the Arts, Letters, and Sciences. *Report*. Chair V. Massey. Ottawa: King's Printer, 1951.

"Canada's Foreign Aid Falls Short of Promises." *CTV.ca* 19 Apr. 2005. CTVglobemedia. 14 June 2005 <http://www.ctv.ca/servlet/ArticleNews/story/CTVNews/ 1113915824477_52/?hub=Canada>.

Canadian Alliance of Student Associations. "Policy Statement: Increasing SSHRC Granting Opportunities." 15 Nov. 2002. *Canadian Alliance of Student Associations*. <www.casa.ca/documents/INCREASING%20SSHRC%20GRANTING %20OPPORTUNITIES%20colour.pdf>.

Canadian Council on Social Development. Fact sheet. 2002. <http://www.ccsd.ca/fact sheets/fs_pov9099.htm>.

"Canadian Security: Security Certificates and Secret Evidence." *CBC News* 23 Feb. 2007 <http://www.cbc.ca/news/background/cdnsecurity/securitycertificates _secretevidence. html>.

Carens, Joseph H., ed. *Democracy and Possessive Individualism: The Intellectual Legacy of C.B. Macpherson*. Albany: State U of New York P, 1993.

Carter, Adam. "Kingdom of Ends: Nation, Post-Nation, and National Character in Northrop Frye." *English Studies in Canada* 29.3–4 (2003): 90–115.

CASA. *See* Canadian Alliance of Student Associations.

Castoriadis, Cornelius. *World in Fragments: Writings on Politics, Society, Psychoanalysis, and the Imagination*. Ed. and trans. David Ames Curtis. Stanford: Stanford UP, 1997.

Cavell, Richard. "Introduction: The Cultural Production of Canada's Cold War." *Love, Hate, and Fear in Canada's Cold War*. Ed. Richard Cavell. Toronto: U of Toronto P, 2004. 3–32.

———. *McLuhan in Space: A Cultural Geography*. Toronto: U of Toronto P, 2003.

Centre for Peace Studies [home page]. 2006. Centre for Peace Studies, McMaster University. 14 June 2005 <http://www.humanities.mcmaster.ca/~peace/>.

Chakrabarty, Dipesh. *Provincializing Europe: Postcolonial Thought and Historical Difference*. Princeton, NJ: Princeton UP, 2000.

Chamberlin, J. Edward. *If This Is Your Land, Where Are Your Stories? Finding Common Ground*. Toronto: Alfred A. Knopf, 2003.

Chambers, Ross. "The Unexamined." *The White Issue*. Spec. issue of *Minnesota Review* 47 (1996): 141–56.

Cheah, Pheng. "Given Culture: Rethinking Cosmopolitical Freedom in Transnationalism." *Cosmopolitics: Thinking and Feeling beyond the Nation*. Ed. Bruce Robbins and Pheng Cheah. Minneapolis: U of Minnesota P, 1998. 290–328.

———. "Introduction Part II: The Cosmopolitical—Today." *Cosmopolitics: Thinking and Feeling beyond the Nation*. Ed. Bruce Robbins and Pheng Cheah. Minneapolis: U of Minnesota P, 1998. 20–41.

————. *Spectral Nationality: Passages of Freedom from Kant to Postcolonial Literatures of Liberation*. New York: Columbia UP, 2003.

Cho, Lily. "Asian Canadian Futures: Diasporic Routes and the Routes of Indenture." *Essays on Canadian Writing* 85. Forthcoming.

Christenson, Deanna. *Atahkakoop: The Epic Account of a Plains Cree Head Chief, His People, and Their Struggle for Survival, 1816–1896*. Shell Lake, SK: Atahkakoop, 2000.

Chryssis, Alexander. "The Cunning of Production and the Proletarian Revolution in the *Communist Manifesto*." *The Communist Manifesto: New Interpretations*. Ed. Mark Cowling. New York: New York UP, 1998.

Clarke, A. *Growing Up Stupid under the Union Jack*. Toronto: McClelland and Stewart, 1980.

Clarke, George Elliott. "Contesting a Model Blackness: A Meditation on African-Canadian African Americanism, or the Structures of African-Canadianité." *Essays on Canadian Writing* 63 (1998): 1–55.

————. *Odysseys Home: Mapping African-Canadian Literature*. Toronto: UTP, 2002.

————. "What Was Canada?" *Is Canada Postcolonial? Unsettling Canadian Literature*. Ed. Laura Moss. Waterloo: Wilfrid Laurier UP, 2003. 27–39.

Cockburn, Bruce. "All Our Dark Tomorrows." *You've Never Seen Everything* [Album]. Rounder, 2003.

Coleman, Daniel. *The Scent of Eucalyptus: A Missionary Childhood in Ethiopia*. Fredericton, NB: Goose Lane, 2003.

————. *White Civility: The Literary Project of English Canada*. Toronto: U of Toronto P, 2005.

Coleman, Daniel, and Donald Goellnicht. "'Race' … Into the Twenty-First Century." Spec. issue of *Race*. Ed. Daniel Coleman and Donald Goellnicht. *Essays on Canadian Writing* 75 (2002): 1–35.

Colley, Linda. *Britons: Forging the Nation 1707–1837*. London: Vintage, 1992.

Collier, Stephen J., and Aihwa Ong. "Global Assemblages, Anthropologica Problems." *Global Assemblages: Technology, Politics, and Ethics as Anthropological Problems*. Ed. Aihwa Ong and Stephen J. Collier. Oxford: Blackwell, 2005. 3–21.

————, eds. *Global Assemblages: Technology, Politics, and Ethics as Anthropological Problems*. Oxford: Blackwell, 2005.

Compton, Wayde. *Performance Bond*. Vancouver: Arsenal Pulp, 2004.

Coste, Didier. "Votum mortis." *Literary Research / Recherche Littéraire* 20.39–40 (2003): 49–57.

Crawford, Robert. *Devolving English Literature*. Oxford: Clarendon P, 1992.

Crémazie, Octave. "Lettre à l'abbé Casgrain sur la littérature (29 Janvier 1867)." *Essais québécois, 1837–1983*. Ed. Laurent Mailhot. Ville LaSalle: Hurtubise HMH, 1984. 55–67.

Curtis, David Ames. Foreword. *Philosophy, Politics, Autonomy: Essays in Political Philosophy*. By Cornelius Castoriadis. Trans. and ed. David Ames Curtis. New York: Oxford UP, 1991. i–xxxix.

Damasio, Antonio. *Descartes' Error: Emotion, Reason, and the Human Brain*. New York: Putnam, 1994.

Davey, Frank. *Post-National Arguments: The Politics of the Anglophone-Canadian Novel since 1967*. Toronto: U of Toronto P, 1993.

Davidson, Arnold E. "Canada in Fiction." *The Columbia History of the American Novel*. Ed. Emory Elliot. New York: Columbia UP, 1991. 558–85.

Day, Richard J. F. *Multiculturalism and the History of Canadian Diversity*. Toronto: U of Toronto P, 2000.

de Beauvoir, Simone. *The Second Sex*. Trans. and ed. H.M. Parshley. New York: Knopf, 1957.

"Deepa Mehta's *Fire* Creates Controversy and Protests in India." *Sawnews: News about South-Asian Women*. 19 Aug. 1999. SAWNET: South Asian Women's NETwork. 4 Apr. 2005 <http://www.sawnet.org/news/fire.html>.

Delanty, Gerard. *Citizenship in a Global Age: Society, Culture, Politics*. Philadelphia: Open UP, 2000.

Delany, Martin R. *Blake; or, The Huts of America*. Introd. Floyd J. Miller. Boston: Beacon, 1970.

Deleuze, Gilles, and Felix Guattari. *Anti-Oedipus: Capitalism and Schizophrenia*. Pref. Michel Foucault. Trans. Robert Hurley, Mark Seem, and Helen R. Lane. Minneapolis: U of Minnesota P, 1983.

Delphy, Christine. "Our Friends and Ourselves: The Hidden Foundations of Various Pseudo-feminist Accounts." *Close to Home: A Materialist Analysis of Women's Oppression*. Ed. and trans. Diana Leonard. Amhert: U of Massachusetts P, 1984.

Denning, Michael. *Culture in the Age of Three Worlds*. London: Verso, 2004.

Derrida, Jacques. *Ethics, Institutions and the Right to Philosophy*. Trans. P. Trifonas. Lanham, MD: Rowman and Littlefield, 2002.

———. *Of Hospitality*. Trans. R. Bowlby. Stanford, CA: Stanford UP, 2000.

———. *On Cosmopolitanism and Forgiveness*. Trans. Mark Dooley and Michael Hughes. London: Routledge, 2001.

Dewart, Edward Hartley. "Introductory Essay to *Selections from Canadian Poets*." 1864. *Towards a Canadian Literature: Essays, Editorials and Manifestos*. Ed. Douglas M. Daymond and Leslie G. Monkman. Vol. 1. Ottawa: Tecumseh, 1984. 50–59.

Diène, Doudou. *Racism, Racial Discrimination, Xenophobia and All Forms of Discrimination: Mission to Canada*. Commission on Human Rights, 60th session. Geneva: Office of the United Nations High Commissioner for Human Rights, 2003. United Nations Economic and Social Council. 1 March 2004 <www.unhchr.ch/huridocda/huridoca.nsf/Documents?OpenFrameset>.

Dimock, Wai Chee. "Literature for the Planet." *Globalizing Literary Studies*. Spec. issue of *PMLA* 116.1 (2001): 173–88.

Doane, Mary Ann. *The Desire to Desire: The Woman's Film of the 1940s*. Bloomington: Indiana UP, 1987.

Dorland, Michael, and Maurice Charland. *Law, Rhetoric, and Irony in the Formation of Canadian Civil Culture*. Toronto: U of Toronto P, 2002.

Dyer, Richard. *White*. New York: Routledge, 1997.

Eagleton, Terry. "The Pope Has Blood on His Hands: The Pope Did Great Damage to the Church, and to Countless Catholics." *Guardian* 4 Apr. 2005. Guardian Unlimited. 20 Apr. 2005 <http://www.guardian.co.uk/comment/story/0,3604, 1451484,00.html>.

Edwards, Brent Hayes. "Uses of Diaspora." *Social Text* 19.1 (2001): 45–73.

Eisin, Engin F. "The Neurotic Citizen." *Citizenship Studies* 8.3 (2004): 217–35.

Elliott, Lorris. *Literary Writings of Blacks in Canada: A Preliminary Survey*. Ottawa: Department of the Secretary of State, 1988.

Emberley, Julia. "The 'Bourgeois Family,' Aboriginal Women, and Colonial Governance in Canada: A Study in Feminist Historical and Cultural Materialisms." *Signs: Journal of Women in Culture and Society* 27.1 (2001): 59–85.

———. "Colonial Governance and the Making and Unmaking of the Bourgeois Eskimo Family in Robert Flaherty's *Nanook of the North*." *Indigeneity: Constructions and (Re)Presentations*. Ed. James Brown and Patricia Sant. Comock, NY: Nova Science Press, 1999. 96–117.

———. "Colonial Phantasms: Aboriginality in the Photographic Archive." *Recalling Early Canada*. Ed. Jennifer Blair, Daniel Coleman, Kate Higginson, and Lorraine York. Edmonton: U of Alberta P, 2005. 301–34.

———. *The Cultural Politics of Fur*. Ithaca: Cornell UP, 1997.

———. *Defamiliarizing the Aboriginal: Cultural Practices and Decolonization in Canada*. Toronto: U of Toronto P, 2007.

———. "Fantasies of Contact in a Transnational Frame: A Transactional Reading." *Tessera* 17 (1994): 52–74.

———. "The Power in Written Bodies: Gender, Decolonization, and the Archive." *Genders* 23 (1996): 184–211.

Engels, Friedrich. *Ludwig Feuerbach and the End of Classical German Philosophy*. Vol. 26 of *The Collected Works of Marx and Engels*. Moscow: Foreign Languages Publishing House, 1950.

Engels, Friedrich, and Karl Marx. *The Communist Manifesto*. Ed. L. M. Findlay. Peterborough, ON: Broadview, 2004.

Enloe, Cynthia. "Updating the Gendered Empire." *The Curious Feminist: Searching for Women in a New Age of Empire*. Berkeley: U of California P, 2004.

ESC: English Studies in Canada. "Readers' Forum: Always Indigenize!" (Spec. Issue) 30.2 (June 2004).

ESC: English Studies in Canada. "Readers' Forum, Part II: Always Indigenize!" (Spec. Issue) 30.3 (September 2004).

Esthero. "We R in need of a musical reVoLuTIoN." *We R in Need of a Musical reVoLuTIoN*. Reprise/Wea, 2005.

Fanon, Franz. *The Wretched of the Earth*. 1963. Trans. Richard Philcox. New York: Grove, 2004.

Faulks, Keith. *Citizenship*. New York: Routledge, 2000.

Fiedler, Leslie. *Love and Death in the American Novel*. New York: Stein and Day, 1966.

Findlay, L. M. "Always Indigenize! The Radical Humanities in the Postcolonial Canadian University." *Ariel* 31.1–2 (2000): 307–26.

———. "Intent for a Nation." *English Studies in Canada* 30.2 (2004): 39–48.

———. "Memory's Hegelian Estate: Class, 'Race,' Treaty, and the Canadas of Alexander Morris (1826–1829)." *Essays in Canadian Writing* 80 (2003): 217–42.

———. "When I Hear the Word 'Culture': State Syntax, Cultural Vocabularies, and Violence." *Nationalisms.* Ed. James Gifford and Gabrielle Zezulka-Mailloux. Vol. 3 of *Culture and the State.* Edmonton: U of Alberta CRC Humanities Studio, 2003. 7–24.

Fire. Dir. Deepha Mehta. New Yorker Video, 1996.

A First Nations–Federal Crown Political Accord on the Recognition and Implementation of First Nations Governments. Assembly of First Nations. 30 May 2005. Assembly of First Nations. 7 June 2005 <http://www.afn.ca/cmslib/general/PolAcc.pdf>.

Fleming, Patricia Lockhart, Gilles Gallichan, and Yvan Lamonde, eds. *History of the Book in Canada, Vol. 1: Beginnings to 1840.* Toronto: U of Toronto P, 2004.

Foreign Affairs Canada. *Canada's International Policy Statement: A Role of Pride and Influence in the World.* Ottawa: Queen's Printer, 2005.

Foster, Thomas. *The Souls of Cyberfolk: Posthumanism as Vernacular Theory.* Minneapolis: U of Minnesota P, 2005.

Foucault, Michel. "Governmentality." Trans. Rosi Braidotti. *The Foucault Effect: Studies in Governmentality with Two Lectures and an Interview with Michael Foucault.* Ed. Graham Burchell, Colin Gordon, and Peter Miller. Chicago: U of Chicago P, 1991. 87–104.

———. *The History of Sexuality: An Introduction.* Vol. 1. Trans. Robert Hurley. New York: Vintage, 1990.

———. "Nietzsche, Genealogy, History." *Language, Counter-memory, Practice: Selected Essays and Interviews by Michel Foucault.* Ed. Donald F. Bouchard. Trans. Donald F. Bouchard and Sherry Simon. Ithaca: Cornell UP, 1977. 139–64.

Frankenberg, Ruth. *White Women, Race Matters: The Social Construction of Whiteness.* Minneapolis: U of Minnesota P, 1993.

Fraser, Nancy. "Rethinking the Public Sphere: A Contribution to the Critique of Actually Existing Democracy." *Habermas and the Public Sphere.* Ed. Craig Calhoun. Cambridge: MIT Press, 1992. 109–42.

The Fraser Institute [home page]. 2006. Fraser Institute. 14 June 2005 <http://www.fraserinstitute.ca/index.asp>.

Freud, Sigmund. *Civilization and Its Discontents.* Ed. and trans. James Strachey. New York: Norton, 1961.

Frye, Northrop. *Anatomy of Criticism.* Princeton, NJ: Princeton UP, 1957.

———. *The Bush Garden: Essays on the Canadian Imagination.* Toronto: Anansi, 1971.

———. "Conclusion." *Literary History of Canada.* Ed. Carl F. Klinck. Toronto: U Toronto P, 1965. 825–55.

Fung, Richard, and Monika Kin Gagnon. *13 Conversations about Art and Cultural Race Politics.* Montreal: Artextes, 2002.

Gagnon, Monika Kin. *Other Conundrums: Race, Culture, and Canadian Art.* Vancouver: Artspeak Gallery, Arsenal Pulp, and the Kamloops Art Gallery, 2000.

Galabuzi, Grace-Edward, and Cheryl Teelucksingh. "New CRRF Report Confirms Significant Barriers to Fair Employment for Racialized Groups and Immigrants." 17 May 2005. *Canadian Race Relations Foundation.* 19 Oct. 2005 <http://www.crr .ca/Load.do?section=4&subSection=6&id=371&type=2>.

Garand, Dominique. *La Griffe du polémique.* Montréal: Hexagone, 1989.

Garber, Marjorie. *Vested Interests: Cross-dressing and Cultural Anxiety.* New York: Routledge, 1992.

Gates, Henry Louis Jr. "Writing, 'Race,' and the Difference It Makes." *The Critical Tradition.* 2nd ed. Ed. David Richter. New York: Bedford, 1998. 1575–88.

Gauvin, Lise. "From Octave Crémazie to Victor-Lévy Beaulieu: Language, Literature, and Ideology." *Yale French Studies* 65 (1983): 30–49.

Gerson, Carole, and Jacques Michon, eds. *History of the Book in Canada, Vol. 3: 1918–1980.* Toronto: U of Toronto P, 2007.

Gezerlis, Alexandros. "Castoriadis and the Project of Autonomy: A Review of *The Imaginary Institution of Society.*" *Democracy and Nature* 7.3 (2001): 469–87.

Giddens, Anthony. *Runaway World.* New York: Routledge, 2000.

Gikandi, Simon. "Globalization and the Claims of Postcoloniality." *South Atlantic Quarterly* 100.3 (2001): 627–58.

Gillmor, Don, with Achille Michaud and Pierre Turgeon. *Canada: A People's History.* Vol 2. Toronto: McClelland and Stewart, 2001.

Gilroy, Paul. *Against Race: Imagining Political Culture beyond the Color Line.* Cambridge: Belknap, 2005.

———. *The Black Atlantic: Modernity and Double Consciousness.* Cambridge: Harvard UP, 1993.

———. *Postcolonial Melancholia.* New York: Columbia UP, 2005.

———. "'Where ignorant armies clash by night': Homogeneous Community and the Planetary Aspect." *International Journal of Cultural Studies* 6.3 (2003): 261–76.

Giroux, Henry A. "Education after Abu Ghraib: Revisiting Adorno's Politics of Education." *Cultural Studies* 18.6 (2004): 779–815.

Godbout, Patricia. *Traduction littéraire et sociabilité interculturelle au Canada (1950–1960).* Ottawa: Ottawa UP, 2004.

Goldberg, David Theo. *Racist Culture: Philosophy and the Politics of Meaning.* Oxford: Blackwell, 1993.

Goldsmith, Oliver, Jr. *The Rising Village and Other Poems.* Ed. Gerald Lynch. London, ON: Canadian Poetry Press, 1987.

Goodale, Ralph. "The Budget Speech 2004." 23 March 2004. *Department of Finance Canada.* 4 Apr. 2005 <http://www.fin.gc.ca/budget04/speech/speeche.htm>.

Gramsci, Antonio. *Further Selections from the Prison Notebooks.* Ed. and trans. Derek Boothman. Minneapolis: U of Minnesota P, 1995.

Granatstein, J. L. *Who Killed Canadian History?* Toronto: HarperPerennial, 1999.

Grant, George. *Lament for a Nation.* 1965. Montreal: McGill-Queen's UP, 2005.

Grewal, Inderpal, and Caren Kaplan. "Introduction." *Scattered Hegemonies: Postmodernity and Transnational Feminist Practices.* Minneapolis: U of Minnesota P, 1994. 1–30.

Guillory, John. *Cultural Capital: The Problem of Literary Canon Formation.* Chicago: U of Chicago P, 1994.

Habermas, Jürgen. *The Postnational Constellation: Political Essays.* Ed. and trans. Max Pensky. Cambridge, MA: MIT P, 2001.

Hall, Anthony J. *The Bowl with One Spoon.* Vol. 1 of *The American Empire and the Fourth World.* McGill-Queen's UP, 2003.

Hall, Stuart. "Conclusion: The Multi-cultural Question." *Un/settled Multiculturalisms: Diasporas, Entanglements, Transruptions.* Ed. B. Hesse. London: Zed Books, 2000. 209–36.

———. "The West and the Rest: Discourse and Power." *Formations of Modernity.* Ed. Stuart Hall and Bram Gieben. Cambridge: Polity P, 1992. 275–331.

———. "When Was the 'Post-colonial'? Thinking at the Limit." *The Post-Colonial Question.* Ed. Iain Chambers and Lidia Curti. London: Routledge, 1996. 242–60.

Hall, Stuart, and David Held. "Citizens and Citizenship." *New Times: The Changing Face of Politics in the 1990s.* Ed. Stuart Hall and Martin Jacques. London: Verso, 1990. 173–88.

Hampson, Sarah. "Sly Mr. Nice Guy." *Globe and Mail* 10 January 2004: R3.

Hanh, Thich Nhat. *The Heart of the Buddha's Teachings.* New York: Random House / Broadway, 1999.

Hardt, Michael. "The Withering of Civil Society." *Social Text* 45 (1995): 27–44.

Hardt, Michael, and Antonio Negri. *Empire.* Cambridge: Harvard UP, 2000.

———. *Multitude: War and Democracy in the Age of Empire.* New York: Penguin, 2004.

Harootunian, H. D. "Postcoloniality's Unconscious / Area Studies' Desire." *Learning Places.* Ed. Miyoshi Masao and H. D. Harootunian. Durham, NC: Duke UP, 2002. 150–74.

Härting, Heike. "The Poetics of Vulnerability: Diaspora, Race, and Global Citizenship in Dionne Brand's *Thirsty* and A.M. Klein's *The Second Scroll.*" *Poetics and Public Culture.* Ed. Diana Brydon, Manina Jones, Jessica Schagerl, and Kristen Warder. Spec. issue. Forthcoming.

Haver, W. "Another University, Now; A Practical Proposal for a New Foundation of the University." *Equity and How to Get It: Rescuing Graduate Studies.* Ed. K. Armatage. Toronto: Inanna Publications and Education, 1999. 25–37.

———. "Of Mad Men Who Practice Invention to the Brink of Intelligibility." *Queer Theory in Education.* Ed. William Pinar. Mahwah, NJ: Lawrence Erlbaum, 1998. 349–64.

Heater, Derek. *What Is Citizenship?* Cambridge: Polity P, 1999.

Hegel, G. W. F. *Philosophy of Right.* Trans. T. M. Knox. Oxford: Oxford UP, 1952.

Hemmings, Clare. "Invoking Affect: Cultural Theory and the Ontological Turn." *Cultural Studies* 19.5 (Sept. 2005): 548–67.

Henderson, Ailsa, and Nicola McEwan. "Do Shared Values Underpin National Identity? Examining the Role of Values in National Identity in Canada and the United Kingdom." *National Identities* 7.2 (2005): 173–91.

Henderson, James Sakej. "*Sui Generis* and Treaty Citizenship." *Citizenship Studies* 6.4 (2002): 415–40.

Henderson, Jennifer. *Settler Feminism and Race Making in Canada.* Toronto: U of Toronto P, 2003.

Hill, Lawrence. *Black Berry, Sweet Juice: On Being Black and White in Canada.* Toronto: HarperFlamingo, 2001.

Hindess, Barry. "Citizenship for All." *Citizenship Studies* 8.3 (2004): 305–15.

Hoffman, John. *Citizenship beyond the State.* Thousand Oaks, CA: Sage, 2004.

Hohendahl, P. U. *Prismatic Thought: Theodor Adorno.* Lincoln: U of Nebraska P, 1995.

Huhndorf, Shari. *Going Native: Indians in the American Cultural Imagination.* Ithaca, NY: Cornell UP, 2001.

———. "Indigeneity, Colonialism and Literary Studies: A 'Transdisciplinary, Oppositional Politics of Reading.'" *ESC: English Studies in Canada* 30.2 (2004): 29–38.

———. "Rituals of Citizenship: Going Native and Contemporary American Identity." *Going Native: Indians in the American Cultural Imagination.* Ithaca, NY: Cornell UP, 2001. 199–202.

Hutcheon, Linda. *The Canadian Postmodern: A Study of Contemporary English-Canadian Fiction.* Toronto: Oxford UP, 1988.

———. *Irony's Edge: The Theory and Politics of Irony.* New York: Routledge, 1995.

———. *Splitting Images: Contemporary Canadian Ironies.* Toronto: Oxford UP, 1991.

Hutcheon, Linda, and Marion Richmond, eds. *Other Solitudes: Canadian Multicultural Fictions.* Toronto: Oxford UP, 1990.

Huntingdon, Samuel. *Clash of Civilizations and the Remaking of the World Order.* New York: Simon and Schuster, 1996.

Huws, Ursula. *The Making of a Cybertariat: Virtual Work in a Real World.* New York: Monthly Review P, 2003.

Ignatieff, Michael. *Empire Lite: Nation-building in Bosnia, Kosovo and Afghanistan.* Toronto: Penguin Canada, 2003.

———. *The Rights Revolution.* Toronto: Anansi, 2000.

———. *Human Rights as Politics and Idolatry.* Ed. and intro. Amy Guttman. Commentary by Kwame Anthony Appiah, David A. Hollinger, Thomas W. Laqueur, and Diane F. Orentlicher. Princeton: Princeton UP, 2001.

Ihimaera, Witi. *The Whale Rider.* Toronto: Harcourt, 1987.

"Indirect Cost of Research." 2000. *Canadian Federation for the Humanities and Social Sciences.* Canadian Federation for the Humanities and Social Sciences. 14 June 2005 <http://www.fedcan.ca/english/fromold/indirectcostresearch.cfm>.

Innis, Harold A. *The Bias of Communication.* Toronto: U of Toronto P, 1951.

Irigaray, Luce. *This Sex Which Is Not One.* Trans. Catherine Porter and Carolyn Burke. Ithaca, NY: Cornell UP, 1985.

Isin, Engin F. "The Neurotic Citizen." *Citizenship Studies* 8.3 (2004): 217–35.

Iyer, Pico. *The Global Soul: Jet Lag, Shopping Malls, and the Search for Home.* New York: Vintage, 2000.

James, C. L. R. *The Black Jacobins: Toussaint L'Ouverture and the San Domingo Revolution.* 2nd ed. 1963. New York: Vintage, 1989.

Jay, Gregory. *American Literature and the Culture Wars.* Ithaca: Cornell UP, 1997.

———. "The End of 'American' Literature: Toward a Multicultural Practice." *College English* 53.3 (1991): 264–81.

Juro, Andrea, and V. Vale, eds. *Angry Women.* San Francisco: RE/Search Publications, 1991.

Kamboureli, Smaro, ed. *Making a Difference: Canadian Multicultural Literature.* Toronto: Oxford UP, 1996.

———. *Scandalous Bodies: Diasporic Literature in English Canada.* Toronto: Oxford UP, 2000.

Kandahar. Dir. Mohsen Makhmalbaf. Avatar, 2001.

Kant, Immanuel. *The Critique of Judgement.* Ed. and trans. James Creed Meredith. Oxford: Clarendon Press, 1969.

———. *Kritik der Urteilskraft.* Vol. 5 of *Kants Werke: Akademie-Ausgabe.* Ed. Paul Natorp and Wilhelm Windelband. Berlin: Walter de Gruyter, 1968.

"Kashechewan: Water Crisis in Northern Ontario." 4 Nov. 2005. *CBC News Online.* 8 Nov. 2005 <http://www.cbc.ca/news/background/aboriginals/kashechewan .html>.

Kernerman, Gerald, and Philip Resnick, eds. *Insiders and Outsiders: Alan Cairns and the Reshaping of Canadian Citizenship.* Vancouver: U of British Columbia P, 2005.

Kertzer, Jonathan. *Worrying the Nation: Imagining a National Literature in English Canada.* Toronto: U of Toronto P, 1998.

Khoo, Tseen-ling. *Banana Bending: Asian-Australian and Asian-Canadian Literature.* Kingston: McGill-Queen's UP, 2003.

Kipnis, Laura. *Against Love: A Polemic.* New York: Vintage, 2004.

Kirby, William. *The U.E.: A Tale of Upper Canada.* 1859. Toronto: U of Toronto P, 1973.

Kiyooka, Roy K. *Transcanada Letters.* Ed. Smaro Kamboureli. Afterword by Glen Lowry. 1975. Edmonton: NeWest, 2005.

———. *Pacific Rim Letters.* Ed. Smaro Kamboureli. Afterword by Smaro Kamboureli. Edmonton: NeWest, 2005.

———. *Pacific Windows: Collected Poems of Roy K. Kiyooka.* Ed. Roy Miki. Afterword by Roy Miki. Vancouver: Talonbooks, 1997.

Klein, Naomi. *Fences and Windows: Dispatches from the Front Lines of the Globalization Debate.* Toronto: Vintage Canada, 2002.

———. "The Rise of Disaster Capitalism." *Nation* 2 May 2005 <http://www .thenation.com/doc/20050502/klein>.

Klinck, Carl F. *Wilfred Campbell: A Study in Late Provincial Victorianism.* Ottawa: Tecumseh, 1977.

Kogawa, Joy. *Obasan*. Toronto: Lester and Orpen Dennys, 1981.

———. *The Rain Ascends*. Toronto: Alfred A. Knopf Canada, 1995.

Kokotailo, Philip. "The Bishop and His Deacon: Smith vs. Sutherland Reconsidered." *Journal of Canadian Studies* 27.2 (1992): 63–81.

Kristeva, Julia. *Powers of Horror: An Essay in Abjection*. Trans. Leon S. Roudiez. New York: Columbia UP, 1982.

———. *Strangers to Ourselves*. Trans. Leon S. Roudiez. New York: Columbia UP, 1991.

Kroetsch, Robert. "The Moment of the Discovery of America Continues." *The Lovely Treachery of Words: Essays Selected and New*. Toronto: Oxford UP, 1989. 1–20.

Kuokkanen, Rauna. "The Responsibility of the Academy: A Call for Doing Homework." Canadian Political Science Association Meeting. University of Western Ontario, 4 June 2005.

Kureishi, Hanif. *Sammy and Rosie Get Laid: The Screenplay and the Screenwriter's Diary*. Toronto: Penguin, 1988.

Kurtz, Hilda, and Katherine Hankins. "Guest Editorial: Geographies of Citizenship." *Space and Polity* 9.1 (2005): 1–8.

Kushner, Tony. *Angels in America, Part I: Millennium Approaches*. New York: Theatre Communications Group, 1993.

Lafitau, Joseph-François. *Customs of the American Indians Compared with the Customs of Primitive Times*. Ed. and trans. William N. Fenton and Elizabeth L. Moore. 2 vols. Toronto: Champlain Society, 1974.

Laguerre, Michel. *Diasporic Citizenship: Haitian Americans in Transnational America*. New York: St. Martin's, 1998.

Lai, Larissa. Lecture. Literary Readings Segment, TransCanada: Literature, Institutions, Citizenship Conference. Vancouver, 23 June 2005.

Lamonde, Yvan, Patricia Lockhart Fleming, and Fiona A. Black, eds. *History of the Book in Canada, Vol. 2: 1840–1918*. Toronto: U of Toronto P, 2005.

Lamore, Jean. "Transculturation: Naissance d'un mot." *Vice Versa* 21 (1987): 18–19.

Lampman, Archibald. "Two Canadian Poets." 1891. *Towards a Canadian Literature: Essays, Editorials, and Manifestos*. Vol. 1. Ottawa: Tecumseh, 1984. 133–37.

The Last Temptations of Christ. Dir. Martin Scorcese. Universal, 1988.

Laurence, Margaret. *The Diviners*. Toronto: McClelland and Stewart, 1973.

Lawson, Alan. "Postcolonial Theory and the 'Settler' Subject." *Testing the Limits: Postcolonial Theories and Canadian Literatures*. Ed. Diana Brydon. Spec. issue of *Essays on Canadian Writing* 56 (1995): 20–36.

Lecker, Robert. *Making It Real: The Canonization of English-Canadian Literature*. Toronto: Anansi, 1995.

Lee, Dennis. "Cadence, Country, Silence: Writing in Colonial Space." *Towards a Canadian Literature: Essays, Editorials and Manifestos*. Ed. Douglas M. Daymond and Leslie G. Monkman. Vol. 2. Ottawa: Tecumseh, 1985. 497–520.

———. *Civil Elegies*. Toronto: Anansi, 1968.

Lee, Jo-Anne, and John Lutz, eds. *Situating "Race" and Racisms in Space, Time, and Theory: Critical Essays for Activists and Scholars*. Montreal: McGill-Queen's UP, 2005.

Lee, Peggy. "Fever." *Things Are Swingin'.* Capitol Records, 1959.

Lee, SKY. *Disappearing Moon Cafe*. Vancouver: Douglas and McIntyre, 1990.

Lenin, Vladimir. "What Is to Be Done." 1902. *Lenin Collected Works*. Moscow: Foreign Languages Publishing House, 1961. 5: 347–530. *Lenin Internet Archive*. 2005. Marxists Internet Archives. 14 June 2005 <http://www.marxists.org/archive/lenin/works/1901/witbd/>.

Leonard, Mark. "The Left Should Love Globalization." *New Statesman* 28 May 2001. *New Statesman*. 19 June 2006 <http://www.newstatesman.com/200105280024>.

Lequin, Lucie. "Quelques mouvements de la transculture." *Writing Ethnicity: Cross-Cultural Consciousness in Canadian and Québécois Literature*. Ed. Winfried Siemerling. Toronto: ECW P, 1996. 128–44.

Lewis, Stephen. Report on Racism in Ontario to the Premier—Summer 1992. <http://www. Geocities.com/capitolhill/6174/lewis.html.>

Lockhart Fleming, Patricia, Gilles Gallichan, and Yvan Lamonde, eds. *History of the Book in Canada: Beginnings to 1840*. Vol. 1. Toronto: U of Toronto P, 2004.

Logan, John E. [writing as Barry Dane]. "National Literature." *The Search for English-Canadian Literature: An Anthology of Critical Articles from the Nineteenth and Early Twentieth Centuries*. Ed. Carl Ballstadt. Toronto: U of Toronto P, 1975. 114–17.

Lopez, Alfred. "The Repeating Apocalypse: Magic Realism and the Future(s) of Comparative Literature." *Literary Research / Recherche Littéraire* 20.39–40 (2003): 69–80.

Lorde, Audre. "Age, Race, Class, and Sex: Women Redefining Difference." *Sister Outsider: Essays and Speeches*. Trumansburg, NY: Crossing, 1984. 114–23.

Lyotard, Jean-François. *The Postmodern Condition: A Report on Knowledge*. Trans. Geoff Bennington and Brian Massumi. Minneapolis: U of Minnesota P, 1984.

Mackey, Eva. *The House of Difference: Cultural Politics and National Identity in Canada*. London: Routledge, 1999.

Macpherson, C. B. *The Political Theory of Possessive Individualism: Hobbes to Locke*. Oxford: Oxford UP, 1962.

Magrath, C. A. *Canada's Growth and Problems Affecting It*. Ottawa: Mortimer, 1910.

"Major Victory against Secret Trials at Canada's Supreme Court." February 23, 2007. <http://www.homesnotbombs.ca/scvictory.htm.>

Makhmalbaf, Mohsen. "Interview with Mohsen Makhmalbaf." DVD booklet. *Kandahar*. Dir. Mohsen Makhmalbaf. Avatar, 2001.

Malcomson, Scott L. "The Varieties of Cosmopolitan Experience." *Cosmopolitics: Thinking and Feeling beyond the Nation*. Ed. Bruce Robbins and Pheng Cheah. Minneapolis: U of Minnesota P, 1998. 233–45.

Mandeville, Bernard. *The Fable of the Bees, or Private Vices, Public Benefits*. 1714. Ed. and intro. Philip Harth. Harmondsworth: Penguin, 1970.

Marchand, Philip. *Marshall McLuhan: The Medium and the Messenger*. Toronto: Random House, 1989.

Martí, José. "Nuestra América (1891)." *Por Nuestra América*. Ed. José Martí. La Habana: 2003. 223–32.

———. "Our America." *Heath Anthology of American Literature*. Ed. Paul Lauter II. Vol. 2. 4th ed. Lexington: Heath, 2002. 879–86.

Maslan, Susan. "The Anti-Human: Man and Citizen before the Declaration of the Rights of Man and of the Citizen." *SAQ: South Atlantic Quarterly* 103.2–3 (2004): 357–74.

Massey, Doreen. "A Global Sense of Place." *Marxism Today* 35.6 (1991): 24–29.

Matthews, John. *Tradition in Exile: A Comparative Study of Social Influences on the Development of Australian and Canadian Poetry in the Nineteenth Century*. Toronto: U of Toronto P, 1962.

McKillop, A. B. *Matters of Mind: The University in Ontario 1791–1851*. Toronto: U of Toronto P, 1994.

McLuhan, Marshall. *Culture Is Our Business*. New York: McGraw-Hill, 1970.

Merleau-Ponty, Maurice. *Phenomenology of Perception*. Trans. Colin Smith. New York: Humanities P, 1962.

Meszáros, Istvan. *Beyond Capital: Towards a Theory of Transition*. London: Merlin Press, 1995.

Mignolo, Walter D. "Globalization, Civilization Processes, and the Relocation of Languages and Cultures." *The Cultures of Globalization*. Ed. Fredric Jameson and Masao Miyoshi. Durham: Duke UP, 1998. 32–53.

———. "The Many Faces of Cosmo-polis: Border Thinking and Critical Cosmopolitanism." *Public Culture* 12.3 (2000): 721–48.

Miki, Roy. "Inter-Face: Roy Kiyooka's Writing; A Commentary/Interview." *Broken Entries: Race, Subjectivity, Writing*. Toronto: Mercury, 1998. 54–76.

Mitchell, W. O. *Who Has Seen the Wind*. 1947. Toronto: Macmillan of Canada, 1969.

Miyoshi, Masao. "Ivory Tower in Escrow." *Learning Places*. Ed. Masao Miyoshi and H. D. Harootunian. Durham, NC: Duke UP, 2002. 19–60.

Mochizuki, Cindy. "Artist Talk: Leaving It Be: Apathy, Activism, and Ethnicity in Contemporary Practice [panel]." Emily Carr Institute, Vancouver, BC. 20 Oct. 2004.

Monkman, Leslie. "Canadian Literature in English 'Among Worlds.'" *Home-Work: Postcolonialism, Pedagogy, and Canadian Literature*. Ed. Cynthia Sugars. Ottawa: U of Ottawa P, 2004. 117–33.

Moodie, Susanna. *Roughing It in the Bush; or, Life in Canada*. Ed. Elizabeth Thompson. Ottawa: Tecumseh, 1997.

Morris, Alexander. *The Treaties of Canada with the Indians of Manitoba and the North-West Territories, Including the Negotiations on Which They Were Based, and Other Information Relating Thereto*. 1880. Saskatoon: Fifth House, 1991.

Morris, Meaghan. *Too Soon Too Late: History in Popular Culture*. Bloomington: Indiana UP, 1998.

Morrison, Toni. *Playing in the Dark: Whiteness and the Literary Imagination*. Cambridge: Harvard UP, 1992.

Moses, Daniel David. "Inukshuk." *The White Line*. Calgary: Fifth House, 1990.

Mosionier, Beatrice Culleton. *In Search of April Raintree*. Winnipeg: Pemmican, 1983.

Moss, John. *Sex and Violence in the Canadian Novel: The Ancestral Present*. Toronto: McClelland and Stewart, 1977.

————, ed. *Future Indicative: Literary Theory and Canadian Literature*. Ottawa: Ottawa UP, 1986.

Moss, Laura, ed. *Is Canada Postcolonial? Unsettling Canadian Literature*. Waterloo: Wilfrid Laurier UP, 2003.

Mouré, Erin. "The Anti-Anaesthetic." *Open Letter* 9.3 (1995): 13–24.

————. *O Cidadán*. Toronto: Anansi, 2002.

————. "Poetry, Memory and the Polis." *Language in Her Eye: Views on Writing and Gender by Canadian Women Writing in English*. Ed. Libby Sheier, Sarah Sheard, and Eleanor Wachtel. Toronto: Coach House, 1990. 201–208.

————. *Sheepish Beauty, Civilian Love*. Montreal: Véhicule, 1992.

Moyes, Lianne. "'Global/Local': Montréal dans la poésie de Robyn Sarah, Mary di Michele et Erin Mouré." *La littérature anglo-québécoise*. Spec. issue of *Voix et images* 90 (2005): 113–32.

————. "Global / local : Montreal in the Poetry of Robyn Sarah, Mary di Michele and Erin Mouré." *Language Acts: Anglo-Quebec Poetry, 1976 to the 21st Century*. Ed. Jason Camlot and Todd Swift. Montreal: Véhicule, 2007. 254–71.

Muir, Alexander. "The Maple Leaf Forever." 1868. Nordheimer, 1871.

Nafisi, Azar. *Reading Lolita in Tehran: A Memoir in Books*. New York: Random House, 2003.

Nancy, Jean-Luc. *The Sense of the World*. 1993. Trans. Jeffrey S. Librett. Minneapolis: U of Minnesota P, 1997.

Nepveu, Pierre. *L'Ecologie du réel: Mort et naissance de la littérature québécoise contemporaine*. Montréal: Boréal, 1988.

————. "Qu'est-ce que la transculture?" *Paragraphes* 2 (1989): 15–31.

New, W. H. *Borderlands: How We Talk about Canada*. Vancouver: U of British Columbia P, 1998.

Niro, Shelly, dir. *Honey Moccasin*. Canada, 1998.

Northey, Margot. *The Haunted Wilderness: The Gothic and Grotesque in Canadian Fiction*. Toronto: U of Toronto P, 1976.

Nussbaum, Martha C. *For Love of Country: Debating the Limits of Patriotism*. Boston: Beacon, 1996.

O'Hagan, Jacinta. "Beyond the Clash of Civilisations?" *Australian Journal of International Affairs* 59.3 (2005): 383–400.

Ong, Aihwa. *Flexible Citizenship: The Cultural Logics of Transnationality*. Durham, NC: Duke UP, 1999.

Ortiz, Fernando. *Contrapunteo cubano del tabaco y azúcar*. La Habana, 1940.

"Our Goal." *Centre for Cultural Renewal*. 14 June 2005 <http://www.culturalrenewal.ca/qry/page.taf?id=16>.

Palmer, Bryan. *Cultures of Darkness: Night Travels in the Histories of Transgression.* New York: Monthly Review P, 2000.

Palmer, Howard. "Strangers and Stereotypes: The Rise of Nativism, 1880–1920." *The Prairie West: Historical Readings.* Ed. R. Douglas Francis and Howard Palmer. Edmonton: Pica Pica, 1985. 309–33.

Parry, Benita. "Signs of Our Times: A Discussion of Homi Bhabha's *The Location of Culture.*" *Learning Places.* Ed. Miyoshi Masao and H. D. Harootunian. Durham, NC: Duke UP, 2002. 119–49.

Pennee, Donna Palmateer. "Literary Citizenship: Culture (Un)Bounded, Culture (Re)Distributed." *Home-Work: Postcolonialism, Pedagogy, and Canadian Literature.* Ed. Cynthia Sugars. Ottawa: U of Ottawa P, 2004. 75–85.

———. "Looking Elsewhere for Answers to the Postcolonial Question: From Literary Studies to State Policy in Canada." *Is Canada Postcolonial?* Ed. Laura Moss. Waterloo: Wilfrid Laurier UP, 2003. 78–94.

"Percentage and Number of Persons in Low Income/Poverty, by Age, Sex and Family Characteristics,Canada, 1990 and 1999." *Canadian Council on Social Development.* 2002. Canadian Council on Social Development. 14 June 2005 <http://www.ccsd.ca/factsheets/fs_pov9099.htm>.

Philip, M. NourbeSe. "Trying Tongues, E-raced Identities, and the Possibilities of Be/longing: Conversations with NourbeSe Philip." Interview with Patricia J. Saunders. *Journal of West Indian Literature* 14.1–2 (2005): 202–19.

———. "Why Multiculturalism Can't End Racism." *Frontiers: Essays and Writings on Racism and Culture.* Toronto: Mercury, 1992. 181–86.

Piper, Martha. "Building a Civil Society: A New Role for the Human Sciences." Killam Lecture. 24 Oct. 2002. University of British Columbia. 10 May 2005 <www.president.ubc.ca/president/ speeches/24oct02_killam.pdf>.

Porter, Carolyn. "What We Know That We Don't Know: Remapping American Literary Studies." *American Literary History* 6.3 (1994): 467–526.

Porter, John. *The Vertical Mosaic: An Analysis of Social Class and Power in Canada.* Toronto: U of Toronto P, 1965.

Posner, Michael. "Our Storied Literary Landscape." *Globe and Mail* 2 May 2005: R1–R2.

"Poverty Rates, All Persons, Canada, 1980–1995." *Canadian Council on Social Development.* 1995. Centre for International Statistics, Canadian Council on Social Development. 14 June 2005 <http://www.ccsd.ca/factsheets/fs_pvall.htm>.

Powell Street Festival. Promotional material. "Leaving It Be: Apathy, Activism, and Ethnicity in Contemporary Practice [panel]." Emily Carr Institute, Vancouver, BC. 20 Oct. 2004.

Pratt, Mary Louise. "Comparative Literature and Global Citizenship." *Comparative Literature in the Age of Multiculturalism.* Ed. Charles Bernheimer. Baltimore: Johns Hopkins UP, 1995. 58–65.

———. *Imperial Eyes: Travel Writing and Transculturation.* New York: Routledge, 1992.

Raddall, Thomas. *Roger Sudden*. Toronto: McClelland and Stewart, 1944.

Radway, Janice. "What's in a Name? Presidential Address to the American Studies Association, 20 November 1998." *American Quarterly* 51.1 (1999): 1–32.

Rancière, Jacques. *The Philosopher and His Poor*. Ed. and intro. Andrew Parker. Trans. John Drury, Corinne Oster, and Andrew Parker. Durham, NC: Duke UP, 2003.

Razack, Sherene H. *Dark Threats and White Knights: The Somalia Affair, Peacekeeping, and the New Imperialism*. Toronto: U of Toronto P, 2004.

———. *Looking White People in the Eye: Gender, Race, and Culture in Courtrooms and Classrooms*. Toronto: U of Toronto P, 1998.

Readings, Bill. *The University in Ruins*. Cambridge: Harvard UP, 1996.

Richardson, John. *Wacousta: A Tale of the Pontiac Conspiracy*. Toronto: Musson, 1924.

Richler, Mordecai. *The Incomparable Atuk*. Toronto: McClelland and Stewart, 1963.

Robbins, Bruce. "Introduction Part I: Actually Existing Cosmopolitanism." *Cosmopolitics: Thinking and Feeling beyond the Nation*. Ed. Bruce Robbins and Pheng Cheah. Minneapolis: U of Minnesota P, 1998. 1–19.

Rosaldo, Renato. "Cultural Citizenship, Inequality, and Multiculturalism." *Latino Cultural Citizenship: Claiming Identity, Space, and Rights*. Ed. William V. Flores and Rina Benmayor. Boston: Beacon, 1997. 27–38.

Rose, Jonathan. *The Intellectual Life of the British Working Classes*. New Haven: Yale UP, 2001.

Rose, Nikolas, and Carlos Novas. "Biological Citizenship." *Global Assemblages: Technology, Politics, and Ethics as Anthropological Problems*. Ed. Aihwa Ong and Stephen J. Collier. Oxford: Blackwell, 2005. 439–63.

Ross, Malcolm, ed. *Our Sense of Identity: A Book of Canadian Essays*. Toronto: Ryerson, 1954.

Roy, Anindyo. "Introduction 'Subject to Civility': The Story of the Indian Baboo." Spec. Issue on *Civility and the Pleasures of Colonialism*. Ed. Anindyo Roy. *Colby Quarterly* 37.2 (2001): 113–24.

Roy, Camille. "La Nationalisation de notre littérature." 1907. *Essais sur la littérature canadienne*. Montréal: Librairie Garneau / Librairie Beauchemin, 1913.

Russell, Peter H. "Citizenship in a Multinational Democracy." *Insiders and Outsiders: Alan Cairns and the Reshaping of Canadian Citizenship*. Ed. Gerald Kernerman and Philip Resnick. Vancouver: U of British Columbia P, 2005. 273–85.

Sakamoto, Kerri. "Bombard/Invade/Radiate: Witness." Catalogue Essay on Aiko Suzuki. Toronto: A Space, 2005.

Said, Edward. *Culture and Imperialism*. New York: Vintage, 1994.

———. *From Oslo to Iraq and the Road Map: Essays*. Intro. Tony Judt. Afterword Wadie E. Said. New York: Vintage, 2004.

———. *Humanism and Democratic Criticism*. New York: Columbia UP, 2004.

———. "Reflections on Exile." *Out There: Marginalization and Contemporary Culture*. Ed. Russell Ferguson, Martha Gever, Trinh T. Minh-ha, and Cornel West. Cambridge: MIT Press, 1990. 357–66.

————. *The World, the Text and the Critic*. Cambridge: Harvard UP, 1983.

Sammy and Rosie Get Laid. Dir. Stephen Frears. Cinecom, 1987.

Sandbrook, Richard, ed. *Civilizing Globalization: A Survival Guide*. Albany: State U of New York, 2003.

"Sask. Natives Sign Historic Land Claims Deal." *Saskatoon Star Phoenix* 24 June 2002: A1.

Sassen, Saskia. "The Repositioning of Citizenship: Emergent Subjects and Spaces for Politics." *Berkeley Journal of Sociology* 46 (2002): 41–66.

Saunders, Patricia. "Trying Tongues, E-raced Identities, and the Possibilities of Be/longin: Conversations with NourbeSe Philip." *Journal of West Indian Literature*. Special issue Rooting and Routing Caribbean Canadian Writing. Eds. Michael Bucknor, Daniel Coleman, John Corr, and Elizabeth Jackson. 14.1–2 (November 2005): 202–19.

Saussy, Haun, ed. *Comparative Literature in an Age of Globalization*. Baltimore: Johns Hopkins UP: 2006.

Schild, Véronica. "Neo-liberalism's New Gendered Market Citizens: The 'Civilizing' Dimension of New Market Programmes in Chile." *Citizenship Studies* 4.3 (2000): 275–305.

Scholes, Robert. "Presidential Address 2004: The Humanities in a Posthumanist World." *PMLA* 210.3 (2005): 724–33.

Scott, David. *Conscripts of Modernity: The Tragedy of Colonial Enlightenment*. Durham, NC: Duke UP, 2004.

————. *Refashioning Futures: Criticism after Postcoloniality*. Princeton: Princeton UP, 1999.

Scott, F. R. "Trans Canada." *A New Anthology of Canadian Literature in English*. Ed. Donna Bennett and Russell Brown. Don Mills, ON: Oxford UP, 2002. 337–38.

Sedgwick, Eve Kosofsky. *Epistemology of the Closet*. Berkeley: U of California P, 1990.

————. *Touching Feeling: Affect, Performativity, Pedagogy*. Durham, NC: Duke UP, 2003.

Shadd, Mary A. *A Plea for Emigration; Or, Notes of Canada West*. 1852. Ed. and introd. Richard Almonte. Toronto: Mercury, 1998.

Shohat, Ella. "By the Bitstream of Babylon: Cyberfrontiers and Diasporic Vistas." *Home, Exile, Homeland: Film, Media, and the Politics of Place*. New York: Routledge, 1999. 213–32.

Siemerling, Winfried. "'May I See Some Identification?': Race, Borders, and Identities in *Any Known Blood*." *Canadian Literature* 182 (2004): 30–50.

————. *The New North American Studies: Culture, Writing, and the Politics of Re/Cognition*. New York: Routledge, 2005.

————. "Rereading the Nation: Cultural Difference, Transculture, and Literary History in Canada and Quebec." Ed. Brook Thomas. *Literature and the Nation*. Spec. issue of *REAL: Yearbook of Research in English and American Literature* 14 (1998): 179–200.

Simon, Paul. "Gumboots." *Graceland*. Warner Bros., 1986.

Simon, Sherry. *Hybridité culturelle*. Montreal: L'île de la Tortue, 1999.

Singer, P. W. *Corporate Warriors: The Rise of the Privatized Military Industry*. Ithaca: Cornell UP, 2003.

Singh, Rama. Conversation with Stephen Slemon. 11 June 2005.

Sirois, Antoine, Pamela Grant, David M. Hayne, Gregory J. Reid, Winfried Siemerling, and Maria van Sundert. *Bibliography of Comparative Studies in Canadian, Québec and Foreign Literatures / Bibliographie d'études comparées des littératures canadienne, québécoise et étrangères 1930–1995*. Sherbrooke: Les Éditions GGC, 2001. Départment des lettres et communications, Université de Sherbrooke <http://compcanlit.usherbrooke.ca/> and <http://www.compcanlit.ca>.

Slemon, Stephen. "Lament for a Notion: Gayatri Chakravorty Spivak's *Death of a Discipline*." *English Studies in Canada* 29.1–2 (2003): 207–18.

Smith, A. J. M. "Introduction." *The Book of Canadian Poetry: A Critical and Historical Anthology*. Ed. A. J. M. Smith. Chicago: U of Chicago P, 1943. 3–31.

Smith, Adam. *An Inquiry into the Nature and Causes of the Wealth of Nations*. 1876. Ed. R. H. Campbell, A. S. Skinner, and W. B. Todd. 2 vols. Indianapolis: Liberty Classics, 1981.

Social Sciences and Humanities Research Council. "SSHRC Transformation." 7 Nov. 2006. *Social Sciences and Humanities Research Council* <http://www.sshrc.ca/web/whatsnew/initiatives/transformation>.

Sormin, Linda. "Artist Talk: Leaving It Be: Apathy, Activism, and Ethnicity in Contemporary Practice [panel]. Emily Carr Institute, Vancouver, BC. 20 Oct. 2004.

Spivak, Gayatri Chakravorty. Afterword. *Imaginary Maps: Three Stories by Mahasweta Devi*. Trans. Gayatri Chakravorty Spivak. New York: Routledge, 1995. 197–205.

———. "Can the Subaltern Speak?" *Marxism and the Interpretation of Culture*. Ed. C. Nelson and L. Grossberg. Chicago: U of Illinois P, 1988. 271–313.

———. *A Critique of Postcolonial Reason*. Cambridge: Harvard UP, 1999.

———. *Death of a Discipline*. New York: Columbia UP, 2003.

———. "French Feminism in an International Frame." *Other Worlds: Essays in Cultural Politics*. New York: Methuen, 1987. 134–53.

———. "Guest Column: Roundtable on the Future of the Humanities in a Fragmented World." *PMLA* 120.3 (2005): 718–21.

———. "Harlem." *Social Text* 22.4 (2004): 113–39.

———. *Outside in the Teaching Machine*. New York: Routledge, 1993.

SSHRC. *See* Social Sciences and Humanities Research Council.

Stael, Germaine de. *Considérations sur les principaux événements de la révolution française*. 2 vols. 1817. Ed. and intro. Jacques Godechot. Paris: Taillandier, 1983.

Stanford Friedman, Susan. "Locational Feminism: Gender, Cultural Geographies, and Geopolitical Literacy." *Feminist Locations: Global and Local, Theory and Practice*. Ed. Marianne Dekoven. Piscataway, NJ: Rutgers UP, 2001. 13–36.

Steele, Charles, ed. *Taking Stock: The Calgary Conference on the Canadian Novel*. Downsview, ON: ECW, 1982.

Stein, Janice Gross. *The Cult of Efficiency*. CBC Massey Lectures 2001.Toronto: Anansi, 2001.

Stone, Andrea. "Behind Every Good Newspaper: Women's Rights in Canadian Black Abolitionist Publishing, the Provincial Freeman, 1853–1855." Paper Presented at Congress of the Canadian Federation for the Humanities and the Social Sciences, London, ON. 30 May 2005.

Stone, Marjorie. Letter to Keith Wilson. 7 Feb. 2005.

Stowe, Harriet Beecher. *Uncle Tom's Cabin*. New York: Oxford UP, 1998 (1852).

Sugars, Cynthia. "Can the Canadian Speak?" *Ariel* 32.2 (2001): 115–52.

———, ed. *Home-Work: Postcolonialism, Pedagogy, and Canadian Literature*. Ottawa: U of Ottawa P, 2004.

———, ed. *Unhomely States: Theorizing English-Canadian Postcolonialism*. Peterborough: Broadview, 2004.

Sundquist, Eric J. *To Wake the Nations: Race in the Making of American Literature*. Cambridge: Belknap, 1993.

Szeman, Imre. "Belated or Isochronic? Canadian Writing, Time, and Globalization." *Where Is Here Now?* Spec. issue of *Essays in Canadian Writing* 71 (2000): 186–94.

———. *Zones of Instability: Literature, Postcolonialism, and the Nation*. Baltimore: Johns Hopkins UP, 2003.

Taylor, Laurie. "Suddenly, A Reputation at Stake, Mr. Nice Guy." *Toronto Star* 28 Aug. 2005, D9.

"Terror Trading Terrible Tactic." *Saskatoon Star Phoenix* 5 Aug. 2003: A8.

Tomkins, Silvan. *Affect, Imagery, Consciousness*. 3 vols. New York: Springer, 1962.

Tomlinson, John. *Globalization and Culture*. Chicago: U of Chicago P, 1999.

Tompkins, Jane. *Sensational Designs: The Cultural Work of American Fiction, 1790–1860*. New York: Oxford UP, 1985.

Torpey, John. "Introduction." *Politics and the Past: On Repairing Historic Injustices*. Ed. John Torpey. Oxford: Rowman and Littlefield, 2003.

Traill, Catherine Parr. *Canadian Crusoes: A Tale of the Rice Lake Plains*. Montreal: McGill-Queen's UP, 2002 (1852).

TransCanada: Literature, Institutions, Citizenship. University of Guelph / Simon Fraser University. <http://www.transcanadas.ca/transcanada1/index.shtml>.

Trouillot, Michel-Rolph. *Global Transformations: Anthropology and the Modern World*. New York: Palgrave/Macmillan, 2003.

Tsang, Henry. "Artist Talk: Leaving It Be: Apathy, Activism, and Ethnicity in Contemporary Practice [panel]." Emily Carr Institute, Vancouver, BC. 20 Oct. 2004.

Tully, James. "Introduction." *Multinational Democracies*. Ed. Alain-G. Gagnon and James Tully. Cambridge: Cambridge UP, 2002. 1–34.

Turk, James L., ed. *The Corporate Campus: Commercialization and the Dangers to Canada's Colleges and Universities*. CAUT Series. Toronto: James Lorimer, 2000.

Turner, Bryan S. "Contemporary Problems in the Theory of Citizenship." *Citizenship and Social Theory*. Ed. Bryan S. Turner. London: Sage, 1993. 1–18.

Ullman, Victor. *Martin R. Delany: The Beginnings of Black Nationalism.* Boston: Beacon, 1971.

United Nations. "Progress Towards the Millennium Development Goals, 1990–2005." *United Nations Statistics Divison.* 13 June 2005. United Nations Statistics Division. 14 June 2005 <http://millenniumindicators.un.org/unsd/mi/mi_coverfinal.htm>.

———. "United Nations Millennium Declaration." *Office of the United Nations High Commissioner for Human Rights.* 8 Sept. 2000. Office of the United Nations High Commissioner for Human Rights. 14 June 2005 <http://www.ohchr.org/english/law/millennium.htm>.

Virgo, Clement (dir.). *Rude.* Conquering Lion Productions, 1994.

Wah, Fred. *Diamond Grill.* Edmonton, AB: NeWest, 1996.

Walcott, Rinaldo, ed. *Rude: Contemporary Black Canadian Cultural Criticism.* Toronto: Insomniac, 2000.

Wallace, Paul A. *The White Roots of Peace.* 1946. Saranac Lake, NY: Chauncy, 1986.

Wallerstein, Immanuel, and Armand Clesse, eds. *The World We Are Entering: 2000–2050.* Amsterdam: Dutch UP, 2002.

Walters, William. "Secure Borders, Safe Haven, Domopolitics." *Citizenship Studies* 8.3 (2004): 237–60.

War Party. *The Resistance.* War Party Productions Studios, 2004.

Warkentin, Germaine, and Heather Murray. "Introduction: Reading the Discourse of Early Canada." *Discourse in Early Canada.* Spec. issue of *Canadian Literature* 131 (Winter 1991): 7–13.

Warner, Marina. *Fantastic Metamorphoses, Other Worlds.* Oxford: Oxford UP, 2002.

Watts, Charles, and Edward Byrne, eds. *The Recovery of the Public World: Essays on Poetics in Honour of Robin Blaser.* Vancouver: Talonbooks: 1999.

Wellek, René, and Austin Warren. *Theory of Literature.* San Diego, New York, London: Harcourt Brace Jovanovich, 1956 (1948).

Welsh, Jennifer. *At Home in the World: Canada's Global Vision for the 21st Century.* Toronto: HarperCollins, 2004.

West, Cornell. "A Genealogy of Modern Racism." 1982. *Race Critical Theories.* Ed. Philemena Essed and David Theo Goldberg. New York: Oxford UP, 2002. 90–112.

Whale Rider. Dir. Niki Caro. South Pacific Pictures, 2002.

Where the Spirit Lives. Screenplay by Keith Ross Leckie. Dir. Bruce Pittman. CBC, 1987.

Williams, Jeffrey J., ed. *The Institution of Literature.* Albany: State U of New York P, 2002.

———. "The Life of the Mind and the Academic Situation." *The Institution of Literature.* Ed. Jeffrey J. Williams. Albany: State U of New York P, 2002. 203–25.

Wittig, Monique. "The Straight Mind." *The Straight Mind and Other Essays.* Boston: Beacon Press, 1992.

Woodsworth, J. S. *Strangers within Our Gates, or Coming Canadians.* 1909. Toronto: U of Toronto P, 1972.

Womack, Craig. *Red on Red: Native American Literary Separatism.* London: U of Minnesota P, 1999.

World Bank. "Global Poverty Down by Half since 1981 but Progress Uneven as Eco-
    nomic Growth Eludes Many Countries." Press release. 23 April 2004. *World Bank.*
    The World Bank Group. 14 June 2005 <http://go.worldbank.org/R3SKHZRZ30>.
Wynter, S. "Rethinking 'Aesthetics': Notes Towards A Deciphering Practice." *Ex-Iles:*
    Essays on Caribbean Cinema. Ed. M. Cham. Trenton: Africa World P, 1992. 237–79.
————. "The Pope Must Have Been Drunk, the King of Castile a Madman: Culture
    as Actuality, and the Caribbean Rethinking Modernity." *The Reordering of Cul-*
    ture: Latin America, the Caribbean and Canada, in the Hood. Ed. A. Ruprecht
    and C. Taiana. Ottawa: Carleton UP, 1995. 17–41.
Young, Iris. *Inclusion and Democracy.* Oxford: Oxford UP, 2002.

CONTRIBUTORS

DIANA BRYDON is Canada Research Chair in Globalization and Cultural Studies at the University of Manitoba, where she specializes in Australian, Canadian, and Caribbean literary studies. Recent publications include a five-volume anthology, *Postcolonialism: Critical Concepts in Literary and Cultural Studies* and a co-edited book, *Shakespeare in Canada* (with Irena Makaryk). *Renegotiating Community: Interdisciplinary Perspectives, Global Contexts* (co-edited with William D. Coleman) is forthcoming from the University of British Columbia Press.

RICHARD CAVELL is the Founding Director of the International Canadian Studies Centre at UBC, the author of *McLuhan in Space: A Cultural Geography* (2002), the editor of *Love, Hate and Fear in Canada's Cold War* (2004), the co-editor, with Peter Dickinson, of *Sexing the Maple: A Canadian Sourcebook* (2006), and, with Imre Szeman, founding editor of the *Cultural Spaces* series at the University of Toronto Press, and co-editor of the *Review of Education, Pedagogy and Cultural Studies* (29.1/2 2007) on Cultural Studies in Canada today.

LILY CHO is an Assistant Professor of English at the University of Western Ontario. Her research interests include work on diaspora, postcolonial studies, cultural studies, food culture, citizenship, and affect. She is currently completing a book-length study of diaspora and Chinese restaurants in small-town Canada. She is also pursuing a project on Pacific Genealogies, which examines the role of indenture and piracy in the emergence of Asian diaspora subjectivity. Her recent publications include "Asian Canadian

Futures: Indenture Routes and Diasporic Passages," in *Essays in Canadian Writing* 85 (2006) and "The Turn to Diaspora," in *Topia* 17 (2007).

DANIEL COLEMAN is a Canada Research Chair in Diversity in Canadian Literature and Culture who teaches in the Department of English and Cultural Studies at McMaster University. His most recent publications include *White Civility* (U of Toronto P, 2006) and *Recalling Early Canada* (co-edited, U of Alberta P, 2005).

PETER DICKINSON is Associate Professor in the Department of English at Simon Fraser University. He is the author of *Here is Queer: Nationalisms, Sexualities, and the Literatures of Canada* (U of Toronto P, 1999) and *Screening Gender, Framing Genre: Canadian Literature into Film* (U of Toronto P, 2007). With Richard Cavell, he has also co-edited *Sexing the Maple: A Canadian Sourcebook* (Broadview, 2006).

JULIA EMBERLEY is Associate Professor of English at the University of Western Ontario. She is the author of *Defamiliarizing the Aboriginal: Cultural Practices and Decolonization in Canada* (University of Toronto Press, 2007), *The Cultural Politics of Fur* (Cornell University Press, 1997), and *Thresholds of Difference: Native Women's Writing, Feminist Critique, and Postcolonial Theory* (University of Toronto Press, 1993). She has recently published articles in *The Journal of Visual Culture, Topia,* and *Fashion Theory,* and contributed a book chapter on Gertrude Bell in *Literature, Empire and Travel: In the Margins of Anthropology* (I.B. Tauris, 2007).

LEN FINDLAY is Professor of English and Director of the Humanities Research Unit at the University of Saskatchewan. Educated at Aberdeen and Oxford, he came to Canada in 1974. Widely published in nineteenth-century European topics and increasingly in Canadian Studies, his recent work includes a new edition of *The Communist Manifesto* (Broadview, 2004), "Spectres of Canada: Image, Text, Aura, Nation" (*UTQ*, 2006), "Towards Canada as Aesthetic State: François-Xavier Garneau's *Canadien* Poetics (*ECW*, 2006), and collaborative projects for the *Australian Journal of Aboriginal Education* (special issue on *Thinking Place*) and for the Office of the Treaty Commission of Saskatchewan. He is currently writing a polemic in the vein of George Grant's, entitled *Intent for a Nation,* and an intellectual biography of Alexander Morris.

SMARO KAMBOURELI is the founder and Director of TransCanada Institute and Canada Research Chair in Critical Studies in Canadian Literature at the University of Guelph, where she specializes in Canadian literature and diaspora studies. Her recent publications include *Scandalous Bodies: Dias-*

poric Literature in English Canada (Oxford, 2000), which received the Gabrielle Roy prize for Canadian criticism, a second edition of her earlier anthology, *Making a Difference: Multicultural Literatures in English Canada* (Oxford, 2006), and Roy Kiyooka's *Pacific Rim Letters* (NeWest Press), which she edited, with an afterword. The Editor of the TransCanada Series (Wilfrid Laurier UP) and of the Writer as Critic Series (NeWest Press), she is currently co-editing, with Daniel Coleman, *The Culture of Research: Retooling the Humanities.*

LEE MARACLE was born in North Vancouver and is the author of seven novels, a collection of short stories, poetry, and non-fiction works. She has published widely in scholarly journals and fiction/poetry anthologies. Maracle is currently teaching at the University of Toronto. Her awards include the J. T. Stewart Voices of Change Award, the American Book Award from the Before Columbus Foundation, and the Wordcraft Circle Writer of the Year Award.

ASHOK MATHUR is a Canada Research Chair in Cultural and Artistic Inquiry at Thompson Rivers University (Kamloops, BC). He directs the Centre for Innovation in Culture and the Arts in Canada, working with artist-researchers on projects and explorations surrounding the intersection of artistic practice and social/political engagement. His creative and critical work includes fiction, poetry, essays, and cultural organizing around art, performance, and writing.

ROY MIKI is a writer, poet, and editor who teaches contemporary literature at Simon Fraser University. He was born in Winnipeg but relocated to the West Coast in the late 1960s. He is the author of *Justice in Our Time* (co-authored with Cassandra Kobayashi) (Talonbooks, 1991), a documentary history of the Japanese Canadian redress movement in which he actively participated, two books of poems, *Saving Face* (Turnstone, 1991) and *Random Access File* (Red Deer College Press, 1995), and a collection of critical essays, *Broken Entries: Race, Subjectivity, Writing* (Mercury Press, 1998). His third book of poems, *Surrender* (Mercury Press 2001), received the Governor General's Award for Poetry. His two most recent publications are *Redress: Inside the Japanese Canadian Call for Justice* (Raincoast, 2004), a work that explores the Japanese Canadian redress movement through a creative blend of personal reflection, documentary history, and critical examination, and *There* (New Star Books, 2006), a book of poems. He received the Order of Canada in 2006.

LIANNE MOYES is Associate Professor of English at Université de Montréal, where she specializes in Canadian and Quebec literatures. She is editor of *Gail Scott: Essays on Her Works*, co-editor of *Adjacencies: Minority Writing in*

Canada, and, from 1993 to 2003, was co-editor of the bilingual feminist journal *Tessera*. Her work on Anglo-Montreal writing has appeared in *Études canadiennes*, *Voix et images*, and *Canadian Literature* as well as in the collections *Un certain genre malgré tout*, *Pour une réflexion sur la différence sexuelle à l'oeuvre dans l'écriture* (Nota Bene), and *Language Acts: Anglo-Québec Poetry, 1976 to the 21st Century* (Véhicule).

WINFRIED SIEMERLING is Professor of English and Comparative Literature in the Graduate Programs in Comparative Canadian Literature at the Université de Sherbrooke and affiliated with the W. E. B. Du Bois Institute for African and African American Research at Harvard University. His books include *The New North American Studies: Culture, Writing, and the Politics of Re/Cognition* (Routledge, 2005), the *Bibliography of Comparative Studies in Canadian, Québec, and Foreign Literatures, 1930–1995* (2001, co-author), *Cultural Difference and the Literary Text: Pluralism and the Limits of Authenticity in North American Literatures* (1996/97, co-editor), *Writing Ethnicity: Cross-Cultural Consciousness in Canadian and Québécois Literature* (1996, editor), and *Discoveries of the Other: Alterity in the Work of Leonard Cohen, Hubert Aquin, Michael Ondaatje, and Nicole Brossard* (1994). He is currently co-editing *Canada and Its Americas: Transnational Navigations*, and working on African- and Asian-Canadian writing in the context of a SSHRC-funded project on transculturalism and double consciousness.

STEPHEN SLEMON is Professor in English and Film Studies at the University of Alberta and a student of imperial and postcolonial representations. His current research focuses on how social understandings of "criminality" circulated in British India from the mid-nineteenth century onwards, and on the literature of mountaineering, through which he attempts to understand some parts of the cross-cultural and gendered politics of the colonial past and the globalizing present.

RINALDO WALCOTT is an Associate Professor of Black Diaspora Cultural Studies at OISE/UT and the editor of *New Dawn: The Journal of Black Canadian Studies*, an online open-access journal. Recent essays include "Black Men in Frocks: Sexing Race in a Gay Ghetto (Toronto)" in *Claiming Space: Racialization in Canadian Cities* (Wilfrid Laurier University Press, 2006), and "Homopoetics: Queer Space and the Black Queer Diaspora" in *Black Geographics and the Politics of Place* (Between the Lines/South End Press, 2007). He is working on a book called *Black Diasporic Faggotry: Frames, Readings, Limits*.

INDEX

149–50; as resistance, 175; religious fundamentalism as, 156, 158; white civility as, 30, 31, 39

cultural studies: and CanLit, as discipline, 3, 7, 132, 192n7

culture: and civility, 26, 28; as discourse, 7, 87; First nations, 58, 92; institutional, 72, 80; and hospitality, 90; literary, and nation, 34, 35, 41, 42, 88, 89, 94, 139; public, 16, 91, 92, 169, 170; settler, 40, 41; transculture, 138, 139

D

Dallaire, Roméo, 33

decolonization, 7, 133, 136, 165, 172

democracy, 38–40, 176; and citizenship, 9, 10, 16; limits in fundamentalism, 156, 157

democratic: citizenship, 133, 135, 140, 165; deficits, 133–34

democratization, 77, 133, 134, 183

Denning, Michael, 4, 89

Department of Canadian Heritage, 14

Department of Foreign Affairs and International Trade, 91, 92, 185

Derrida, Jacques, 18, 20, 90

diaspora: Black, 18; and CanLit, ix, 3, 12, 98, 106, 107, 108, 195n4; and citizenship, 87, 94, 96, 99–109, 144; colonizers as, 55, 56, 59; and majoritized/minoritized communities, 98, 100, 144; studies, as discipline, 12, 136; and subjectivity, 99

difference, 156, 184; in CanLit, ix, 89, 93, 99; and civility, 31, 32; linguistic, 131, 136, 139; racial, 20, 35, 154, 155; within, 124

Dimock, Wai Chee, 12

disciplinarity: changes in, x, 6, 12, 15, 52, 76–84

discipline: CanLit as, xiv, ix, x, 2, 3, 6, 12, 71, 75, 82; change in humanities, 72, 83, 134, 151; methods in CanLit as 71, 76; postcolonialism as, 76, 77, 87

Dyer, Richard, 30

E

economics, 90, 155, 160, 174, 178; as hegemony, 183–85

economy: knowledge, 180

education, 29, 52; in colonization, 182; problem as discipline, 18

elsewhere/ness, x, xiv, 99, 100, 117, 155, 166

Enlightenment, 31, 49, 126, 170, 192n8

epistemology, x, 47, 113, 155; First Nations, 55–58, 63, 69, 185

essentialism, 87, 129, 132, 133

ethics, xi, 29, 90, 146, 154, 170; and citizenship, 117, 125; cosmopolitan, 12, 18, 22; and planetarity, 16

ethnicity, 32, 143, 144, 145; and nationalism, 116, 117

Eurocentrism, 39, 47, 55, 56. *See also* civility

Europe, 127, 167; as civilized, 30, 39, 125, 167; colonizing, 55, 56, 106

F

family: as institution, 73, 154, 161, 168, 171; familialism, 155–59, 169

Fanon, Franz, 114, 119, 120, 126, 136

feminism, 124, 154, 155

film, 156, 164, 165, 167

First Nations: citizenship, 100–103, 106; democracy, 39, 40; relationships to colonizers, 68, 75, 82, 91, 92; resistance, 22, 37; treaty rights, 99, 179, 181, 182, 185. *See also* Aboriginal; Native

Foucault, Michel, 47, 72, 153–54

Frye, Northrop, 48, 85, 87, 89, 136, 138

Fugitive Slave Law, 137

fundamentalism: consequences of, 8, 156, 169, 170; and family, 161, 162; and institutions, 154, 155; and materialism, 158; and nationalism, 167; and women, 16, 164

G

gay/lesbian, 53, 113, 118, 156, 170; marriage, 53, 154, 158, 197n1; nation, 89, 124

gender: and citizenship, 113, 114, 124; in film, 164, 165, 169, 170; and performance, 50, 51, 54; and subjectivity, 113, 114

Giddens, Anthony, 8–11

Gilroy, Paul, 16, 20, 22, 106, 191n33